SUPERVISORY SKILLS

SUPERVISORY SKILLS

Harold M. Emanuel, CPCU
Patricia E. Gould, CPCU, AIM
William F. Simpson, CPCU

Coordinating Author
James Gatza, D.B.A., CPCU

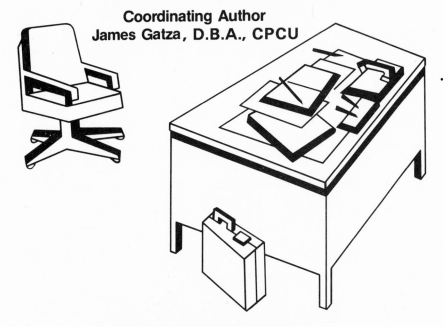

First Edition ▪ 1985
Insurance Institute of America
720 Providence Road, Malvern, Pennsylvania 19355-0770

Preface

This book is the second of two texts in the Insurance Institute of America's two-course Program in Supervisory Management. The first text, *Essentials of Supervision*, presented the ideas of greatest immediate use to a new supervisor. This book builds upon that base to deepen your understanding of critical supervisory activities.

The authors brought to their writing a rich and broad experience in supervising insurance work. They sought the practical: recommendations of immediate value on matters of everyday importance. The tricky part is providing you not with answers, but with guidelines that you can use in finding answers that will work for you.

Harold Emanuel's direct and consulting expertise are amply reflected in the chapters on automation and work management. Pat Gould accepted responsibility for two very different chapters: the diverse Chapter 2 (management functions) and the action-oriented final chapter on developing teamwork. Bill Simpson's extensive experience in supervisory training is visible in his chapters on problem solving and time management. George Khoury wrote the chapter on performance appraisal, and Ray Normann authored the chapter on training. Frank Herberg's Chapter 7 plays a unifying role as it provides problem situations for you to diagnose and solve.

We are grateful to the following reviewers who gave generously of their time and insight:

Richard G. Becker, CPCU
Director—Personnel Development
PRUPAC

Lawrence W. Brochhausen
Assistant Vice President—Training and Development
The Home Insurance Company

Eliot M. Daniels, CPCU, CLU
Vice President
Johnson & Higgins

Thomas E. Green, CPCU, CLU, AIM
Director of Production and Personnel Development
Training
Wausau Insurance Companies

William I. Grogg
Manager—Education and Training Division
State Farm Insurance Companies

Steven M. Horner, CPCU, CLU, AIM
Assistant Secretary—Training
Harleysville Insurance Companies

Daniel P. Hussey, Jr., CPCU, ARM, AAI
Vice President
Joseph A. Rigg Insurance Agency, Inc.

Alfred L. King, Jr., CPCU, AIC, AIM
Regional Training Manager
Denny's, Inc.

Moira J. Murray
Vice President
St. Paul Service, Inc.

Louis A. Oberle
Secretary of Personnel
Royal Insurance Company

William E. Painter, CPCU, ARM, AIM
Retired
Mount Laurel, NJ

Eleanor Raye, CPCU
Vice President
AMGRO, Inc.

Robert A. Ross, CPCU
Assistant Vice President-Claims Operation
Crum & Forster Underwriters Group

Gerald D. Seidl, J.D., CPCU, CLU, AIC
Legal Counsel
United Fire & Casualty Company

Roger L. Smith, CPCU
President
Insurance Educational Association

Homer O. White, CPCU
Retired
Berwyn, PA

As an insurance supervisor, you hold the power to affect important outcomes: organizational results and the personal satisfaction and career development of the persons who produce those results. We hope that the ideas in this book magnify the good you do for your organization and for the persons who look to you for leadership.

James Gatza, D.B.A., CPCU
Vice President
Insurance Institute of America

Contributing Authors

The Insurance Institute of America acknowledges with deep appreciation the help of the following contributing authors:

Frank J. Herberg, CPCU
Vice President—Sales and Marketing
Worcester Insurance Company

George F. Khoury
President
George F. Khoury Communications

Raymond M. Normann, M.B.A., CPCU, AIM
Commercial Training Director
Allstate Insurance Company

Table of Contents

CHAPTER 1

Problem Solving

INTRODUCTION

Supervisory problem solving is a basic, underlying activity that will often precede many of the other actions described later in this book. These include time management, developing employee performance standards, and using office automation effectively. Problem solving is intertwined with all of your supervisory functions.

Examples of Problems

You will find yourself using a problem-solving approach with two general types of problems, operational and "people" problems. The first concerns the specific, practical work or task that your unit or department performs. For example, these can include billing, underwriting, coding, rating, selling, claim processing, auditing, filing, and automation.

The second type, people problems, deals with the human element in the work situation. This factor is one that all supervisors, new or experienced, will recognize intuitively, albeit wryly. It is the propensity of the employee, properly trained and with adequate resources, not to perform the task at all or to perform it incorrectly. Such task failure is often accompanied by employee frustration or demotivation. Further, as supervisor, you can't instinctively blame the employee and stop there. Rather, a problem exists and you must unsnarl it. You may even find that your behavior has contributed to the problem as it now exists.

The Supervisor As Problem Solver

The insurance business today at both the agency and company level is often characterized by vigorous competition including, at times, severe price

1

competition. Nontraditional competitors such as financial conglomerates have entered the marketplace adding to the pressure to perform.

Since people expenses (pay and benefits) are such a key factor in insurance operations, the organization that is task effective and relatively "lean" in its staff has a decided advantage over one that is inefficient in the use of human resources.

As an example, a survey of twenty-five large metropolitan area brokers showed that most had increased their total revenues in two successive years, along with revenues generated per employee. While this in and of itself might not be particularly noteworthy, what is significant is that one-third of the brokers surveyed were producing the increased revenues with a smaller staff than a year before.

Agencies and brokers often consolidate in an attempt to get more favorable performance ratios including commission income per employee. Similar actions continue at the company level as a casual reading of financial news or the insurance trade press will show. In recent years carriers have consolidated offices and staff in an attempt to become more cost competitive.

How does all this affect you as supervisor? In brief, survival and success of insurance organizations (agency, brokerage, company or other types), require the supervisor to be professionally competent in all aspects of the supervisory role. While management may not always explicitly state in a position description or in performance standards that it expects the supervisor to be a proficient problem solver, in practice that expectation is there. Management wants the supervisor to solve, or at least reduce, the continuing operational and people problems that challenge the department or unit.

Reciprocally, as employees see increased demand for performance, tighter control of expenses and staff reductions, they, more than ever before, are likely first to want a competent supervisory leader. In addition, employees want to feel that the supervisor can help them to identify and solve their own everyday problems.

Operational Problems

What are some operational problems that you are likely to encounter as a supervisor? Here are a few:

1. Poorly designed jobs.
2. Poorly designed workflows and work processes.
3. Ineffective control procedures that either do not control at all or control the wrong things.
4. Poorly conceived and implemented office automation applications.
5. Missing or obsolete job aids such as procedural bulletins, guides, and training manuals.
6. Ineffective communication between "provider" departments (such as rating function) and "user" departments (such as an underwriting unit).

As front line supervisor, your role in solving such problems can vary depending on such factors as the size of your company or organization, the scope of your authority, and the needs of the situation. For example, in a small company or in an agency, you may be expected to learn enough about microcomputer rating programs to recommend a choice of software. In addition, you may have to select or recommend who is to be trained and to what extent.

People Problems

What are some people problems that you are likely to meet in your supervisory role? (Note that here we are going to focus on such problems in a collective sense rather than an individual one since such skills as appraising the performance of the individual employee are dealt with elsewhere in this text). Here are some problems often encountered by supervisors:

1. Employees' activities fail to support the achievement of the department or unit objectives.
2. Employees do not meet performance standards.
3. Excessive absenteeism.
4. Failure to use current job procedures.
5. Taking too much time for lunch and breaks.

In all of the above problems, we are going to assume that you or other supervisors or managers have communicated the appropriate objectives, performance standards, absenteeism policies, and so on beforehand. For whatever reason, employees are either failing to perform or failing to perform properly. Hence, you confront a people problem rather than an operational one.

Placing the blame rarely helps in solving people or operational problems. You would usually be right if you said, in each case, "I helped make this problem what it is." Perhaps you made a small problem worse by ignoring it. Maybe you should have reorganized it sooner. Don't look for the guilty parties; attack the problem as it stands.

KEY DEFINITIONS AND FACTORS

Quiz

At this point, in order to further develop the subject of problem solving, we will ask you to complete a short quiz either here or on separate scratch paper. After you complete the quiz, we will review each of your answers and then explore each point more completely.

1. A problem may be generally defined as a question raised for consideration, inquiry, or solution.

    ____Agree   ____Disagree

2. A problem usually has both an intellectual and an emotional aspect.

    ____Agree   ____Disagree

3. Creative people usually solve problems better than other people.

    ____Agree   ____Disagree

4. Problem solving is best categorized as a supervisory

_____Function _____Skill

5. The supervisory skill of decision making is uniquely related to problem solving.

_____Agree _____Disagree

6. Problem solving is more directly related to the supervisory functions of planning and controlling than it is to those of organizing and directing.

_____Agree _____Disagree

7. Rapid, pervasive change increases the need for supervisory problem solving.

_____Agree _____Disagree

8. Supervisory problem solving requires the possession of special aptitudes.

_____Agree _____Disagree

9. The increasing use of automation and systems specialists will tend to relieve the supervisor of the responsibility to become a proficient problem solver.

_____Agree _____Disagree

10. Theoretical knowledge of problem solving by itself is probably insufficient to develop a supervisor as a problem solver.

_____Agree _____Disagree

Now, let's review your answers. We will give the preferred answer and then follow with some comments on the specific point being considered.

1. A problem may be generally defined as a question raised for consideration, inquiry, or solution.

_X_ Agree _____Disagree

You should have agreed with the statement.

2. A problem usually has both an intellectual and an emotional aspect.

_X_ Agree _____Disagree

The emotional aspect of a problem may be more difficult for the supervisor to cope with than the purely intellectual side. As an example among the aforementioned operational problems, inadequate job aids such as bulletins or training manuals can result in frustrated or discouraged employees.

In approaching such a problem, you should be sensitive to both intellectual and emotional factors. You might discover through active listening that a claims representative is perplexed by an apparent contradiction in a memo containing claim processing guidelines. If you can clarify the memo's intent to the employee's satisfaction, the emotional aspect of the problem is likely to be eliminated or at least reduced. In some other cases the supervisor may have to develop some appropriate, understandable written examples of policies and procedures in order to address an employee's emotional distress.

    3. Creative people usually solve problems better than other people.

       ____Agree   _X_Disagree

There is little evidence to suggest that certain personality or occupational types are better problem solvers than others. For example, many people think that painters, sculptors, musicians, and others with artistic talents are more skillful problem solvers than people in other vocations. This has not been proven.

What is more accurate to say is that researchers on problem solving have identified the process of finding solutions to problems as an essentially creative act.[1] In this sense, creativity means reorganizing present facts into a new order or outlook. Incidentally, this creativity is an ability or aptitude believed to be widely distributed among people.

Senior or experienced managers sometimes pride themselves on their ability to sense this creative potential in their subordinates and, through training and coaching, to develop their employees into proficient problem solvers. In addition, business schools and colleges often include problem solving training in their courses.

What does this mean to you? It means simply that the average supervisor with the appropriate training and adequate opportunity to practice can become a proficient problem solver.

    4. Problem solving is best categorized as a supervisory

       ____Function   _X_Skill

You may recall from the first chapter of *Essentials of Supervision* that the supervisor applies certain skills, such as communication, listening, counseling, motivation, leadership, and training in order to support his or her main supervisory functions of planning, organizing, directing, and controlling. Problem solving is such a skill since it involves the ability to use one's knowledge effectively in performance. A skill connotes action.

Note that these supervisory skills can have a linear relationship in the sense that they may be used in a sequence. In an earlier example we saw that it was first necessary for a supervisor to listen to an employee's perplexity about unclear processing guidelines before the supervisor could intelligently approach the problem.

    5. The supervisory skill of decision making is uniquely related to problem solving.

       _X_Agree   ____Disagree

While decision making is identified as a separate supervisory skill by some management writers, others see it as one step in an overall problem-solving process. For example, one such approach considers decision making as the third step in a multi-step process after the problem and causes have been defined and various alternative solutions have been generated.[2] This third step, decision making or the selection of a solution, is essentially a choice among alternatives.

We raised this question so that we could comment on terminology. As usually used, decision making is a narrower idea than problem solving.

6. Problem solving is more directly related to the supervisory functions of planning and controlling than it is to those of organizing and directing.

  ____Agree   _X_Disagree

We will examine the supervisory functions in more detail later in this text. At first problem solving might appear to be more directly related to planning than to organizing and directing since planning is essentially determining ways to achieve organizational objectives. Failure to plan properly beforehand can often dramatically signal a need for remedial problem solving. An example might be the failure to identify a suitable annual expense control objective prior to the beginning of the year. By April the expenses could be too high, and the trend too threatening, thus triggering often frantic attempts to solve, reduce, or conceal the problem.

Similarly, failure in the control function is often highly visible in a unit or department. An example can be making a major change in a billing procedure without later evaluation of the change in terms of such factors as meeting the needs of customers or users, timeliness, error rate, and cost effectiveness. Failure to follow up could conceivably intensify any negative results which, in turn, could precipitate another round of problem solving.

While the relationship of problem solving to planning and controlling is often graphic, it can be just as directly related to organizing and directing. Under the heading of organizing decisions are the choices made when dividing the unit's workload by policy line, by territory, or on some other basis. Other organizing decisions involve which jobs will be changed when a new procedure is required.

An example of the directing function might be how work assignments are made within a unit or department. These could be at random (first work in, first assigned), by job category (whether technical, paratechnical or clerical), or by experience level within a job family. Failure of the supervisor to correctly direct employees on a continual basis can often result in both operating and people problems.

In summary, on an everyday basis, problem solving serves all of the supervisory functions.

7. Rapid, pervasive change increases the need for supervisory problem solving.

  _X_Agree   ____Disagree

Changes in operations and their subsequent effect on people continue at all levels in the industry. As supervisor you are often at the lead point of organizational change and such technological change as automation. As such you must understand the change and be able to apply skillful problem solving in order to adapt your department to it. Such changes can involve consolidation of an operation, upgrading automation equipment, or absorbing a task or process that may have been done elsewhere.

8. Supervisory problem solving requires the possession of special aptitudes.

_____Agree   _X_ Disagree

This question is related to the earlier one about whether or not so-called creative people can solve problems better than others. Are there special aptitudes that can equip a supervisor to solve problems? For example, do supervisors from such number-oriented disciplines as accounting, finance, data processing, and systems analysis have an advantage over others? Are supervisors from such fields as sales, marketing, public relations, and personnel who tend to approach problems intuitively at a disadvantage when compared to their systematic peers? According to problem-solving authorities, both approaches have their advantages, but apparently neither has a significant overall advantage over the other.[3] For example, the number-oriented people are likely to rule out alternative solutions only after careful analysis, and this is often highly desirable. But not all supervisory problems are of this nature.

With some problems, the easiest way to a solution is for the supervisor to explore alternative solutions quickly and to discard those that appear inappropriate. Intuitive problem solvers can apparently do this more easily than those who favor quantitative approaches.

In practice, many supervisors will often use a blend of both techniques though they may tend to lean toward one approach or the other. Later in this chapter, we will describe a relatively structured approach to solving operational and people problems. If you already tend toward systematic problem solving, you will find that this reinforces and expands what you have been doing naturally. If, however, you are an intuitive thinker, you may find that you will probably modify the structured approach after you master it.

9. The increasing use of automation and systems specialists will tend to relieve the supervisor of the responsibility to become a proficient problem solver.

_____Agree   _X_ Disagree

If anything, the necessity to work with such specialists can increase the need for such a proficiency on the supervisor's part. Such specialists are often employed by large and medium-sized companies and organizations to help line operating units decide on computer and office automation applications.

In practice, the supervisor will have to analyze workflows and work processes beforehand to determine if they are rationalized, that is, free of redundancies and gaps. Such an analytical activity is definitely related to problem-solving skill. Even when a smaller organization or agency considers an automation application, an outside consultant or vendor will often require the office manager (or a supervisor) to first analyze how work is processed.

10. Theoretical knowledge of problem solving by itself is probably insufficient to develop a supervisor as a problem solver.

_____Agree   _X_ Disagree

This answer is implied in an earlier one in which it was pointed out that problem solving is a skill and requires the possessor of such knowledge to use it effectively in action. Practice is essential in obtaining and sharpening skills. Early practice is likely to be more beneficial if there is coaching help from one's manager.

Let's illustrate. Assume that you are confronted with an unacceptable error ratio in a renewal billing function for which you are responsible. Further assume that the item or document is processed by three employees before the final product is created. Through your manager, this course, or some other training, you learn that the technique of analysis consists of separating a whole into its component parts. Analysis can help you isolate the part or, in this case, the step in the billing process that is either causing the problem or contributing to it.

You may understand this intellectually or conceptually. However, by itself, this understanding will probably not solve the error problem. To solve it, you will have to apply the knowledge by some specific action such as observing employees as they process the bills or inspecting their work product. In brief, you will have to practice the skill for it to be effective.

Conclusions

Let's summarize what we have learned about problem solving up to this point:

1. Problems are of two main types: operational or people.
2. A problem usually has both an intellectual and an emotional side.
3. Problem solving is a familiar, though often haphazard, experience for most supervisors.
4. Problem solving is a key supervisory skill that supports the various supervisory functions and must be practiced.
5. Decision making is seen as a critical step in a broader problem-solving process.
6. Management and employee expectations of the supervisor, coupled with the effect of rapid change and the use of automation specialists, stress the need for the supervisor to be a proficient problem solver.
7. The systematic and intuitive approaches to problem solving are both useful.

We solve problems every day in our work lives. What will this chapter add to our repertoire or to our abilities? Simply this. It will introduce a structured, relatively disciplined approach to problem solving which will enable the supervisor to systematically address the relatively more complex operating and people problems which he or she faces every day. It will build on and strengthen the relatively automatic, intuitive approach to solving problems that you use naturally.

MAJOR STEPS IN PROBLEM SOLVING

Now, let's identify nine steps and illustrate them with the typical thoughts or actions of the supervisor at each step.

Step 1—Describe the Apparent Problem

Supervisor's thoughts or actions—"Last week's error rate is too high. I'll bet the staff is not applying the new procedure correctly."

Reminders—This statement of the problem at this point could be illusory or misleading. For our purposes here we can accept as fact that the error rate is too high. However, we do not know that it is because the staff is not applying the new procedure correctly.

Step 2—Gather Facts

Supervisor's thoughts or actions—"I tried to determine who is making the mistakes. I spent much of this morning talking to employees and watching them as they did their jobs. Of the eight employees, two of them appear to be making the majority of the mistakes. Later, I remembered that one of them was out ill for two days during the procedural change, and the other apparently has forgotten some of the new procedures."

Reminders—Notice the techniques used in this fact-gathering step. They are:

a. Analyzing work measurement or output in order to determine who is making the errors.
b. Interviews—talking to each employee.
c. Observation—recognizing and noting facts or behavior.

In addition there are other fact-gathering techniques that might be used:

- Feedback from customers or internal "user" units or departments as to the correctness of or their satisfaction with the work or service being provided.
- Surveys, if time is available.
- Brainstorming—a group problem-solving technique that involves spontaneous contributions from all participants, or other group problem solving.

Step 3—Identify the Root Cause

Supervisor's thoughts or actions—"Two of the eight employees are making most of the errors. Now the problem is to correct the actions of these two persons quickly and with a minimum of disruption to the operation."

Reminders—The supervisor is now responding to the root cause, that is, to correct the errors being made by the employees in question. In a general sense, a root cause is something that is an origin or source of an effect or result. Now the focus of your attention is narrowed to the two employees. A unit-wide solution would waste at least some of your efforts since most of the staff are performing correctly.

How do supervisors and managers determine root causes? They use two general techniques: analysis and synthesis. Let's examine them in order.

Analysis   Analysis is defined as dividing a whole into its parts. Thus, in the fact-gathering step, the supervisor talked to each employee in the workflow, observing how each did the job and as a result, was able to pinpoint which employees were causing the increase in the error rate.

Often it will be necessary for you to break a larger problem down into its smaller parts in order to gain a starting point. Another example of analysis would be a workers' compensation underwriting supervisor charged with the responsibility of an acceptable loss ratio for a given area, say California. For the supervisor to control the underwriting results practically, he or she would need more finely drawn objectives. The supervisor might use categories based on size of premium, amount of premium produced by broker or agent for some period, and relative premium generated by metropolitan producers in Los Angeles and San Francisco, compared with those from other areas in the territory.

Analysis, in general, can facilitate later control and, indeed, can prevent or reduce future problems. For example, if the supervisor determines that the loss ratio for policies produced by one Los Angeles producer is deteriorating, he or she can specifically correct that problem rather than waste time addressing the policies and producers that are meeting underwriting requirements.

Synthesis   The second general problem-solving technique that you should master is synthesis, which essentially combines components or elements into a whole and, of course, is the opposite of analysis. A commercial underwriting example of synthesis might be the critical question:

> What is an acceptable response time for agents' requests for price quotation on simple commercial property risks?

In a particular market, competitors may be supplying such quotes in ninety minutes. You are going to have to meet or surpass their performance if this is a critical factor in ultimately getting submissions. You determine that two employees are involved in assembling this information, let's say an underwriter and an underwriting assistant. Each needs a certain time to make his or her contribution to the final product. Let's assume that you determine that their combined time needs are 100 minutes.

Your practical ceiling is ninety. You cannot go above this and still match competitors' response time. So you go back and analyze how the underwriter and the assistant perform their parts of the task. Perhaps they are not doing some tasks efficiently, and a saving of ten minutes can be made by changing the sequence of tasks and their allocation between underwriter and assistant.

Here we have an example of how synthesis and analysis are combined.

There was an analysis of the individual detailed tasks performed by the two employees, followed by a synthesis of a new work flow.

Step 4—Identify Alternative Solutions

Supervisor's thoughts or actions—"I'll have to see that the two employees are trained in the new procedure and at the same time minimize the impact on unit productivity. Maybe I should train them myself. Another possibility is to create a checklist for the operation. Maybe we could all work up a checklist, or at least a few of us could do it. I could ask some of the experienced employees to help out while the two are being trained."

Reminders—Here you should avoid two pitfalls:

a. Uncritically accepting and using the first one or two solutions that present themselves.
b. Over-analyzing by continuing to seek alternative solutions beyond the point of task and cost effectiveness. In practice, you may have to arbitrarily limit the number of alternative solutions in order to solve the problem within a time deadline or some other restriction.

Step 5—Evaluate Alternative Solutions

Supervisor's thoughts or actions—"Basically I have three alternatives—either to train the two employees myself, get help from senior employees who know how to do job training, or develop a checklist. I'll analyze the pluses and minuses of each approach."

Reminders—Here you can construct or adapt a worksheet similar to the one in Exhibit 1-1. You can assign a point value to each criterion and then total the points for each alternative.

Step 6—Select the Best Alternative

Supervisor's thoughts or actions—"I think I'll do the training myself. The checklist might help, and people might enjoy creating it. I'm not sure that the two employees will change their methods even if they were involved in developing the checklist. I would rather have the senior employees concentrate on making up actual production during the training."

Reminders—You do not always have to select the alternative with the greatest number of total points. Other factors may govern. For example, you may want to have a senior employee gain job training experience. The point difference between the two training alternatives is small enough to permit choosing the second best action for an outside reason.

Step 7—Implement the Best Alternative

Supervisor's thoughts or actions—"Now, let's see...I have to set up a training schedule for the two employees and notify them, and so on."

Exhibit 1-1
Evaluation Worksheet

Scale: 4. Excellent
3. Good
2. Acceptable
1. Poor

Criterion	Alternatives		
	I Train	Others Train	Checklist
Probability of success	4	4	3
Cost	2	2	2
Amount of time needed	1	3	1
Simplicity	4	2	1
Possible side effects	4	2	4
(Other criteria can be added as appropriate)			
Total Points	15	13	11

Reminders—It is easy to neglect careful implementation. Sometimes making the choice in a complex problem leads to a letdown. Selecting the best course of action is not the end of the story, although it may be the emotional climax.

Step 8—Evaluate the Results

Supervisor's thoughts and actions—"Well, I have trained the new employees and the error rate is back down where it should be."

Reminders—It may be necessary for you to take intermittent corrective action in order to "fine tune" and reinforce the solution chosen.

Step 9—Document the Results

Supervisor's thoughts and actions—"Now, I want to note how I trained the two employees on the new procedure. Also, I learned that when I introduce a change in the future I want to be certain that everyone knows it and how to do it correctly."

Reminders—This documentation is particularly important with complex problems and complicated answers. Documentation helps overcome the natural tendency to solve new problems by repeating answers that worked for similar problems in the past by directing attention to the specifics of the past situation.

As was pointed out earlier, the intent here is to equip you with a structured problem-solving approach to use with operational and people problems. As you use the process and become proficient in it, you will find yourself doing some of the steps automatically. However, for large, more complex problems you should consciously perform each step.

Benefits of Structured Problem Solving

While specific problem-solving pitfalls will be treated in more detail later in the chapter, at this point it is appropriate to identify several pitfalls encountered in the training and coaching of nearly a thousand managers, supervisors, and technicians in using the structured approach. These problems included relocating a unit or department within an office, moving an office to a new location, integrating automation into a work flow, and absorbing relatively new positions such as full-time word processing operators into an existing department. The lessons learned follow.

Focus on Root Cause Without following a structured approach, supervisors and managers tended to respond to the apparent problem rather than to the root cause, frequently wasting time and other resources before getting back on the track.

Avoid Shortcuts Supervisors and managers were tempted to shortcut the step of identifying alternative solutions, often to the detriment of the overall process. While a supervisor should not interminably try to identify additional alternatives, he or she should be able to honestly assess whether this step has been completed thoroughly.

Documentation Supervisors or managers are reluctant to document results, drawn as they often are to new, more immediate concerns. This can be shortsighted. Often the supervisor or another key employee is transferred or promoted. If the problem reappears, it might be necessary to retrace all the steps, with the related waste in time, money, and other resources, not to mention the possible negative impact on customers and employees.

At this point you may want to apply the structured approach to an operational or people problem you face. For your convenience the steps are summarized on the accompanying worksheet, Exhibit 1-2.

CASE: ROBERTA McCARRAN

Situation

Roberta has been a commercial property underwriting supervisor for a year. Her department is located in the Chicago regional office of a national multi-line insurer. She reports to Marilyn Ferguson, the office's commercial property underwriting manager who directs Ms. McCarran and several other supervisors. The Chicago regional office processes business produced in nearly a dozen midwestern and north central states. The company's business is produced by independent agents and brokers.

Exhibit 1-2
Problem-Solving Worksheet

Major Steps	How Applied to My Problem
1. Describe the apparent problem.	1.
2. Gather facts.	2.
3. Identify the root cause.	3.
4. Identify the alternative solutions.	4.
5. Evaluate the alternative solutions.	5.
6. Select the best alternative.	6.
7. Implement the best alternative.	7.
8. Evaluate the results.	8.
9. Document the results.	9.

Roberta's unit underwrites business produced in Michigan, Indiana, and Illinois. She supervises four underwriters and two underwriting assistants. Clerical support is furnished by a separate service unit also reporting to Ms. Ferguson. Roberta's boss favors general rather than close supervision of her immediate subordinates. Because of changes in market conditions and the attractiveness of the company's pricing program for good grade risks, submissions to Roberta's unit have risen an overall 10 percent in the last six months. As a result, she finds herself spending a third of her time supervising and the remainder underwriting and doing other technical tasks. Roberta believes that if she spends any less time supervising, the overall unit will suffer.

Roberta occasionally suspects that she and some of her staff are not setting priorities effectively. She is particularly concerned now since one of her underwriters will begin an eight-week maternity leave in a month. Under company guidelines, Roberta's unit cannot hire a replacement for this period. While Roberta received formal supervisory training when appointed, she still does not feel skillful at some supervisory tasks. She wonders whether she should ask her manager for help on these matters. However, she hopes that she will have more time for other aspects of supervision once her newest underwriter becomes fully trained in three or four weeks. Another perceived

Exhibit 1-3
Unit Organizational Chart

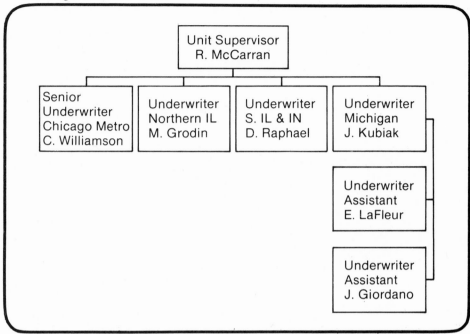

plus is the fact that the new underwriting assistant is halfway through the training period of approximately eight months.

Each underwriter in the unit is responsible for a specific territory, serving a number of producers in that territory. Over the years, for a variety of reasons, including economic, some underwriters have underwritten in more than one of the unit's territories. This has apparently been a successful tactic, meeting both the unit's operating needs and the employee's training and motivational needs. Each underwriter assistant serves two underwriters. Following the company's promote-from-within policy, an underwriting assistant has occasionally been promoted to underwriter either within the unit or in another one.

Before being appointed supervisor a year ago, Roberta was an underwriter in the same unit for four years. She started with the Southern Illinois and Indiana territory and took over the Chicago Metro desk two years later. She has completed nine of the ten parts of the CPCU program.

Roberta's unit organizational chart appears in Exhibit 1-3.

Thumbnail sketches of the staff follow. Carla Williamson, Senior Underwriter. Territory: Chicago Metro. Submissions in this territory have grown 12 percent in the last six months. Work Experience: Carla is the unit's most experienced underwriter. She has been a commercial property underwriter for ten years, five of them with a competitor. Ms. Williamson joined the unit five years ago, underwriting the Michigan territory. A year ago, she succeeded Roberta McCarran at the Chicago Metro desk.

She manages her time well. Though her territory has experienced significant growth in the last six months, she has absorbed the additional work. In fact, before the business increase, Carla told her supervisor that she felt somewhat underutilized. Carla and Roberta agree that the senior underwriter now has enough challenges. Other Information: Carla wants to remain in professional underwriting and has no desire to become a supervisor. She has completed half of the requirements for the CPCU designation.

Michael Grodin, Underwriter. Territory: Northern Illinois. Because of changes in agency representation in his territory, Michael's submissions have grown only 5 percent in the last six months. Work Experience: Michael is in his mid-twenties and came into the unit four years ago directly from a community college. He worked for fifteen months as an underwriting assistant. Mr. Grodin was promoted to underwriter and was trained on the Northern Illinois desk. In addition to his company training, he has completed the Program in General Insurance of the Insurance Institute of America. Other Information: Michael is ambitious and energetic. He hopes that his territory will eventually match the others in the increase in business. In the interim, he has asked Roberta several times if he could help in training either the newest underwriter or underwriting assistant since he has practical experience in both jobs. Grodin has done training in the unit before and is effective at it. He is somewhat puzzled by his supervisor's lack of response but puts it down to her preoccupation with the many demands on the unit that have occurred lately.

Debra Raphael, Underwriter. Territory: Southern Illinois and Indiana. Debra's submission increases have been the same as the unit average of 10 percent. Work Experience: She is in her late twenties and has six years' experience in underwriting commercial property business. Three years ago, Debra transferred into the unit as an experienced underwriter from another regional office and was assigned the Southern Illinois and Indiana territory. Many of her producers generate smaller and medium-sized risks unlike those of Carla Williamson of Chicago Metro. Ms. Raphael is considered a solid underwriter by her supervisor and her peers. Other Information: Debra is expecting her first child and has requested an eight-week maternity leave to begin in three to four weeks. Her work is current now and she expects it to be current when she begins her leave.

John Kubiak, Underwriter. Territory: Michigan. John's territory has the largest percentage increase in submission, approximately 13 percent. Work Experience: John is the newest underwriter in the unit, having joined it around a year ago. Roberta has been devoting much of her time to training him and helping him underwrite his increase in business. She believes that he will be fully trained in the next month. Kubiak is a college graduate with a bachelor's degree in business administration from a large midwestern university. Other Information: Roberta believes that John is bright and is progressing satisfactorily in his job. On his part, John is eagerly looking forward to having somewhat more autonomy in doing his underwriting work.

Elizabeth LaFleur, Underwriting Assistant. Territories: Elizabeth assists

Carla Williamson and Michael Grodin, the underwriters for Chicago Metro and Northern Illinois respectively. Work Experience: Elizabeth has been in the job for four years. Before that, she had another job in the regional office. Ms. LaFleur has been able to help Carla Williamson absorb her 12 percent business increase. In fact, Elizabeth can do much of the processing for smaller, less complex risks in both territories, freeing the underwriters to address tasks that only they can do. With her experience, Elizabeth still has discretionary time available. Other Information: As of now, she enjoys her job. She has not completely decided whether or not she wants to be an underwriter though she has completed the first part of the Program in General Insurance of the Insurance Institute of America.

James Giordano, Underwriting Assistant. Territories: Jim assists Debra Raphael and John Kubiak in underwriting the Southern Illinois, Indiana, and the Michigan territories respectively. Work Experience: Jim is the unit's newest member, having joined it four months ago. Before this, he had worked for a year in a bank but decided he wanted to get into the commercial part of the property and casualty insurance business. Mr. Giordano feels particularly challenged by the fact that the Michigan territory has had the largest percentage increase in submissions in the unit. Other Information: He is understandably wondering how Debra Raphael's upcoming two-month leave of absence will affect his role as underwriting assistant for that territory.

It is time now to analyze these facts. We suggest that you use the Problem-Solving Worksheet. Accordingly, your first challenge is to determine the major problems faced by Roberta McCarran.

Analysis

Now let's analyze the case. You should compare your analysis with the one that follows. We'll comment on each of the major problem-solving steps in turn.

1. Describe the apparent problem

There are actually several apparent operational and people problems here:

    a. How to continue to process the increase in submissions that has occurred in the unit over the last six months.

    b. How to underwrite the Southern Illinois and Indiana territory during Ms. Raphael's two-month leave without hiring a replacement.

    c. How to ensure that John Kubiak completes his underwriter training and Jim Giordano completes his training as an underwriting assistant.

2. Gather the facts

As you analyzed the case, you should have noted certain points, including these:

    a. Carla Williamson is apparently fully challenged now and appears capable of staying up with the increase in business in her territory.

    b. Michael Grodin's submission increase is below the unit's average for various reasons. He apparently has time available to perform other tasks and seems willing to do so.

        (1) He is competent to help on several facets of the problem because
- (a) he has training experience.
- (b) he has prior experience as an underwriting assistant and could conceivably help train Jim Giordano, the new assistant.
- (c) his experience as an underwriting assistant included the Southern Illinois and Indiana territory. This is the territory currently underwritten by Debra Raphael, who will be going on leave in three or four weeks.

  c. John Kubiak, the newest underwriter, will complete his training in a month.

  d. Elizabeth LaFleur, the experienced underwriting assistant for the Chicago Metro and Northern Illinois territories, is capable of doing much of the processing for smaller, less complex risks. Further, she appears to have occasional free time available.

  e. Jim Giordano, the newer underwriting assistant, should complete his training in approximately four months.

3. Identify the root cause

Roberta already intuitively suspects that she and some of her staff are not setting priorities and following up on them as well as they could. Incidentally, this is not an uncommon experience. The person involved in the problem often experiences vague feelings of unease that can point in the right direction for solving or reducing the problem. This is the root cause, masked by the increase in the unit's business, the need to train Kubiak and Giordano, and the upcoming maternity leave for Ms. Raphael.

4. Identify the alternative solutions

Basically, Roberta has two main alternatives:

  a. She can increase her technical involvement in the unit by underwriting a large share of the business in Debra Raphael's Southern Illinois and Indiana territory until Raphael returns. She can also continue her role as the primary trainer for John Kubiak and Jim Giordano or,

  b. She can increase her ability to identify unit priorities and increase her discretionary time by such tactics as
- (1) determining if she can delegate to Michael Grodin some of Raphael's underwriting while she's away.
- (2) determining if she can delegate to Elizabeth LaFleur the processing of some smaller risks of which there are a number in Raphael's territory.
- (3) exploring the possibility of whether Michael Grodin can help to train John Kubiak during the last month of the latter's training.
- (4) exploring the possibility of whether Grodin and/or LaFleur can assume the primary role for training John Giordano under Roberta's general direction.
- (5) finally, and this might be the first thing to do, seek coaching help on setting priorities, delegating, and managing time from her

manager, Marilyn Ferguson. It's not unusual for a supervisor with a year's experience to need such coaching.

5. Evaluate the alternative solutions

Referring to the earlier example of an evaluation worksheet, Roberta's second main alternative, that is, identifying priorities, delegating as much as possible, and having others take over the primary responsibility for the training of the newer people, seems preferable to deeper technical involvement on her part.

This preferred alternative should meet most criteria—probability of success, cost, amount of time needed, and simplicity. Further, if Ms. McCarran does not challenge the obvious skills and abilities of Grodin and LaFleur, she could run the risk of demotivating them to some degree, further adding to her problem.

6. Select the best alternative

At this point, let's assume that Roberta selects the second main alternative, that of identifying priorities and delegating tasks including training. In a sense, if a supervisor has done the prior steps thoroughly, this step, the decision itself, can often seem relatively straight-forward, even anti-climactic.

7. Implement the best alternative

Here, Ms. McCarran would have to meet with staff members, individually and as a group, to pin down the specific accountabilities that will be changed. This includes fully utilizing Michael Grodin and Elizabeth LaFleur's abilities in underwriting and processing tasks while Raphael is away. Similarly, if the two people are to take on expanded training roles concerning Kubiak and Giordano, this will have to be spelled out in detail. Further, Roberta will want to ensure that Debra Raphael's work remains current up to the time she begins her leave. Finally, she will want to communicate with her manager as to which employees are responsible for what tasks, what authority they have, and any applicable time targets established. As part of this communication, Roberta should seek appropriate coaching from her boss.

8. Evaluate the results

This will be an ongoing process through the period of the increase in business, Raphael's leave of absence, and the training of the newer people. Again, this will demand continued communication among the supervisor, her staff, and her manager. While many of the reports will be informal, oral ones, it is conceivable that the people involved will occasionally report significant happenings in writing.

9. Document the results

Key events or information should be noted in written form. At the end of the period, Roberta should give a brief written report to her manager, Ms. Ferguson. This will be a ready reference for use when similar problems occur.

To summarize, the problems that Roberta McCarran faces are representative of those challenging many supervisors every day in the contemporary insurance environment of vigorous competition and the necessity to accomplish objectives with a lean staff and the prudent use of other resources.

INTUITION AND LOGIC IN PROBLEM SOLVING

In addition to the major steps of problem solving and the supporting techniques of analysis and synthesis, you should be aware of your unique personal orientation to problem solving, that is, whether you tend to follow a logical or intuitive approach. We pointed out earlier that while no special aptitudes were required to solve problems, supervisors in such number-oriented activities as accounting, statistics, computer, and systems analysis often tend to analyze problems logically or systematically. In contrast, supervisors in such fields as sales and marketing tend toward an intuitive orientation, often applying quick insight to a problem.

Both approaches have their advantages and disadvantages. In the McCarran case, for example, we found that from the very beginning Roberta intuitively suspected that her ability to identify and set unit priorities was not what it should be. Later she complemented this intuition by applying the logic of the structured approach to her problems.

Incidentally, supervisors who freely use an intuitive approach often disconcert their more logically oriented peers. They sometimes inexplicably and correctly respond to hunches. For example, in the earlier analysis of the need for time-competitive rate quotes, an intuitively oriented supervisor could ascertain in an instant that the delay is being caused by the underwriting assistant since the latter tends to double check and triple check the work, sometimes unnecessarily. However, intuitively oriented supervisors can occasionally approach problems in a haphazard way—for example, by failing to adequately explore all reasonable alternative solutions since they initially perceive some solutions as tedious.

Of course, in the everyday world, supervisors like Roberta use both orientations in solving problems. However, many supervisors tend to favor either the intuitive or the logical approach when confronted with a problem. Which do you prefer? Is your preference so strong that your decision making is adversely affected? If so, we suggest two remedies: (1) force yourself to spend a few minutes consciously following the unfamiliar approach on important decisions and (2) check your reasoning with another supervisor or manager who has a different orientation.

INDIVIDUAL VERSUS GROUP PROBLEM SOLVING

The McCarran case illustrates both of these aspects of problem solving. For example, Roberta would have to do some of the prior analysis by herself such as determining how much of her time she was spending training the two newer employees. However, later she would depend on the ideas and actions of others, both her staff and her manager, to solve or address facets of the problem. For example, she would need to get estimates from Michael Grodin and Elizabeth LaFleur as to how much discretionary time they have available. Certainly, she'd need to consider the suggestions or recommendations of her boss on how to approach the problem. Thus, Roberta's problem actually involved, or could involve, a group of people; her manager; herself; and her staff. This is not uncommon.

Not surprisingly, both the individual and group approaches to problem solving have advantages and disadvantages. Let's consider the individual approach first. What do you think the pluses and minuses are?

Individual Approach

Advantages

1. Rapid
   For example, a claim supervisor observes that claim frequency for a certain class of risk is above what it historically has been. He or she can then immediately concentrate on those risks and identify factors contributing to the increased frequency.
2. Direct and focused
   Continuing the example, the claims supervisor, relying on experience and knowledge, need not diffuse efforts by examining the other claims, those that are performing according to expectations.
3. No need to compromise
   Once the claims supervisor has mentally worked through the problem-solving steps, he or she can either take specific remedial action directly or can recommend that it be taken.

Disadvantages

1. May waste time
   In the previous example, the supervisor could initially misdiagnose the problem and then waste time performing the subsequent steps in problem solving. Like flying solo, individual decision making can mean proceeding a great distance before discovering a navigational error.
2. May focus too narrowly on the problem
   Continuing the example, if the supervisor responds exclusively to what is apparently wrong, he or she may overlook other related aspects of the problem such as improper recording of claims or a change in underwriting criteria.
3. The decision maker may be unaware of relevant information. Rarely will any single individual have sufficient knowledge to solve complex problems alone.

Group Problem Solving

Advantages

1. Increased knowledge and skill
2. Varied viewpoints

3. Greater understanding of the problem

One of the techniques that groups can use in addressing operational or people problems is brainstorming. This approach encourages the spontaneous contribution of ideas from all members. Initially, at least, no ideas are ruled out, no matter how improbable. Successful brainstorming, by its very nature, will require a leader or facilitator wise enough not to stifle ideas no matter how unrelated they first appear.

4. Greater probability of accepting the decision

When employees have had a voice in making a decision, they are likely to carry it out more willingly, show imagination in its implementation, and sell it to other employees. For some decisions, acceptance may be as important or even more important than the quality of the decision.

Disadvantages

Now, what are the disadvantages of group problem solving? In some cases they can actually spring from a purported advantage.

1. Aiming for the lowest common denominator
   In an effort to please all or the majority of group members, the group may accept a solution that does not address the problem or please anyone.
2. Time
   Some groups, for a variety of reasons, simply take too long to solve a problem or to make a decision. Even at its best, group decision making takes time, if only because of the time needed to hear all contributions. In addition, groups must work through what are usually called group dynamics issues: power, leadership, ways of behaving and contributing, and how decisions are to be made.
3. Group think
   Some group members may be reluctant to challenge the apparent "consensus" of group thinking with an individual idea that actually might more appropriately address a specific problem. Another factor is the propensity of some newer, less experienced members to be unduly influenced by persons of high status or expertise. Thus, a relatively inexperienced supervisor might be unduly swayed by the glibness of another member or by the formidable technical knowledge displayed by a data processing specialist.

To summarize, you will find that you will use both the individual and group approach to problems, sometimes in combination. When acceptance of a decision is critical, the group method is almost always used.

REPORTING RESULTS

Usually you, either as an individual, or occasionally as part of a group, will have to communicate either how you solved a problem or what recommendations you have to solve it. Very often, in a simple problem, a brief oral report to your manager will suffice. The critical factor here is to first analyze your audience, and then communicate at their level of understanding.

However, in more complex problems, a written report may be required. This in turn will include, or at least refer to, the evaluation and documentation of the result you achieved. Again, you should analyze your audience beforehand. If the report is to be circulated above the level of your manager or laterally to other departments, or to "users" of your product or service, you may want to begin the report with a relatively brief nontechnical summary. You can then follow this with a concise listing of your recommendations and the reasons for them. You should preferably place any technical reference material in an appendix at the end of the report. If appropriate, you may want to include a brief glossary of technical terms or abbreviations along with a bibliography of reference sources.

PITFALLS IN PROBLEM SOLVING

Earlier we briefly mentioned some pitfalls faced by supervisors confronted with a problem. We also identified some of the disadvantages of the individual and the group problem solving methods. Let's now examine these pitfalls in more detail in terms of the major problem-solving steps and then comment on the problem involved.

We will illustrate these pitfalls by eavesdropping. We'll quote statements you might make or hear from other supervisors.

These pitfalls fall into two general types: failure to use knowledge of how to solve problems and failure to accept responsibility for the problem and its solution.

1. Statement

"The loss ratio problem will go away by itself."

You are likely to be making an unwarranted assumption at this point. You have to first thoroughly gather the facts and then determine the root cause. Some problems do fade away, but most remain or get worse.

2. Statement

"This homeowners claim problem is identical to the one we had last year."

This may be only apparently so. Further investigation may identify different circumstances and details of the problem. The highlights may be similar, but two problems are rarely identical.

3. Statement

"We have always typed manuscript policies this way. 'They' would not like it changed."

You have jumped to a solution (or eliminated an alternative) without the analysis.

4. Statement

"We do not have enough marketing information to solve it completely so I won't do anything now."

This appears to be another unwarranted assumption. The quantity and quality of information should be weighed carefully, not assumed quickly.

5. Statement

"I will wait until the collection problem gets worse; then it will be easier to understand."

The problem may become more complex with the possibility that you will have to use much more time and other resources to solve it. It is true that a decision maker often waits for a problem to ripen. However, the justification may be one of two reasons: (1) to verify its existence or (2) to give others a chance to recognize it and, as a result, to accept the solution. If these reasons do not apply, delaying is probably unwise.

6. Statement

"I will wait until everyone else recognizes that it is a problem so that my solution will be accepted more easily."

True, it is often wise to wait for a problem to be widely seen *as a problem*. However, you do not need to wait for everyone. Also, you must recognize that the problem could worsen.

7. Statement

"Once we get the microcomputer and the software package, the error should disappear."

The computer by itself is not a substitute for your applying the various steps. In fact, it could compound the problem unless you do the necessary upfront analytical thinking.

8. Statement

"I will wait until my boss sees the coding problem and gives me an idea of how she would like it handled."

An alert boss knows that you are closer to the problem and he or she will expect your recommendations on how to approach it.

9. Statement

"I do not see it as a communication problem (because I probably caused it)."

Eventually, someone—your manager, peers, employees, or others—will probably link you with the problem. Why not take the initiative now with your analysis and recommendations?

10. Statement

"I did not cause the backlog problem, so why should I handle it now?"

Your boss will realistically expect your constructive suggestions.

11. Statement

"Once the systems analyst gets here, he can take over. I am just a systems user."

Many systems analysts will justifiably expect you, as a user, to frame problems and define objectives.

12. Statement

"It is also happening in the policywriting unit (maybe someone else will handle it)."

Again, your manager expects you to cooperate by making constructive suggestions.

In summarizing this chapter on problem solving, the key is to use what you have learned so that it will become almost a reflex action when you are confronted with a problem. You may want to photocopy the major problem-solving steps listed in this chapter and keep them handy.

Chapter Notes

1. Robert Kreitner, *Management: A Problem Solving Process* (Boston: Houghton Mifflin Co., 1980), p. 55.
2. Kreitner, p. 74.
3. Kreitner, p. 65.

CHAPTER 2

The Functions of Management

INTRODUCTION

Describing what you do as a supervisor is something like describing what an automobile does when it moves. There are so many things happening all at once that the view from any vantage point will always be inadequate. Nonetheless, there is a time-honored way of depicting the work of a manager or supervisor. This classic view sets forth four functions of management. Although the functions are usually called management functions, they fully apply to first level supervision. Indeed, this chapter could have been titled "The Functions of Supervision." We chose to use the word management in the title to emphasize your role in the overall management of the organization.

Four Functions of Management

The four functions of management and supervision are:

- Planning—determining what is to be done
- Organizing—creating the organizational structure and arranging the use of resources to achieve objectives
- Directing—giving instructions that accomplish the work
- Controlling—seeing to it that the planned results are achieved

Management as a Process

These brief statements do not begin to suggest the richness of the four functions of management and supervision. The functions constitute an ongoing process: an unending stream of activities that unify the efforts of others. Indeed, the essence of the functional approach is the emphasis on the continuous and interrelated nature of the things managers and supervisors do when they manage. The subjects treated as separate chapters in this text and its companion volume can all be placed within the four functions or can be said to apply in carrying them out. The four functions, then, serve as an all-encompassing framework that summarizes all of the many things you do as supervisor.

Although it has achieved classic status, the planning-organizing-directing-controlling framework is not the only one to be found in textbooks. Some authors prefer to divide the pie into more slices. Staffing sometimes appears as a fifth function rather than as part of organizing. Communicating is sometimes listed as a basic function. Directing is sometimes called leading or implementing. We think it best to follow the mainstream and will examine the continuous process of managing others in terms of the four major functions.

This chapter will not give equal space to the four functions. Doing so would mean duplication of material elsewhere in this book and in *Essentials of Supervision*. Instead, we will favor topics not covered in other chapters as we examine each major function. Thus hiring and other staffing activities receive particular attention in this survey of the four interwoven functions of managing.

Illustrations of Imbalance

If you overemphasize one function and neglect others, problems are inevitable. Like links in a chain, each function is equally vital. The amount of time you spend on any function is not an accurate indication of overemphasis or neglect. Many supervisors spend half or more of their time directing. Organizing often receives the least amount of time. The proper balance must reflect the particular work and problems of your unit. Let us look at some examples of poor balance.

Too Much Control Pouring over computer printouts and other control reports may be a sign of overconcentration on the control function. Do you spend a good part of each day scanning reports and searching for signs of poor performance? Do you find yourself looking again and again for ways to improve performance reports, perhaps in minute detail?

Tom, an underwriting supervisor, focuses on control to an extreme. He reads most of the files, often staying late to do what he mistakenly considers "work sampling." Members of Tom's unit see him as the EXPERT who wants everything done his way. They think that he ignores them as people because his nose is always buried in paperwork. They rarely stay more than two or three years in Tom's unit before transferring elsewhere. Other supervisors in the company like to have people transfer from Tom's unit. As one said, "Tom's people are well trained and when they get here they are so happy about the way they are treated that they give 120%."

Overly People-Centered Cynthia cares deeply about the members of her unit. She likes to spend ten or fifteen minutes a day with each of her nine subordinates. She thrives on face-to-face communication and is sincerely convinced that employees welcome her interest in them. None has the courage to tell her that her lengthy chats are not always welcomed. On some days they would prefer to concentrate on their duties, especially if backlogs or deadlines are pressing. In making her daily rounds, Cynthia reduces the time they have for deskwork activities. It seems likely that she does not give full attention to planning, organizing, and controlling.

Insufficient Planning   George believes that planning is something done at higher levels of the organization. He perceives the role of supervisor as "making the machine run smoothly." Basically, he believes that managers make changes and supervisors carry them out. George has an excellent reputation as a supervisor—he is a person "who gets things done." Associates commend him for "running a tight ship." What they do not see is that George never innovates.

PLANNING

The major activities of the planning function are these:

1. Forecasting—analyzing internal and external forces that will affect your unit in the future
2. Setting objectives
3. Developing action plans to meet objectives

While these same activities are performed at higher organizational levels, they are essential responsibilities of the first line supervisor. Your forecasts reflect those prepared at levels above your unit. The objectives you set intermesh with those set elsewhere in the organization. If corporate and divisional objectives are to be met, unit objectives must play a role of direct support. If units are to move forward at the same pace, you must coordinate with peer supervisors when setting unit goals.

Forecasting

Forecasting serves two major purposes: it helps you to anticipate changes and it helps you to prepare for formal planning. To highlight the value of forecasting, let us contrast the *proactive* and the *reactive* supervisor. Being proactive means that you take action on your own, before events require you to react. A reactive supervisor is trapped, waiting for outside forces to initiate change. A proactive supervisor asserts initiative and acts in anticipation of changes. For example, Sam, an underwriting unit supervisor, was convinced that computer-assisted underwriting would never come about. Sam was shocked when his manager told him that an automated system would be installed in his unit. Sam was unable to contribute to decisions about the installation process as his resentment added to his lack of knowledge about computers. Later Sam was sorry that he did not become computer literate "just in case." Sam regretted that he seemed to be "out of the picture" when automation arrived in his unit.

How to Forecast

Gather Information   The sources of information are virtually unlimited. For example:

> Magazines and newspaper articles often identify changes in the economy, industry, and society
> Trade publications such as the *National Underwriter* shed light on the future of insurance lines and insurance organizations
> Internal reports suggest trends within your organization
> The people around you, in everyday conversations, portray their expectations and hopes for the days ahead

Obviously there are more sources of relevant information. The trick is not in finding information; it is in recognizing the usefulness of the information that already comes your way.

Analyze the Information   Analysis refines information and assigns it meaning. Analysis puts facts in perspective and applies them to the insurance business, to your organization, and to your unit.

Here are illustrations of the kinds of questions that contribute to an analysis for forecasting purposes:

> What events or changes in society are likely to influence the insurance industry, my firm, the firms with which we do business, my department?
> What are the trends within the insurance industry?
> What are competitors doing now and what do I think they will do in the future?
> What opportunities—and problems—are being created by automation?
> Where is my organization headed? What goals and values drive it?
> What changes do I anticipate within my unit? What do I think my unit will be like in three years?

Analysis, then, is a search for applications of information to your organization and unit. It is a fallacy to think that such analysis is the province of specialists. True, some organizations have "think tanks" inhabited by persons with impressive credentials, imposing vocabularies, and impregnable conclusions. Their number-crunching and horizon-gazing has obvious value. However, they tend to grab the spotlight and hide the fact that managers and supervisors throughout the organization create and use forecasts.

Make Predictions   Making predictions probably seems the most difficult part of forecasting since many of the forces that cause change are not predictable. Perhaps the most useful question is one we have already seen: how will my unit look a few years from now?

A prediction does not have to be presented as a single image. Forecasters often think in terms of three possible futures: pessimistic, probable, and optimistic. They often express an outlook in terms of the probability that something will occur. (It may be pouring outside the studio, but the radio weather forecaster tells us there is an eighty percent chance of rain.) One supervisor thought that there was a sixty to seventy percent chance of unit business declining because of market conditions. He decided not to replace a departing employee immediately, but committed to requesting a replacement if business failed to decline in each of the next three months. His "sixty to seventy percent chance" estimate was the basis for a sound supervisory decision.

Developing Objectives

Objectives stipulate what an organization wants to achieve in the future. Objectives are often based on predictions but they are quite different in nature. If a prediction tells what you *expect* to happen in the future, an objective captures what you *want* to happen in the future. An objective expresses what you want to *make* happen. In most instances an objective will not occur without benefit of the efforts you will mobilize.

Format Objectives are desired end results. They are expressed as written statements that describe a condition which will exist at a stipulated time. For instance, an objective is "to reduce unit expenses by $2\frac{1}{2}\%$ by December 31st." The format for stating an objective is this:

ACTION VERB + NOUN + TARGET DATE

where the NOUN is the desired result.

Is a goal the same thing as an objective? For our purposes, yes. Some planning systems distinguish between objectives and goals by the time frame involved or by the organizational level at which they are established. The business world lacks a uniform vocabulary of planning, and we will consider goals and objectives to be the same.

Performance Standards and Objectives Compared Performance standards bear a resemblance to objectives in that they are also statements of conditions that will exist when efforts have been successful. For example:

A supervisor will have done a good job when he or she:
1. Develops, maintains, and conducts on-the-job training so that all employees perform to standard within six months of hire.
2. Maintains updated performance standards for each position within the unit.

Performance standards define "how well" each important aspect of the job should be performed on an ongoing basis. If the standards are correctly written and the tasks do not change, the standards will remain the same year after year. Objectives have target dates; performance standards do not. (However, both the performance and the performance standards are likely to be evaluated at least once a year.) Consider the following two objectives which have the same subject matter as the performance standards above:

A supervisor will:

1. Revise the on-the-job training program for new employees by June 1.
2. Update all unit performance standards by August 15.

A comparison of these objectives with the performance standards given previously should make clear the distinction between them. It should also highlight the character of objectives as statements of what is to be new and different in the future. In some firms all employees have performance standards, while only supervisors and managers have objectives.

Objectives and Motivation   We use standards and objectives in our personal lives in order to give ourselves direction and a push in that direction. We use both: for example, "I should keep my weight below 165 pounds" and "lose ten pounds by Thanksgiving." That objectives motivate is a key reason for their undisputed value. All of us like having a target to shoot at and we like the satisfaction of hitting it. Organizations capitalize on the motivational power of objectives by giving them a central role in the planning process.

Management by Objectives (MBO)

MBO is an approach to management which requires objectives to be set by each manager and supervisor, from the chief executive to the first-line supervisors. Often technical positions are included if these employees are project oriented or have freedom to select alternatives. At the end of a specific period of time (usually a year), actual results are compared to objectives, corrective action is taken, if necessary, and the cycle is repeated. Quarterly or semi-annual interim reviews are commonly required.

Management by Objectives has other names: Management by Objectives and Results (MOR), Management by Results (MR), and Accountability Management. The basic concepts defined in this chapter for MBO are equally applicable to MOR, MR, and accountability management, although the other varieties of MBO may use a slightly different vocabulary and add certain enhancements. Many firms do not have a formal MBO program, yet they still follow the concepts and process of MBO in their planning.

In practice every organization has its own way of applying the concepts of Management by Objectives. After reading this chapter, find out how your company develops objectives and formulates plans.

DEFINING MBO

Management by Objectives—MBO—is not easy to describe. The concepts of MBO mean different things to different organizations. Some organizations see MBO as a movement, others view it as a procedure, others as a means of motivation; and some organizations consider it a way of life within their organizations.

The core activity in any MBO program is the formulating of objectives. Throughout the organization the key players (those who have the freedom to act within their jobs) are asked to identify a number of major objectives for a period of time, usually a year. These objectives are discussed with one's superior and refined so that they coordinate with objectives being set by others. The final result is a pyramid of goals, each meshing with and contributing to those set elsewhere in the organization. Each individual has a strong say in the objectives that will guide his or her activities for months to come. This should maximize the person's commitment and drive. However, the freedom to set objectives is counterbalanced by the preliminary objectives and planning information that flow down the chain of command and by review discussions with one's manager.

This sounds straightforward and simple. Why, then, has there been controversy over MBO? The power of MBO seems to come from the notion that your objectives become a kind of performance agreement with your boss. When MBO is properly executed, the boss should leave you free to accomplish your objectives in your own way. As long as you follow organizational policies, you are on your own to achieve the results you have committed yourself to produce. The controversy is often over how much freedom superiors allow their subordinates in setting objectives and determining the means of implementing them. Superiors use, monitor, and control objectives in different ways. Some rely heavily on objectives. Unfortunately, a few file them away in desk drawers and review them sporadically. MBO seems to be only as effective as managers want it to be.

MBO can be a way of life and, in a sense, a motivational system. By limiting the number of objectives, MBO forces you to concentrate on the most important job results. As you concentrate your energy on achieving the critical results, you delegate the routine parts of your job to your subordinates, much to their liking. You should find yourself doing better things rather than doing things better. You trust yourself, and your associates, to handle the lesser matters as you focus on critical goals. MBO asks you to believe in yourself and in others.

Does MBO work? Results appear mixed. Some research suggests that MBO often has disappointing results. Since each organization adapts the MBO fundamentals and creates its own version, we should be skeptical of generalizations. Nonetheless, there is no doubt that the spread of MBO systems in the 1950s and 1960s has left a lasting mark on organizational life. That mark is a most welcome one: the idea that it is better for supervisors to concentrate on achieving results rather than on specifying the detailed activities to be performed.

The Planning Cycle

Many organizations start the annual planning cycle in the fall, so that the whole process can be completed by January of the next year. As the planning process begins, the long-range objectives set last year are reviewed and updated. The finished product is usually published, perhaps in booklet form. A common format is this one:

- Forecasts: Trends and conditions, both internal and external are explained. Sometimes the forecast is titled "scenario."
- Long-term or long-range objectives for more than a year usually up to five years.
- Annual objectives: These tend to be more specific than the long-term objectives.
- Action Plans: Action plans show how the long-term and/or annual objectives will be met. Often longer-term plans are called strategies and supporting lower level plans are called tactics, but strategies and tactics are only other names for action plans. Each organization develops its own vocabulary.

As the planning sequence proceeds, top management will usually issue a notebook or booklet containing the tentative corporate plan. Each department, division, region, or branch will also develop a plan, possibly called operating plans.

Combining Top-down and Bottom-up Objective Setting

Objectives, both long- and short-term, are set from the top down and bottom up. This means that the top executives usually start the planning process by developing preliminary long- and short-term corporate objectives. These objectives are then sent to the next level of management to use as a guide in setting objectives. This process continues to the first line supervisors. Then the upward process begins as objectives are sent from the supervisors up through the various levels of management to the corporate level. As information flows up, objectives are reviewed and refined. The end result should be a pyramid of objectives that blends the vision of the top level executives with the practical concerns and commitments of managers and supervisors throughout the firm.

A basic principle in this process is that lower level objectives must support and implement higher level objectives. This is achieved through review by a higher management level and through negotiations. For example, a sales manager says he can only achieve an 8 percent premium growth in a certain line of insurance for the year because of competitive conditions. His manager wants a 14 percent growth in premium. They discuss the specific obstacles, resources, and tactics involved in reaching the sales volume. They may reach a compromise after a probing analysis that is itself a goal of the planning process.

Objectives and plans should be more than an annual writing exercise. The written plans serve as documentation of the agreements reached.

Criteria of Effective Objectives

To be effective, objectives should meet the following criteria:

1. Define specific end results to be achieved
2. State target dates
3. Establish specific measures
4. Are realistic, but challenging
5. Cover critical areas
6. Support higher level objectives

1. Define End Results   Objectives are concise, simple sentences which define the end result to be achieved by a specific target date.

NOT THIS: Design and write an on-the-job training program to train experienced employees how to rate homeowners or auto policies, which ever one they don't know. Select one employee to do the cross training.

BUT THIS: Develop a new cross training program for raters by March 1.
Select and train an employee to assist in the cross training by March 1.
Complete cross training by July 1.

2. State Target Dates   The second set of objectives defines end results and gives a completion date. Target dates are essential or objectives may be postponed or downgraded in priority. Often one objective must be met prior to another objective. Without target dates, objectives are only good intentions.

3. Establish Specific Measures   Objectives should be stated in such a way that it is possible to know if and when the end results were achieved. How measurable are these objectives?

1. Improve productivity within the unit by the end of the year.
2. Reduce turnaround time for new business by July 1.
3. Improve quality by July 1.

How will anyone know when these objectives have been met? They leave too many questions unanswered. For example, how is the supervisor going to measure increases in productivity? What is the desired turnaround time? How is quality going to be measured, or whose opinion of quality will serve as the test?

Since these objectives are so general as to be almost useless, let us add measurements:

1. Increase productivity by 6 percent as measured by transaction per employee by September 15.
2. Achieve a turnaround time of three days for all new business by July 1.
3. Achieve an error ratio of 2 percent by July 1.

These specific measures may be stated in terms of either quantity or quality. Following are examples of quantity and quality measures used in objectives. You add these measures only if necessary.

Quantity Measures.   These measures are stated in terms of percentages, numbers, or dollars.

Quality Measures.   These define how well something is done and can contain numbers. For example:

> Develop and implement a means of improving communications between the clerical and underwriting units by end of the year. This objective will be achieved when there are zero complaints by staff in either unit about the lack of needed information.

4. Are Realistic, But Challenging   To be realistic, objectives must be attainable. To stimulate personal growth, they must present some challenge and require extra effort. Objectives set too low can be easily achieved and support the status quo, not growth. Sometimes supervisors are afraid to set objectives which they might have difficulty meeting because they are afraid of failure. This is unfortunate because objectives set too low fail to bring out the best in a person.

Objectives consistently set too high are also meaningless and can become discouraging. As a rough rule of thumb, you should achieve about seventy percent of your objectives over the year. As in target practice, if you keep hitting the bull's-eye you are standing too close. Sure-thing goals also do not bring out the best in you.

5. Cover Critical Areas   Objectives can never cover the entire job of a supervisor. Objectives need to be set only in those critical areas where increased effort will make a difference. Areas where critical objectives are commonly set by supervisors are:

- Support for higher level objectives
- Work processing time
- Quality improvement
- Training
- Expense reduction
- Staffing
- Methods and work flow improvements
- Service
- Updating, revising or developing manuals and forms
- Conducting research and submitting reports

If the supervisor has a sales responsibility, the premium volume, new business, and renewal business will always be a critical area for setting objectives.

There are a variety of ways to determine the critical areas where objectives are needed.

- Review objectives your manager is setting for the year and identify those objectives you must directly support.
- Ask unit members to identify those things which hamper their work efforts.
- Ask unit members to recommend improvements which would allow them to get better results.
- Ask yourself what would constitute optimal results in your unit and choose one or more obstacles which need to be overcome to reach these results.

6. Support Higher Level Objectives If all the objectives of supervisors and managers form the corporation's annual and long-range plan, then lower level objectives must support and implement higher level objectives. For example, a manager sets these three objectives which must be supported and implemented by the technical and clerical supervisors:

1. Improve turnaround time for new business to seven days by July 1.
2. Increase renewal rate by 8 percent over last year by sending out renewal notices 60 days before due date, to be accomplished by December 31.
3. Reduce error ratio to 2 percent by March 1.

Clerical supervisor's objectives:

1. Implement a productivity study and analysis and submit recommendations for improving turnaround time by March 1.
2. Achieve a turnaround time of three days for all new business by July 1.
3. Design and pilot test a new cross training program for raters by March 31.
4. Select and train an employee to be able to assist in cross training by March 31.
5. Complete cross training by July 1.

Technical supervisor's objectives:

1. Achieve a turnaround time of four days for new business by July 1.
2. Have all renewals prepared and mailed at least 60 days before due date by July 1.
3. Design and implement a new quality control program by February 1.
4. Achieve an error ratio of 2 percent by March 1.

As you can see, the manager will not meet her objectives unless the two supervisors also meet their objectives. Note also that the clerical and technical supervisor's objectives support each other.

Developing Action Plans

Unless action plans are developed to implement objectives, the objectives are likely to remain only good intentions.

Some objectives may require only a one-step action plan, while others may be more detailed and complex. An action plan should:

- Define tasks or activities to be completed.
- Identify who is to do what.
- Identify check points and target dates.

Common Pitfalls in Planning

Following is a list of the common pitfalls to avoid when planning and formulating objectives.

Creative Writing Exercise   If objectives are not discussed and integrated, and participation is not encouraged, the objectives are likely to be annual creative writing exercises and nothing more.

Cast in Concrete   If objectives are not revised when priorities change during the year, they will be evaluated as irrelevant and ignored.

Failure to Develop Action Plans   Without action plans, objectives are only good intentions.

Failure to Reflect Long-Term Needs   There is a tendency to favor short-term objectives and those which are easily measured, sometimes to the point of neglecting long-range issues.

Failure to Provide Rewards for Meeting Objectives   Salary and promotion decisions should reflect accomplishment of objectives.

Objectives as a Way of Managing

Supervisors often use objectives in ways that are not part of their organization's MBO or planning program. Some examples follow.

Objectives in Giving Assignments   Whenever you give an assignment to a subordinate, you should first define the objectives: the end result the subordinate is to achieve.

Developmental Objectives   As you will see in the chapter on performance appraisal, a formal appraisal system often results in developmental objectives which define what the employee should do to improve present performance or prepare for future career growth.

Improvement Objectives   One of the results of a disciplinary discussion should be an improvement objective which defines what the subordinate must do to bring performance up to an acceptable level. An action plan should show what steps the subordinate must take and what the supervisor will do to assist the subordinate in meeting the objective. A review date must be established to define the time the subordinate has for improving performance.

Instructional Objectives All training programs, on-the-job training, classroom or self-study courses should have objectives which define what the "student" should be able to do as a result of the training course. For example, note the instructional objectives at the beginning of each assignment of the Course Guide which accompanies this text.

Summary on Planning

Rather than thinking "What activities should I perform or should my subordinates perform?" the supervisor should look at every opportunity in terms of "What results are needed?" Setting objectives establishes a cycle of managing which also includes action plans, monitoring progress, and taking corrective action when needed. This serves as the basis for the control function which we will discuss next. An organization-wide system of planning by establishing objectives:

1. Provides the organization with integrated short and long range plans to help cope with change, to grow, and to innovate.
2. Helps managers and supervisors to plan and control results in their departments.
3. Encourages participation and involvement and encourages employees to be committed to achieving results.
4. Encourages managers and supervisors to communicate about expected results rather than activities.
5. Encourages creativity and innovation, because objectives are future oriented.

ORGANIZING

Some organizations do not have organization charts or position guides, yet everyone knows what the formal structure looks like, what titles people have, and what tasks and responsibilities employees perform. Organizing is a process of coordinating resources, and these visible signs should not be confused with the process itself.

As a supervisor, you are required to work within an existing formal structure and have little say about how your firm is designed. However, you do have extensive organizing responsibilities. You must maintain and improve, if not develop, work flows and methods for getting the work out. Often you must update position guides, clarify what needs to be done, assign work, and recommend expanding or reducing staff. Thus you take part in the process of organizing.

We consider staffing part of the organizing function, although some management books classify it as a fifth managerial function. Staffing involves recruiting, interviewing, and selecting new employees and selecting employees for promotion.

Organization Structure

Organization Charts   The formal structure defines, often in writing, the way the parts fit together to form the whole organization. The organization chart is the most obvious depiction of the structure of an organization. It serves as a snapshot of a moving object. It shows:

1. Authority levels
2. Responsibilities and accountabilities
3. Departments
4. Relationships

A sample organization chart for a small branch office of an insurance company is shown in Exhibit 2-1.

There are other ways that this office might be organized. For example, there might be a personal lines department and a commercial lines department, each combining the underwriting and marketing functions. The rating unit might be part of the underwriting department rather than reporting to the office services manager.

Elements of Organization Structure   The structure of any organization reflects these factors:

1. Centralization
2. Number of layers of management
3. Narrow or broad span of management control
4. Role of staff

Centralization.   Centralized authority means that authority to make decisions is concentrated at the top. Decentralized authority means that decision making is delegated to lower management levels. The degree of centralization is not obvious and may not be shown at all on an organization chart.

No company or agency is totally centralized or decentralized. The major advantage of centralization is the uniformity which it provides throughout the organization. The critical disadvantage is that managers do not obtain the necessary decision making experience needed to prepare them for higher level jobs.

Layers of Management.   Unlike centralization, the number of layers of an organization is readily seen on the organization chart. Some firms favor a "flat" structure, with few levels. The main reason may be communication. In a flat structure, there are relatively fewer levels through which messages must pass and be interpreted or colored. On the other hand, some firms prefer a "tall" structure with, necessarily, more managerial positions. Units and departments receive closer supervision under a tall organizational structure.

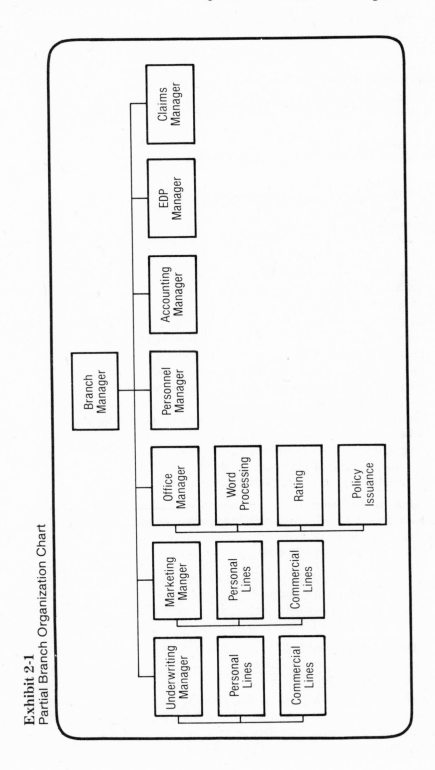

Exhibit 2-1
Partial Branch Organization Chart

Span of Management. Closely related to the number of levels in the organization is the span of management, also called the span of control. This term refers to the number of subordinates reporting to a manager or supervisor. A narrow span of management, say two to four subordinates reporting to all the supervisors and managers in a company, means that the organizational structure tends to be vertical and have many layers. Five to ten subordinates reporting to all the supervisors and managers in a company means that the organizational structure has a much more horizontal appearance. Since it is difficult for managers to closely supervise ten subordinates, managers are forced to delegate authority extensively in horizontal organizations.

Whether a narrow or wide span of management on the supervisory level is best, depends upon the experience and knowledge of the staff members and how much guidance and direction they need from the supervisor. A narrow span of management has the advantage of allowing the supervisor to spend more time with each subordinate. If staff members are trainees or need a great deal of supervision, then a narrow span of management is desirable. If staff members are experienced and are self-starters, then a wider span of management is best.

Use of Staff. Staff departments provide service to line departments. In insurance, line departments are those departments which directly sell the policies, underwrite and service them, and settle the claims. Staff departments do not directly sell, service, underwrite, or settle claims. Rather the staff departments provide service to the line departments. For example, the home office personnel department sets employment policies and procedures and monitors compliance. A home office underwriting or sales department might also be considered staff because it provides guidance and services to underwriting and sales lines managers who report to branch managers. The number, scope, and location of staff units is determined in the organizing process and wide variations among organizations are common.

Job or Position Guides   A job or position guide defines reporting relationships, job tasks, responsibilities, accountabilities and qualifications for a job. An example of a generic supervisory position guide is given in Exhibit 2-2.

Position guides are used to:

1. Clarify what each employee is expected to do.
2. Aid in recruiting and selecting employees.
3. Identify areas where performance standards should be established.
4. Evaluate jobs for salary purposes.

Organizing Your Unit   As supervisor, you may have a certain amount of control over an organizational structure within the unit. Here are some guidelines you can follow.

The Employee Who Has the Title Should Also Have the Responsibility and Authority. The most common error is to hold back some of the authority when assigning a task. You may believe that the control function justifies this action, yet the result is usually to tie the hands of an employee. The employee

Exhibit 2-2
Sample Position Guide for Supervisors

Principal Objective of Position:

Under direction, plans, organizes, directs, and controls the work activities of two or more full-time clerical and/or technical employees. Reports to the_____ manager.

Principal Responsibilities and Accountabilities

Directs and motivates employee

1. Conducts interviews of prospective employees and selects most qualified candidate.
2. Develops an on-the-job training program for new employees, conducts or monitors the training and reviews progress to assure that new employees are brought up to the appropriate effectiveness and efficiency in the prescribed time.
3. Conducts performance appraisals and recommends salary adjustments.
4. Formulates plan for continued development of all staff members.
5. Counsels and coaches employees as needed.
6. Provides guidance and assistance to staff to assure that the work is accurate and complete.
7. Conducts unit meetings.
8. Recommends transfers, and promotions.

Plans and Schedules the Work

9. Schedules work to meet production goals.
10. Formulates or assists in formulating performance standards for the work unit.
11. Prepares objectives and budgets.

Organizes the Work

12. Recommends methods and procedures to improve workflow and work distribution.
13. Recommends staffing requirements and plans.
14. Assigns work to assure a balanced and even work distribution.

Controls the Work

15. Reviews completed work to assure accuracy and completeness.
16. Develops control procedures and quality control programs to assure an acceptable quantity of work.
17. Controls expenses according to guidelines established.

Desirable qualifications

Has at least two years of clerical or technical experience related to the work in the unit to be supervised and has demonstrated an ability to meet performance standards. Has the human relations skills to interact with other employees in a cooperative and constructive manner.

Can communicate effectively and diplomatically with a wide variety of people.

who has the title should be performing the tasks defined in the position guide and have full authority to accomplish those tasks.

Unit Structure Should Be Flexible and Capable of Absorbing Changes in Staffing. You should expect employee turnover in your unit. What can you do to reduce the effects of turnover? Train, cross train and develop employees. In addition, avoid getting "locked in" to an inflexible unit structure.

Staff for Productivity. Why is it that two departments or units doing substantially the same amount of work will differ in the number of employees? Insurance organizations look at staffing very carefully as expense control is a continuing corporate objective. What causes overstaffing?

- Work tends to expand to meet the time and number of people available to do the work—the work is done more slowly and carefully or perhaps with unnecessary steps.
- Technical employees do clerical work and supervisors do technical work inefficiently.
- Poor or inefficient work methods, procedures and work flows.
- Lack of proper supervision.
- Lack of cross training and personnel development.
- Empire building—the supervisor believes that many subordinates mean higher status.

To staff for productivity, you should do the following:

- Train, cross train, and develop employees so that you will always have qualified employees to replace anyone who leaves or is promoted.
- Don't overstaff, even in times of expansion. Best staffing level is 90 percent of apparent need. When an employee leaves, re-assign work to determine if the unit could function with one fewer employee.
- Use temporary employees to handle peak load periods. You might make an agreement with other units to borrow and loan employees, or draw on a central pool of floating employees.
- Plan staffing needs. Set contingency plans for staffing if the work load increases, decreases, or remains the same.
- Maintain efficient work methods, procedures, and work flows.
- Spend adequate time supervising and make certain that employees are doing the work they should be doing and are doing it as well as they can.
- Do not promote someone to a higher job grade just to be able to pay him or her more. Promote only on the basis of qualifications for the job.
- Publicize unit productivity and periodically ask employees for ideas to improve it.
- Clarify authority, responsibilities, and tasks with each employee.

If reductions in staff are necessary, do not take this as a lowering of your status. You can allow normal voluntary terminations, transfers, and promotions to reduce your staff if your work load is down. Do not wait for management to tell you to reduce staff if you believe a cutback is inevitable.

Forced staff cuts can be very painful for you and for your employees. One proactive supervisor believed that staff reductions were coming in the future. Because the work load was light, he did not replace employees. When the reductions did come, he was not required to let anyone go. Other supervisors who had continued to replace had to go through the painful process of deciding who was to be terminated. Naturally you cannot predict every rise or drop in staff levels. However, you can respond when you think the evidence is strong. Favor a lean staff rather than overstaffing.

Staffing

The central task of staffing is matching the person to the job. Activities involved in staffing are:

1. Recruiting, interviewing, and selecting new employees.
2. Selecting employees from within the company to transfer to your unit.
3. Selecting and promoting employees for positions within your unit.
4. Recommending employees for promotions outside of your unit.

Recruiting, interviewing, selecting, and promoting employees are considered employment decisions. Employees and potential employees are protected by fair employment laws and regulations covered in *Essentials of Supervision*, companion volume to this text. We will not repeat these laws here.

The Selection Process   The major steps in selecting an employee from outside of your organization are these:

1. Recruiting or finding job candidates to interview. In a large organization, a personnel department usually does this.
2. Job application. The application is the key document that personnel counselors and supervisors use for screening applicants and for structuring the job interview.
3. Screening interview. A personnel counselor usually interviews the job candidates to determine who is qualified. The best candidates are then submitted to the supervisor for the secondary or supervisory interview.
4. Secondary or supervisory interview. The supervisor interviews the candidates and decides who is the best qualified for the job.

We will concentrate upon the secondary or supervisory interview. The process is much the same for screening interviews.

The steps we will discuss are:

1. Defining job qualifications
2. Reviewing applications
3. Preparing for the interview
4. Conducting the interview
5. Accepting and rejecting job candidates

Defining Job Qualifications   First define the qualifications for the job.

1. Review the position guide.

2. Write two lists: *Need-to-have* qualifications and *nice-to-have* qualifications.

You may want to put the *need-to-have* items in order of importance.

For example, Bob Ruffus is hiring an underwriting assistant. He would prefer an experienced employee, but he thinks he may be forced to take a trainee.

Need-to-Have Qualifications	Nice-to-Have Qualifications
1. Types 40 wpm	1. Types 60 wpm
2. Good English skills	2. Excellent English skills
3. Can communicate with a variety of people	3. Good knowledge of personal lines
4. Basic knowledge of insurance	4. Knows how to rate personal lines
5. Math skills to learn how to rate	5. Eighteen months to two years as a rater
6. Two years of business experience	6. Has worked on word processing or data processing equipment

The supervisor will often find two or three candidates who meet most of the *need-to-have* and some of the *nice-to-have* qualifications. From then on it is a matter of trade-offs and judgment. For example, one candidate does not have one of the *need-to-have* qualifications: two years of business experience. But the candidate types 60 wpm, has excellent English skills, and has an associate degree in word processing. This candidate might appear to be better than someone who has all of the *need-to-have* qualifications.

The supervisor faces two special problems in applicant interviews: (1) the tendency to be overly impressed by one or two talents; and (2) the tendency to settle for a poorly qualified applicant rather than continue the search.

Reviewing Applications The application is a critical document. First, it is a screening device. You look over the application and decide if the person meets enough of the qualifications to make it worthwhile to interview. Second, the application helps you to formulate questions to ask the job candidate.

Beth Howard is applying for the job of underwriting assistant in Bob Ruffus's unit. She has filled in the company's employment application form. Here are the guidelines which Bob followed as he reviewed Beth's application.

1. Education. A person could be overqualified as well as underqualified in education. The education of young people with limited work experience is usually more important than for experienced employees. (Beth has two years of college. Bob determines she is neither under or overqualified.)
2. Experience. How much job experience does the person have? How closely does the experience relate to the job she is applying for? (Beth

did work for an insurance company, but all of her other jobs were unrelated.)

3. Skills. What skills does she have? (Beth can type and has used a word processor and an IBM personal computer.)

4. Employment pattern. How consistent and progressive has the work experience been? Has the applicant gone from job to job? If so, is career progress evident? (Beth has had a number of jobs, but this is typical of students whose main goal is to make money for school.)

5. Are there any unaccounted time lapses in the application? (There are no long periods of unemployment in Beth's application.)

6. How carefully and accurately was the application filled out?

Some applicants may provide resumes. You can follow the same guidelines in examining a resume. Resumes are often prepared with outside assistance and tend to exaggerate a person's accomplishments. You should probe for the substance behind the glowing words. For instance, "coordinate activities of six units in creation of a new file system" may turn out to mean, "received, photocopied and distributed status reports during relocation of files."

Bob reviewed Beth's application and decided to interview her. He believed she might qualify for the assistant position. Bob's decision to interview was based upon his review of other applications. He screened out several because they were either under or overqualified for the job. Being significantly overqualified is as much a detriment as being underqualified. The overqualified person is likely to become discontented quickly and leave the organization.

Preparing for the Job Interview The best predictor of future job performance is past performance. How can a supervisor gain this information about a job applicant?

- Reference Check. You can expect little of value from reference checks. The reason is that often companies, especially large corporations, will only verify dates of employment, position titles, and perhaps salary. Companies do not want to take the risk of a lawsuit filed by a former employee who believes, rightly or wrongly, that a derogatory reference prevented him or her from getting a job. Many persons called for references will not even say whether or not the employee did a good job. If the situation is reversed and you are asked to give an employment reference, it is suggested that you give only the facts mentioned. In some organizations, supervisors are required to refer requests for references to the personnel department.

- Testing. Many organizations will give specific job-related tests such as typing, English, and math. Many kinds of tests have been eliminated to avoid the expense of validating them by proving that they are good indicators of job performance. Pencil and paper tests are not necessarily good predictors of on-the-job performance. For these and other reasons, tests have declined in importance and are rarely decisive in hiring.

Preparing Questions for the Interview. The interview is probably the key source of information, but it puts a burden on you as supervisor to probe and ask a sufficient number of right questions. Most job applicants will provide accurate information if asked, but they certainly will not volunteer all of the information you need.

What kind of information do you need? You need information about the job applicant's knowledge and skills gained through past jobs. The following questions can elicit this information:

1. What were your major job responsibilities? Describe your job to me.
2. What do you believe you did best? Found most difficult?
3. What were your greatest accomplishments?
4. What do you consider your job successes? Problems? Why?
5. Why did you leave this specific job?

The primary objective of such questions is to encourage the applicant to describe each job in detail, even if the job is not relevant to the position you are filling. If the applicant has limited job experience, then ask him or her to describe school experiences, both academic and extracurricular activities.

You also need information about the job applicant's work habits, preferences, and willingness to learn and develop. The following questions can elicit this information:

1. What did you think of your employer or supervisor?
2. In what areas could your supervisor have helped you develop more?
3. What parts of the job did you like best? Least? Why?
4. What is the best job you have had? Worst job? Why?
5. What job goals are most important to you?
6. What are your career goals?

Conducting the Job Interview It is suggested that you set aside a minimum of one hour for the interview. It should be held in a place where you and the job applicant can talk without distractions or interruptions.

Put the Applicant at Ease. When the applicant first comes in, it is your job to put him or her at ease. Use some safe opener and avoid comments or questions about sports (some people are not interested) or current events (some people do not follow the news closely). You might select some item from the application that you feel the applicant would want to talk about. For example, "I noticed you worked in Colorado. How did you like the mountains?" While this may not elicit key information, the applicant can talk about something which is nonthreatening.

Describe the Job in General Terms. While you will need to specifically describe the job eventually, do not go into detail at this point in the interview. The danger is that you will cue the job applicant to what qualifications and kind of person you are looking for. For example, if you say you are looking for a person who likes to learn new things and shows initiative, do not be surprised if the applicant says, "I like to work on my own. I don't like close supervision."

Elicit Key Information. Using the job application and your list of questions, ask the applicant to describe, explain, and evaluate every job he or she has held. Then ask summary evaluation questions at the end.

During this questioning, probe for additional information. Ask for clarification and reflect phrases and words you want further explained. Check your perceptions frequently to assure that you understand what the job applicant is saying. Use nondirective interviewing techniques carefully and cut off discussion that might reveal information forbidden by fair employment guidelines.

What does the supervisor do if the job applicant talks about subjects which are off limits? For example, Beth Howard told Bob Ruffus in the interview that she was getting married in six months and asked if she could have time off. Bob could not ask Beth if she were planning to get married, but he can answer her question. He cannot take this as an open door to ask further off-limits questions, such as questions about plans to have children.

Explain the Job. You can now explain the job in detail. Consider how much you want to sell the job to the applicant. If you know the applicant is not highly qualified, then keep the explanation brief.

If the applicant is someone you would like to hire, do not oversell the job because he or she will have unrealistic expectations and soon be disappointed. Provide the applicant with enough information to make an informed choice.

Define your expectations and the kind of performance you demand. Now is the time you can say, "I expect my people to work with minimal supervision," or "In our unit we usually expect to work overtime for a couple of days at the end of each month."

Encourage the applicant to ask any questions he or she may have about the job.

Discuss Salary. Do not interview someone who has requested a salary out of the range you are willing to offer. Job candidates usually ask about salary. You can say that their request is within your range. When giving the job's salary range, be careful not to imply that you might start the applicant at the high end of the range. Specific salary is usually negotiated when the job offer is made. You may wish to explain how often increases are given according to your organization's salary program.

Closing the Job Interview. Most supervisors and managers do not make a job offer at this point. They like to consider their options, compare qualifications of applicants and think about the proper choice. Job candidates need time to think about the job and perhaps talk it over with someone else.

The usual closing statement is, "I'm interviewing other applicants and I will get back to you in a few days."

Comparing Job Applicants You should interview a minimum of three candidates; perhaps five is ideal. What normally happens is that you screen out two or three as underqualified and are left with two or three possible choices.

Many supervisors write pro and con lists for each possible candidate and compare them to one another and to the original "need-to-have" and "nice-to-have" qualifications.

Bob Ruffus has made up the following comparison list for Beth Howard and Char Ellison, the two leading candidates.

Beth Howard	Char Ellison
1. Types 70 wpm	1. Types 50 wpm
2. Excellent English skills	2. Fair to good English skills
3. Good communicator	3. Good communicator. Has experience talking to banks & financial organizations.
4. Basic knowledge of insurance	4. No knowledge of insurance, but knows property values.
5. Fair math skills	5. Excellent math skills. Had part time job as accountant for real estate office.
6. Eight to twelve months' business experience	6. Seven years as part time real estate dealer and office accountant.
7. Knowledge of data processing and word processing	7. Never worked on a computer terminal before.

Char Ellison has worked for the past seven years in a real estate office. Because of her math knowledge she could easily learn to rate homeowners policies. In addition, her knowledge of real estate would help her learn insurance coverages. She intends to continue part time in real estate, but since she believes the market in her area will be down for the next five years, she wants a stable full-time job. She believes working in underwriting and with homeowners and fire insurance would be interesting. She is used to negotiating with bank officers on loans so she would be effective talking to agents. Her liabilities are her lack of experience with computers and only fair writing skills.

Beth Howard has limited work experience but she has had a clerical job in an insurance company, is experienced with computers and has excellent written skills. Her primary liability is her lack of business experience. Bob is also suspicious that she changes jobs frequently because she does not know what she wants to do.

Note that there are pluses and minuses for both candidates. Neither Beth nor Char meet all of the "need-to-have" qualifications, but each has some of the "nice-to-have" qualifications. The choice is not obvious, so Bob will have to use his judgment. He may well decide to interview more applicants.

Common Errors in Selection

Halo and Horns Effect. While it is normal to have impressions and "gut feelings" which can be valid guidelines, be cautious of the halo and horns effect. In the halo effect, you have an overall positive feeling toward the applicant because he or she appears to have a quality you admire. In the horns effect, you form an overall negative feeling about the applicant because he or she possesses one unattractive quality. To guard against the halo/horns effect, identify your biases before interviewing applicants.

Similar-to-Me Error. Job candidates who are similar to you in age, personality, value system, and life-style may seem appealing. But do you really need someone like you, or do you need someone who will complement you? To build an effective team, hire people with a variety of strengths.

The Ideal Person Error. In making your final selection, remember that you are going to select the best qualified for the job among all the job applicants you have interviewed. Think in terms of the best qualified rather than the ideal person for the job. Selecting the best qualified is much easier than searching for the perfect person.

Accepting and Rejecting Applicants In some large companies, a personnel counselor makes the job offer or notifies an applicant that a job offer will not be made. If you are going to decline the applicants, then your basis for declining must be, "Your qualifications do not match the job," or "I have selected someone who is better qualified." DO NOT go into detail even if the job applicant questions you. There is a danger that you could say something which the applicant could use against you in a formal discrimination charge. For example, "This position calls for a trainee. Someone who is relatively inexperienced and you are over qualified." If the person is 40 years old or older, this reason might be interpreted as, "The supervisor thinks I'm too old. He wants a young person." This can lead to a charge of age discrimination.

In declining a job candidate, the less said the better. You may send a letter or telephone the applicant. Be very careful what you say in a letter of refusal. You may want a personnel specialist or your manager to review the letter.

When you make a job offer, you will probably telephone the person or you may prefer to invite him or her into your office. When making an offer, state the exact salary and gain agreement. Establish a date for the first day of work. Tell the new employee the time and place he or she is to report and where to report. Explain your organization's procedures for the first day since part of the day will be spent on employment paperwork.

New Employee Orientation Do you remember your first day on a job? If the day was unpleasant, you probably remember every detail. Few of us remember exactly what we were told about our jobs or companies on that first day, but we seem to be able to recall its emotional tone. We all tend to ask ourselves these questions:

Do the people seem friendly?

Will I feel comfortable here?

Will co-workers accept me?

The objective of the first-day orientation should be to make the new employee feel comfortable. If possible, avoid difficult training on the first day because most new employees are too concerned about meeting others and the kind of impression they are making to concentrate fully on learning new tasks.

The first thing on the agenda is for you to find a quiet place and talk to the new employee. Set up a checklist of things you want to cover. Here is a sample checklist:

1. Provide names of all people in the department. Some supervisors make up a diagram of the office and label each desk with the names of all co-workers and their telephone numbers.
2. A brief organizational chart showing:
   Who reports to whom.
   Which departments or units your unit relates to.
3. Give a brief description of the mission of the organization, division, department, and unit.
4. Describe benefits which are immediately available to the new employee. You may mention other benefits, but do not go into detail.
5. Have employee fill out any necessary papers. (Steps 4 and 5 may be done in the personnel department before the employee arrives in your unit.)
6. Explain work hours, lunch time, breaks if any, flex hours if you have them.
7. Explain when the employee will be paid.
8. Provide the ground rules for the unit. For example, "If you are sick, you should call me in the morning."
9. Identify holidays and when vacation is available for the new employee.
10. Explain the training schedule.

Next, give the new employee a tour of the immediate office area, lunchroom, and other facilities. As you give the tour, introduce the new employee individually to each employee in your unit. Allow time for brief conversations.

Take the employee to his or her desk. Explain the phone systems and procedure for taking messages. Give the employee materials to read. For example, a benefits manual, employee handbook, or company magazine.

Make arrangements to have lunch with the new employee or to have someone else invite him or her to lunch. You may find that doing this a day or two in advance avoids an awkward situation.

Schedule activities for the afternoon. For example, have one or more employees explain what they do. Allow time for employee to read at his or her desk. You might have someone give the new employee a tour of the entire facility.

Note that the employee does little or no work, and there is as little job training as possible. The benefit of this approach is that it allows the new employee to:

Get to know the people in the office.
Start a relationship with you.
Relax and start to feel comfortable.

Do not delegate new employee orientation. The employee benefits from your doing the orientation because he or she has had the opportunity to build a relationship with you. First impressions are very critical to future relationships.

Plan for additional orientation sessions of one to two hours in two weeks' time. The time to go into detail on such matters as the performance standards, performance appraisal, and the salary program, would be at another conference, perhaps after two months.

A brief performance appraisal at two or three months helps to identify potential problems and further training needs and provides feedback to the new employee. Your active listening skills should be used to encourage the employee to discuss any questions or problems.

DIRECTING

As a basic management function, the term *directing* has a straightforward meaning—giving instructions and getting the work done. Directing involves guiding and influencing subordinates so that they perform their present jobs competently; and helping them grow and develop so they can assume greater responsibilities. Many of the traditional directing activities are discussed in other chapters of this book and its companion volume, *Essentials of Supervision.* These activities include communicating, motivating, training, coaching, conducting meetings, and delegating. The aspect not discussed in detail is directing, as such, which we will concentrate on now. Because many positive suggestions are given elsewhere, our treatment will emphasize the problems you can encounter in directing the activities of subordinates.

For ease of discussion let's separate directing into these activities:

1. Clarifying
2. Giving feedback
3. Being a problem-solving resource
4. Being an information resource

Clarifying

Objectives, action plans, performance standards, work flows, methods and procedures must move from paper into the minds of subordinates. For example, you have formulated objectives for the unit and have written action plans. You must discuss and clarify these objectives and plans. This involves telling and explaining, because what is written is usually only a summary of ideas. Employees want to know what end results are expected, why these end results are needed, and how the action plans are to be implemented. They want specific, concrete details. You will want two-way communication so that employees will be willing to ask questions freely, check their perceptions, and make recommendations.

Giving Feedback

Employees need frequent verbal feedback on how they are doing individually and collectively. The very best control mechanism is self-control, but employees cannot modify or adjust their performance unless they receive feedback or create it themselves. Feedback can be as simple as a word of recognition or a suggestion for doing a task differently. The best feedback is immediate and specific. "You did a fine job on the Clarion application" is far better than "You handle complicated applications well."

Clarifying and giving feedback can be viewed as a planning and control cycle. You can do this for the whole group during a meeting and with individual employees. For example, during monthly staff meetings, you can review unit objectives, report progress toward objectives and clarify what needs to be done and why.

You can also meet with each employee on a regular basis. If your unit is large, you will probably schedule discussions. You should ask each unit member to make up an agenda of all items he or she wants to discuss. In addition, you will identify specific items you want to discuss.

Being a Problem Solving Resource

You need subordinates to identify problems, especially in the early stages. But on the other hand, you do not need or want to hear about every minor problem. To prevent becoming overwhelmed by problems you should identify what kind of problems should be brought to your attention. This could be done in a staff meeting. List problems you feel subordinates should solve themselves and those you want brought to you. To take one conspicuous example, problems that involve other units usually require your personal involvement.

To encourage employees to learn to solve problems, follow problem identification with a question. "What would you recommend as a solution?" The message is that you do not want a problem without a recommended solution. Another approach is to provide the employees with two or three options and ask him or her to select one.

Being an Information Resource

You have greater access to information than do your subordinates. You usually know more about what is going on in the organization and what changes are planned.

As a member of management you need to communicate management's position and explain why changes are necessary. You are also an information resource for technical information. A word of caution: be careful of your role as technical expert. If you are meeting your supervisory responsibilities, you should lose some of your technical expertise because you are not involved in the work on a daily basis. We can put the point more forcefully: if you think you are still the all-around technical expert, you are probably neglecting your supervisory responsibilities or, worse yet, fooling yourself.

Rewarding—Key to Directing

The organization's reward system goes far beyond salary increases, promotions, and any other formal actions you make by virtue of your authority as a supervisor. Every day you reward, fail to reward, or punish others by your response to their requests and actions. A basic psychological principle is that we tend to repeat behavior which is rewarded. We give and accept rewards often without thinking.

No one consciously wants to reward unacceptable behavior or performance, but we all do so at times. The primary purpose of the following material is to give you a framework to follow in analyzing your day-to-day relationships with your subordinates and in choosing appropriate responses.

Boss-Dependent Subordinates   Some employees are boss-dependent. Perhaps it is better to say that some employees become boss-dependent if the boss allows it. This hurts them because they are not growing and developing their career potential. Boss-dependent subordinates demand more than their fair share of your time and emotional energies.

"Reassure me."   Some employees dislike making decisions and frequently ask the supervisor to check work, give reassurance, or make a decision. For example, "Is this right? Is this the way I should do it?" The supervisor takes the time to listen and usually responds, "Good. That's correct," just to get rid of the person. But underneath the supervisor is irritated because this employee is constantly interrupting to ask about things which other subordinates do without questioning.

What are the rewards for the subordinate? Attention, recognition, and reassurance. The supervisor is actually rewarding the subordinate who now comes back on a regular basis for more attention and reassurance.

Suggestions: Stop saying "Good" and other positive words. Rather, respond with a question which shifts the responsibility back to the employee. For example: "What would you recommend?" Or be candid in saying that you want the employee to handle the matter.

Once the positive reward is not forthcoming, the employee will probably reduce the number of interruptions. However, you should watch for signs of stress. If you reward the employee for making decisions on his or her own, a lasting change may be on the way.

"I don't know how. Do it for me."   This employee can come to your desk and within minutes you have five new assignments! The employee seems to be an expert at identifying problems for you to solve or may habitually play the helpless role of "I don't understand." The reward for the employee is obvious: getting out of work by delegating difficult problems to you.

Suggestions: Do not reward the employee by doing work or solving problems for him. Tell the employee to try the task. Set a time for review. Expect the employee to be frustrated and perhaps a little angry because you are not doing what he believes you SHOULD do.

"I have such problems. Don't expect anything of me."   This employee is constantly playing the role of "Poor Me." While all of us do have problems at times, the tip-off for a chronic "Poor Me" role player is responding to your suggestions by saying, "Yes, but that won't work for me." Other clues are that the person's problems never seem to get solved and new ones replace old ones on a regular basis. Compare this employee to others in the unit. If this "problem employee" were another subordinate:

1. Would you take corrective action because of low performance?
2. Would you give constructive criticism?

If you answer yes, then why aren't you treating this employee the same as others?

What is the reward for the employee in this situation? He or she does not have to perform at the standard level because "you understand." In addition, the person is getting attention. You are not playing psychologist when you establish ground rules that stop game playing so long as the rules apply to everyone.

Suggestions: If you suspect that the person has chronic, serious personal problems then he or she should be referred for professional help through your organization's established procedures. If your firm does not have such a program, you should use extreme caution in recommending professional help. You are not trained in such matters and saying "You need professional help" may make matters worse. Stick to job behavior and focus on job performance when dealing with the employee. Treat the person as you would any other employee and require the same job performance.

People Who Need to Control Others   Some people have a high need to be in control. They want to call the shots and give the orders. If you ask, "Where should we go to lunch?" the person with a high control need would have an answer and would try to sell others on the choice. The same is true of business situations: they want others to do things their way. Controllers may be difficult people to get along with. The suggested remedy is obvious: be assertive when a subordinate tries to control you or other unit members.

Analyze Your Reward Behavior

Whenever you identify a pattern of unacceptable behavior, ask yourself how you may be rewarding this behavior. Boss-dependent subordinates are rewarded when you take responsibility, do work for them, or give them attention. Those who seek to control are rewarded when you back down and are not assertive.

We have just looked at four kinds of problem employees. There are many more varieties and you may be eager to add one or two that have caused you particular grief. Our purpose has not been to encourage you to hang labels on people, especially those who deserve your understanding. Rather, our aim has been to stress how you can select behavior that will foster change. In effect, you have a behavioral toolbox. You can select the tools best suited for each troublesome employee. To review, these tools are:

- Giving rewards
- Withholding rewards
- Giving information
- Delegating
- Asking employees for recommendations
- Clarifying expectations

- Recommending professional help
- Sending "I" messages
- Asking open-ended questions
- Using assertive behavior

To continue the toolbox analogy, you will not use all of these tools at the same time. Moreover, you should not expect immediate results. Patience and persistence may not be in your job description, but they are the very essence of directing troublesome employees.

Rewarding does not stop at words of praise or thanks but also includes specific work assignments. Most importantly, it includes providing information to employees. We all want to be "in the know." One of your most powerful rewards is information (not gossip) about matters of interest. Whom you tell and whom you tell first become much-prized honors if done with deliberate intent to reward.

The majority of your subordinates are not difficult people, but conscientious workers who sincerely try to do a good job, sometimes get frustrated, and need to communicate. Reward them by giving them attention, your time, and a "thank you" occasionally. Behavior that is rewarded tends to be repeated.

Overdirecting

Does every employee need constant direction and control? Checking and rechecking on employees breeds boss-dependency in some and frustration in others. Overdirecting is often associated with the authoritarian management style and a supervisor who tends to be highly production-oriented rather than people centered.

There are circumstances in which overdirecting may be necessary. For example, close direction is needed if a supervisor has a group of inexperienced employees or employees who are unmotivated and doing simple tasks which change frequently. However, we suspect that overdirecting is more common than underdirecting as a supervisory excess.

Underdirecting

Underdirecting may be caused by many supervisory attitudes and behaviors. We will examine several.

Some supervisors who are independent and achievement oriented believe all employees want what they want: a great deal of freedom to act and take initiative.

Other supervisors underdirect because of a desire to avoid face-to-face communications. Some supervisors shrink from frequent face-to-face communication out of a sincere conviction that employees grow best if left alone. Others cling to their technical roles—in other words, they have not made the full transition to being supervisors.

Misdirecting

The supervisor can misdirect by concentrating on the needs of boss-dependent subordinates, while avoiding the controlling type of employees and ignoring the good performer. The supervisor who does this may sincerely believe that time should be concentrated on problems, the squeaky wheels. This lack of consistent direction and proper rewards seems to perpetuate the very problems the supervisor is trying to resolve.

Why Influence Is Important

As a supervisor you are delegated the authority to make decisions and to dispense rewards. But today that power alone is rarely sufficient. To your formal power must be added the broader idea of your influence on others: your ability to effect change in their behavior. There are a number of reasons.

Employees tend to reject the authoritarian approach to management. While you may receive minimal compliance by telling subordinates what to do, you will not receive enthusiastic commitment. Employees want to be able to question their supervisor about any decision which affects them and receive honest and complete answers. Education and aspirations of employees are on the rise.

Fewer and fewer employees are likely to be boss-dependent in the future. Employees want you to treat them as co-workers rather than as subordinates. Even the terminology we use in this book, superior and subordinates, is becoming obsolete. Employees no longer think of themselves as being subordinate to their supervisor or anyone else. Perhaps these terms will die out in the coming years and we will have a new terminology.

Settling Grievances

One of the least pleasant roles of supervisors is that of grievance settler. Employees believe that they have the right to bring grievances to their supervisor, be listened to, and then have the supervisor take corrective action. Please note that we are considering informal grievances and exclude formal ones filed under the terms of a union contract. The grievance might concern:

- Something the supervisor did or did not do.
- Something the organization did or did not do.
- A conflict between two or more employees.

As a supervisor, your employees see you as the mediator of disputes and the rectifier of wrongs. Following is a model procedure for handling grievances.

1. Listen and Acknowledge What the Person Is Saying As a supervisor you should maintain an open door policy which allows employees to bring problems to you. Even if you believe the issue is petty or one you should not be involved with, you should listen and respond by acknowledging that the employee is upset, angry, or concerned. Acknowledgment does not mean agreement, but rather a response that says, "I hear what you are saying and I recognize that you feel strongly about the matter."

2. Investigate the Facts Ask open-ended questions and ask for clarification. Also take notes. Notes serve these purposes:

- Help you recall exactly what was said
- Serve as documentation, if needed
- Show the employee you take the situation seriously

If the employee is a chronic complainer and does not want any corrective action, taking notes will emphasize that you are taking the situation seriously. Some grievances may disappear at this point if the employee decides not to pursue the issue.

3. Respond by Checking Your Perceptions Summarize the conversation or read your notes and ask the employee if this is correct. Modify or change your notes based on the employee's comments.

4. Present Your Position or Opinion This might involve explaining policy or giving your opinion of the situation. In many situations you cannot resolve a grievance when first presented but must gather more information.

5. Explain the Corrective Action You Will Take Sometimes the grievance involves a co-worker. If so, ask the employee if you have his or her permission to talk to the co-worker about the grievance. You might ask the employee to meet with the co-workers in your presence to discuss the problem. In some cases you may decide that the best course is to ask the employee to go directly to the co-worker to discuss the situation.

Describe what you intend to do. If the complaint involves only you and the employee, you can act immediately in many instances. Perhaps discussion is itself the remedy. Perhaps you must explain the reason for a decision. (You cannot always give the full story.) Perhaps the only corrective action needed is to say you will communicate about a specific subject more frequently with the employee. Many grievances amount to this plea: "Communicate with me. I have a right to know."

6. Set a Follow-up Date to Review the Situation Some problems wither when exposed to discussion; others flourish. You will want to follow up to determine if the situation has been resolved.

An Example of Grievance Handling Jim Hicky complained to his supervisor, Ruth Nelson, about a co-worker, Janice Webster:

Jim: "Janice absolutely refuses to cooperate with me or anyone else in the unit."

Ruth asked questions and probed to find out that Jim's primary complaint was that Janice talked so loud on the phone neither he nor other employees could concentrate.

Ruth took the corrective action of talking to Janice. Janice complained that Jim and other co-workers refused to answer her phone when she was not at her desk. "I'll tell you what the problem is. Those men don't like working with a woman in a technical position. It's just prejudice on their part."

Next, Ruth met with Jim and Janice together in private. Each one was asked to explain his or her side. In addition, Ruth set up this guideline for the discussion. "Before you defend or explain your side of the situation, you must show that you understand the other person by repeating what you think the other person said or meant." Ruth told Jim and Janice they must reach a compromise and agree upon a solution. After some discussion Jim agreed that he would take messages for Janice if she would keep her voice down.

At the end of the discussion Janice confided to Jim and Ruth that she probably did talk too loud. Both her mother and father were hard of hearing and she had always been yelled at to "speak up," because she had a soft voice. Jim suggested that he might signal her in some way when her voice was too loud. Janice said, "I would appreciate that because I raise my voice automatically. I don't realize I'm doing it." Janice tried to soften her voice, but frequently failed and had to be reminded, but it ceased to be a problem.

As you can see in this example, people often rely on false assumptions about a situation. The truth usually dissolves faulty assumptions. Your supervisory skill makes a great difference in the speed and permanence of the solution. You must accept the feelings that are displayed. Often employees take hardened positions and you must generate new possibilities and help them reach new perceptions and positions.

Sometimes a grievance is extremely serious; for example, sexual harassment or abusive behavior. Such grievances should be reported to your personnel department and to your manager. When there is a possibility that the law is being violated, you should not handle the dispute as a simple clash between two employees.

Summary on Directing

Directing others in a face-to-face situation requires effective human relations skills. These skills involve communications. As a supervisor, you must be aware of what kind of behavior you reward and why. You have the power of the formal reward system, but authority is not enough. You need to build and maintain your influence. The sources of influence are persuasive ability, the willingness to share information and knowledge and the capacity to build and maintain trust.

CONTROLLING

Setting objectives would be an ineffectual activity without follow-up to see that plans are being properly executed. This follow-up has long been called the control process.

The control process consists of these steps:

1. Identify what desired performance is to be achieved: objectives; performance standards; or action plans.
2. Obtain information on results or progress.
3. Compare actual results to desired performance.

4. Take corrective action, if necessary.

Control, then, is the time-honored term for this ongoing four-step process. As a supervisor, you control things (activities, tasks, equipment, and work flow) and people (assignments, behavior, and skill development.) It seems wrong to say that you control people. However, the word control in management means the process of assuring that planned results are obtained and that includes acceptable employee performance.

What Is Controlled

The following are commonly monitored and controlled by supervisors.

Objectives   Any time that you set objectives for assignments, development, or performance improvement, you must follow up, review, and take corrective action, if necessary. Without follow-up, employees may believe that the objective was not important and your credibility or competency might be questioned.

Individual Performance   What is expected of an employee in accomplishing routine duties is usually defined by performance standards. Individual performance is periodically evaluated formally during performance appraisal sessions and informally on a continuing basis. Both kinds of control require clear and mutually understood ideas of planned results.

Unit Output   The quantity your unit produces should be measured and controlled as well as individual performance. Output is directly related to the productivity of a unit. While productivity is often difficult to measure, it is defined as output divided by the human resources that created it; for example, policies issued per week divided by the number of employee hours available for processing. Increasing productivity has become a key objective for our industry. A modest productivity superiority over competitors means a significant advantage.

The expense associated with producing and servicing policies is critical in an insurer's operations. There are a number of ways to reduce expenses and increase productivity: increased automation, improved methods, altered procedures, and reorganized work flow. With ever-increasing automation as the background, frequent changes are required in unit job procedures. Control measures embrace such changes and their effects on job performance.

Quality   Quality of work is usually monitored through a quality control program which is separate from output or productivity measurements.

Quality control often takes the form of review of underwriting and claim files on a periodic basis. Usually samples are taken instead of reviewing every file. The person doing the review may be a higher level staff person who is responsible for doing a periodic audit. The supervisor may also sample files or a senior employee may be given some quality control responsibilities.

No matter what the product of your unit, you should set up some means of periodically sampling the work to determine its quality. For example, a word processing supervisor picks up outgoing completed work and reads items on a random basis. She checks for typos and misspelled words and format errors. She counts the mistakes and the letters and reports that are error free. She then reviews the results with each employee. This continuous feedback shows employees that she cares about quality and that she expects each person to improve.

Service   Improving the time taken to provide service to agents, policyholders or other departments is a stated goal in many organizations. One such standard is the time it takes a piece of paper to flow through a unit. For example, turnaround time for a policy will be a maximum of four working days. A service standard may also be response time. For example: all quotes from agents will be answered within 24 hours.

As a supervisor you should set reasonable service standards and periodically check to see how closely these standards are being met. Since meeting service standards is usually a cooperative effort, some of the feedback can be given to the employees as a group. Regular meetings on service quality may pay dividends because employees are able to identify problems and recommend solutions.

Budget and Expense   After plans are set, most organizations start budgeting for the year. Budgets are plans expressed in financial terms, usually expenses. Reports, usually monthly or quarterly, compare actual costs with budgeted costs.

Paperwork   With the advent of word processors and computers and their high speed printers, organizations can print volumes of pages, reports, memos, and letters, often in multiple copies. If information overkill is a common problem, you can conduct your own paper control program and minimize the paperwork you receive and create.

Employees who have access to terminals need to learn to use information on the terminals rather than paper copies. Somehow paper copies are so tangible and familiar that employees seem reluctant to give them up. This is a very expensive attachment. One primary objective of automation is to allow the insurance industry to become a paperless industry or nearly so. Your efforts can contribute to this important goal.

Financial Results   The insurance industry uses extensive use of ratios to show results. As a supervisor, you should understand key ratios so that you can identify the strength of a company, office, or line of insurance.

There are three ratios which tell how profitable an insurance company is as a whole and by line of insurance. In simplified form, they are:

Loss Ratio:

The loss ratio is the percent of premiums that goes to pay claims. The loss ratio is a simple fraction multiplied by 100 to put it in the form of a percentage:

$$\frac{\text{losses (dollars)}}{\text{premiums (dollars)}} \times 100 \ = \ \text{loss ratio (in percent)}$$

Expense Ratio:

The expense ratio is the percent of premiums that goes to pay the insurance company's operating expenses.

$$\frac{\text{expenses (dollars)}}{\text{premiums (dollars)}} \times 100 \ = \ \text{expense ratio (in percent)}$$

Combined Loss and Expense Ratio:

The combined loss and expense ratio is simply the sum of the loss ratio and the expense ratio.

$$\text{loss ratio} \ + \ \text{expense ratio} \ = \ \text{combined ratio}$$

When the combined ratio is exactly 100 percent, every premium dollar has been used to make loss payments and cover operating costs, with nothing left for profit and contingencies. When the combined ratio is greater than 100 percent, an underwriting loss occurs; more dollars are being paid out than are being taken in as premiums. When the combined ratio is less than 100 percent, an underwriting gain, also called an underwriting profit, occurs, because all premium dollars taken in are not being used for claims and expenses.

While an insurance company's profits from investments can make up the difference, a combined ratio over 100 percent means that the company is losing money selling insurance. Sustained high investment earnings have made it commonplace for insurers to lose money on insurance operations and recoup it on investments. The danger is obvious: the insurance company cannot control the stock market or the movement of interest rates. Company success depends on what it can control or partially control: premiums, expenses, and losses.

The combined ratio can become more favorable because of these changes:

1. Increase in premium dollars
2. Decrease in expenses
3. Decrease in money paid out in losses through better underwriting and claim practices.

As a supervisor you can help the combined ratio of your company by:
1. Reducing costs
2. Improving productivity
3. Improving quality of service and products so that more insurance is sold.

Policies and Procedures   Policies are written statements that provide guidelines for supervisory or managerial decisions.

Procedures specify how policies should be implemented.

As a supervisor, you administer policies and procedures. You teach them to employees, you interpret them and you take action when they are violated. While you may not have much to say about organization-wide policies and procedures, you are the control officer.

Guidelines for Controlling

Employees will resist and reject controls if they feel that they are being overcontrolled or believe that the wrong indicators are being monitored and evaluated. Following are some guidelines to keep in mind as you develop or administer controls.

Control Should Be a Positive Force Whether control programs are perceived as positive or negative depends largely on how you use them. If you only identify failures or errors and only communicate the negative, your employees will have a negative attitude toward controls. On the other hand, if subordinates are given recognition for doing a good job as individuals and as a group, they will more readily accept corrective action when needed.

Feedback Should Be a Motivator All of us need feedback, both negative and positive, which tells us how we are progressing so that we can regulate our behavior and efforts. Feedback should be immediate and regular.

One characteristic of achievement-oriented people is a high need for immediate feedback. If we are dieting, we need to see how much weight we have lost. When we reach an interim goal, we have a feeling of satisfaction. The satisfaction of reaching goals is a reward in itself.

One company used objectives and feedback to correct a problem. The company was having difficulty with low productivity. The manager explained to every unit why productivity was important. Then weekly objectives were set. Progress toward objectives was charted on a weekly basis. The charts were placed in work areas so that the employees could see their unit's progress.

The simple action of charting progress provided enough incentive for each of the work groups to strive to improve productivity. The only reward was the sense of satisfaction of gradually achieving an objective. The competition and team spirit of the work units added a little spice and excitement.

Controls Should Be Designed to Guide Behavior, not Just to Measure Things What is the primary purpose of a control program? The main purpose is to redirect action so that planned results are achieved. Stating, measuring, and comparing numbers constitute only the first three steps in the control process. They build toward the fourth step, taking corrective action or revising plans. Unless someone acts to change performance or behavior, controls are not meeting their primary purpose.

It is trite to say that change comes from within, but it is nonetheless true. Control programs are designed to provide individuals with feedback and direction so they can adjust their performance. The supervisor who over concentrates in measuring things and computing numbers and neglects the human element is missing the whole point of the function. An effective control does not impose change on employees—it provides them with information that makes them want to change.

How to Design a Control Program

In designing a control program, ask yourself the following questions:

A. What do I need to control?
   1. Progress toward objectives
   2. Individual and/or group productivity (output)
   3. Individual and/or group quality
   4. Conformity to policies and procedures
   5. Turnaround time of service
   6. Expenses
B. What specific things will I monitor to give me the information to determine if we are on target?
C. How am I going to measure results? What mechanism will I use?
   1. Review all items
   2. Sample
   3. Observe
   4. Collect statistics
   5. Obtain computer printouts and reports
D. Who should do the monitoring?
   1. Me, as the supervisor
   2. A designated unit member (a senior of highly qualified employee)
   3. Each employee
E. Who should compare actual results to objectives and recommend corrective action?
   1. Me, as the supervisor
   2. A designated unit member
   3. Each employee
F. Who needs the results of controls?
   1. Me
   2. Each employee
   3. My manager
   4. Staff departments
G. Who should take corrective action when needed?
   1. Me
   2. Employees
H. How can self-control be structured into the program?

Guidelines for Giving Feedback

How   How should the feedback be communicated? On paper or in person? Or both? The answer depends on the nature of the feedback, what you know about the person and whether the feedback is negative or positive. Generally it is a good idea to give feedback verbally even if you give the employee the results in written form.

When   When should the feedback be given? Give performance feedback as soon as you have the information. Avoid making feedback into a *gotcha* system. In a gotcha system, the supervisor collects negative feedback, then dumps it all at once on the unsuspecting subordinate. Much gotcha feedback comes long after the performance.

Avoiding "Gotcha" Feedback   What are the mistakes in a gotcha system? First, most of us can accept and agree to change one or two things, but few of us can cope with a long laundry list of our mistakes. When overwhelmed with negatives, the usual responses are to become defensive or argumentative or to reject the feedback. Second, we tend to forget what we did months ago. So feedback that goes too far back does not seem relevant and is often open to debate. Third, we need both positive and negative feedback to adjust performance. Growth comes from building on strengths as well as overcoming weakness. Fourth, we expect to be treated fairly. Collecting a list of mistakes and dumping them all at once seems grossly unfair. Once this happens, the supervisor has set up a potential win/lose situation with the employee, rather than a win/win situation where both can agree on how to correct the problem or problems.

Who   Even if a senior employee collects the control data, the supervisor should talk to subordinates about performance, especially when performance is below par. Exhibit 2-3 summarizes the control process in terms of the decisions you must make.

Example of a Control Program

Tom Donnelly is a property claim supervisor who supervises five outside property claim adjusters. Tom sets up the claim files and assigns claims on the basis of the adjusters' knowledge, experience, and work load. Tom has set performance standards for his adjusters.

> Service Standards: Maximum time for contacting a claimant, maximum time for responding to the claimant and maximum time for settling the claim.

> Quality Standards: All claims must be looked at, pictures taken and any dollar amount on the claim must be documented. In addition, adjusters must follow all procedures given in the claim manual.

The first control mechanism is settlement authority. Each adjuster has a certain dollar amount of settlement authority. This means he or she can pay the claim and write a check to the policyholder without getting Tom's approval. The amount of settlement authority depends upon the adjuster's knowledge and experience. Every claim file which exceeds the adjuster's settlement authority must be submitted to Tom for his approval.

The second control mechanism is review of the claim files. Tom doesn't

Exhibit 2-3
Decision Flow Chart for Taking Corrective Action

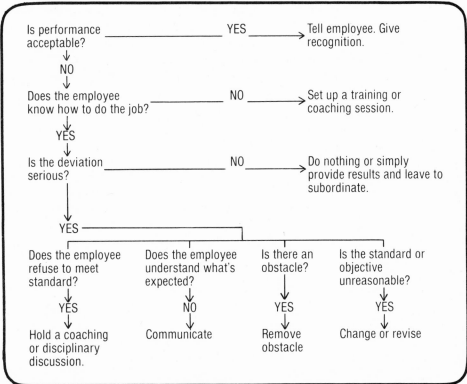

have the time to review every claim file, so he has a come-up system for each claim. The first come-up for every file is 21 days after the file was created. If a claim is not settled within 21 days, Tom reviews it. Many small claims are settled within this time period, and Tom regularly skims a sample of the closed files.

If a claim is reviewed at 21 days, then Tom sets up subsequent review dates at 30 days and every fourteen days after that until the claim is settled.

When Tom reviews the claim files, he evaluates:

Time taken to contact claimant, inspect damage, respond, and settle.

Documentation in the file. Is it complete? Are damage estimates correct? Is the claimant covered for the damages?

Is the adjuster following claim procedures?

If Tom spots a serious problem with a file, he discusses this with the adjuster immediately. Otherwise each quarter he reviews his notes with each adjuster and tells him or her what he or she is doing well and where improvements need to be made.

Tom saves his notes on these files and reviews them at performance appraisal time.

Tom believes this system works well for him. It allows him to sample the work of all of his adjusters on a periodic basis and identify any problems that may be developing. It keeps him mindful of his responsibility to supervise the work of the whole unit and is a safeguard against overconcentration on control.

SUMMARY

All supervisory and managerial activities can be separated into one of the following four managerial functions: planning; organizing; directing; and controlling.

These functions are of equal importance, although different levels of management may spend more time on one function than on others. Higher level managers spend more time on planning than do supervisors, while supervisors spend more time directing and controlling.

These functions of management should be viewed as a cycle of management. To control effectively, supervisors must first plan. To achieve plans, supervisors must organize work and people and provide directions to subordinates. The broadest perspective of the supervisor's role is that of the four continuous and intertwined functions of planning, organizing, directing, and controlling.

CHAPTER 3

Training

INTRODUCTION

Your firm, whether it is an agency or a company, exists to provide a return for its "stakeholders," its owners, its customers and, of course, its employees. Most successful insurance organizations find that their most valuable assets are their human resources. This chapter is devoted to the development of those human resources to their fullest potential by improving their performance for the good of the firm. Most large insurance organizations have formal training departments and training programs. Nonetheless, as a supervisor you are responsible for the training of your unit members. In addition, you provide, directly or indirectly, the on-the-job training that is central in skill development. There is a special challenge in providing adequate training in smaller organizations with limited resources. Being a supervisor means being a trainer and a training manager.

As this chapter unfolds, you will see the supervisor as a determiner of training needs, a presenter of training, and an evaluator of training programs available to meet the needs of employees.

THE SUPERVISOR'S ROLE IN TRAINING

If your employees cannot perform the jobs they have been given, they will most likely need training. Some workers do not know how to do their jobs because they lack knowledge and skill. Others, you will find, will just be careless. You must determine just what each person lacks and then react accordingly.

Importance of Training to the Firm

Experience indicates that some insurance organizations cut back on training when times are difficult. Doing so gives the impression that training is a luxury. In reality, it is a necessity! Indeed, when an organization reduces formal training, it often means that much of the training shifts back to the supervisor.

Employees perform best when the work itself permits them to grow and develop. When an employee is recruited and hired, a large investment is being made with the expectation that the person will perform well. However, training is not just for new employees. It is also for people whose jobs are modified or who are promoted to new responsibilities or transferred within the organization. Good training, you will find, reduces turnover and provides the needed skills when and where they are needed. It also gives the firm the reputation of being a good employer and makes some departments more attractive to employees than others.

Importance of Training to the Employees

People work for monetary rewards and for the satisfaction of doing work in which they are interested. Most want to perform well because it gives them great satisfaction. When people leave school, they do not expect their education to end. They expect to learn the knowledge and skills necessary to perform their life's work. Many hope to move up to better jobs as well.

If an employee does not get an opportunity for growth and development from the work environment, he or she will often lack commitment to the unit and to the company. As first line supervisor, you are the single most important element in providing opportunity for growth and development.

EMPLOYEE TRAINING, EDUCATION, AND DEVELOPMENT

Definitions

The terms training, education, and development are often used interchangeably, but have three different objectives. A popular term for all three is Human Resource Development (HRD). HRD has been defined as any series of organized activities conducted for a specific time and designed to produce behavior change. The change is one that improves job performance. Training has been defined as those activities which are designed to improve performance on the job the employee is presently doing or is being hired to do.[1] Education is directed toward the individual (rather than the job) and is generally designed to prepare a person for promotion. Development is often referred to as those activities that prepare employees for future jobs as the firm changes.

Goal of Training

The goal of training is to build the knowledge and skills needed to do the job the employee now has. It may include training in communication skills, attitude training, and such things as product knowledge, rating, underwriting, selling, or adjusting claims. It involves a process of teaching and a process of learning and focuses on the goal of improving performance.

Goal of Education

The goal of education is to improve the overall competence of the employee in a specific direction and beyond the present job. Education helps to develop individual potential for growth within the firm. Education also equips people with knowledge and skills useful in work life and deliberately goes far beyond the abilities needed for present or expected position requirements.

When Is Training Needed?

Sometimes training is provided simply because management thinks it is a good idea. Other times, it is provided because employees expect it. Still other times, it is available just because somebody has put money in the training budget. However, good business practice dictates that training be provided for good reasons. Some experts argue that there are only three good reasons for training:

1. The employee cannot do the job. (Examples: cannot code a health insurance policy; cannot identify whether the insured has coverage or not.)

2. The employee can do the job but not well enough. (Example: has an unacceptably high ratio of mistakes in rating auto insurance policies.)

3. The employee is doing the job incorrectly. (Example: is confusing the named insured with the beneficiary.)[2]

Learning, in the full sense of the word, covers three components or areas. The first is *knowledge*, that is, knowing what to do and how do it. The second is *skill*, that is, the ability to coordinate the eyes, mind, and body into one action that results in accomplishing a task easily and correctly. The third is *attitude*, that is, the emotional response of a person to a particular job or situation. Training tries to develop employees in all three areas. It must be remembered that learning in one does not *necessarily* guarantee learning in the others.

Improved Knowledge To improve knowledge, the supervisor must first determine what must be known to do the job. Job descriptions, position guides, or performance standards are sources of this information. Some employees simply cannot do the job because they are new to it and have never done it before. Others do not know how to do it well enough. Others simply do it wrong because of misinformation or misunderstanding. Even if your organization provides training through a training department, you must see to it that training is based on a clear picture of what the employee must know to do the job.

Employees can acquire knowledge in many ways. Some work best on a self-study basis—reading books, watching video tape recordings, or working exercises. If a large group of people need the same knowledge, perhaps the best method is classroom training. We will talk more about determining which method is best later in this chapter. A knowledge of the insurance business in general is basic information needed by all employees. Beyond this, specific knowledge regarding each one's job is critical.

Improved Skill To perform adequately, employees need to develop skill in how to do their jobs. Skill is the successful and efficient application of knowledge. If employees are hired at an entry level, they must be given basic training and help in skill development. If, later, they are promoted to new jobs, they may once again need to acquire new skills. Often when experienced employees join a firm, the skills acquired elsewhere must be modified to fit the new position. Skills can be built in a number of ways, but most frequently through demonstration, role playing, and repeated practice until proficiency is reached.

Changed Attitudes Attitudes are intangible. We do not see them directly but reach conclusions about what they are by observing a person's behavior. Attitudes are the positions characteristically taken or emotions shown by people in responding to stimuli. Employees with positive attitudes toward their supervisors, their work, and their firm usually perform the best. As a supervisor, you cannot directly change the attitudes of employees. However, you can create experiences and situations that foster attitude change. Training that seeks attitude change is often needed to build enthusiasm and loyalty, especially for new employees. The goal is to have them say, "I like working here." In addition, the changing composition of the work force, with more minorities and women entering positions of authority, may call for changes in the attitudes of existing employees. If a conflict exists, training may not be the answer and other action may be required. Role modeling of proper attitudes through the use of role playing is often used.

It has been shown that the attitudes of the worker do seem to be related to his survival on the job.[3] Negative attitudes often breed turnover and absenteeism resulting in additional hiring and training costs. If employees are satisfied with their jobs, they tend to be highly motivated and better performers.

Application to Job Performance

You have seen that one of the goals of training is to provide new knowledge, skills, and attitudes. In addition, it is necessary to provide reinforcement for knowledge, skills, and attitudes already possessed by the trainee. You do this by rewarding good performance, sometimes with just a compliment. In addition, it may be necessary to eradicate or redirect existing knowledge, skills, and attitudes that inhibit the growth of the employee. You help bring this about by withholding reinforcement and, at times, by directly discouraging behavior you want to eliminate. Sometimes this is looked upon as being threatening. While it is difficult to accomplish all of these things, the best answer is to provide an open climate so that trainees can express themselves. This is the first step toward improving their knowledge, skills, and attitudes.

HOW ADULTS LEARN

Assumptions About Adult Learners

Training adults to perform their jobs in your agency or your company is very different from the training you received in school. When you entered the work force and got your first job, no doubt you were anxious to perform well and to show the world how good you were. This is one of the first things you should realize about job training. Adults do not want to study "subjects"; they want to know about the real world, its situations, and the problems they will face. The role of the supervisor should be that of a guide rather than a teacher.

Self-Motivation Adults are motivated to learn when they feel the need and see the interests that learning will satisfy. One learns when one wants to learn, and this desire is called motivation. It involves knowing clearly what is to be learned and understanding why the learning is desirable, which creates a sense of urgency. Employees need to feel that they are making valuable contributions.

Application-Centered Adults must feel that training is going to help them immediately, not ten years from now. They want something useful from each session. If you want them to concentrate on learning rather than just paying attention, you must give them practical examples to which they can relate. For instance, you might have them examine actual account files taken from the underwriting or claims departments.

Adults learn best by doing things. They can learn by listening and watching, but it is best to get them actively involved. You have to involve their minds by testing their mental agility, their alertness, and forcing them to stretch to catch facts and ideas. Adults learn mainly as a result of their own efforts and must apply what they have learned or they will quickly forget it. They retain more when they solve real problems. (Much of this is true of children too, of course.)

Experience Base For an adult to learn and retain more, he or she must relate facts and ideas to what is already known. The experience of your trainees is a central resource for learning. Therefore, be sure you analyze your trainees' experience as you plan your training sessions. It is often best to put bits and pieces of information into a logical and meaningful whole and relate it to the experience of your audience. For example, some accounting functions can be taught by showing their similarity or contrast to keeping a personal checking account.

Self-Direction Adults have an important need to be self-directing. Thus, the trainer's role is one of a facilitator encouraging discovery, not simply transmitting information. Adults learn best in an informal climate. Supervisors who have yet to realize this typically train as they were taught, perhaps even as children.

Adult learners like a variety of methods, yet the use of repetition to avoid forgetting is essential. It can be achieved through the use of a variety of visual aids and practice sessions. While adults are self-directing, they need you to emphasize the significant points and their implications and applications on the job. Adults want guidance, not grades. They want to know how well they are progressing, but please remember that a test can be frightening to many people. Since adults want to measure their own progress, you must provide them with ways of doing it such as exercises, case studies, and quizzes.

Personal Differences   Age differences create wide individual differences among people. Some see better than others and some hear better than others. Learning is affected by differences in individual personalities, styles, and attitudes. An individual's ability to learn does not change with age, but learning speed does. Adjust your pace to the level of your employees.

Assumptions About Adult Learning

Dr. Malcolm S. Knowles has written much on the subject of andragogy, the education of adults. He lists four main assumptions of andragogy:

1. Changes in self-concept. As a person grows and matures, his or her self-concept moves from total dependency to one of increased self-directedness.
2. The role of experience. As an individual matures, he or she accumulates an expanding reservoir of experience that causes him or her to become an increasingly rich resource for learning and at the same time providing him or her with a broadening base with which to relate new learning.
3. Readiness to learn. As an individual matures, his or her readiness to learn is decreasingly a product of biological development and academic pressure and is increasingly the product of the developmental tasks required for the performance of his or her evolving social roles.
4. Orientation to learning. Adults tend to have a problem-centered orientation to learning rather than being subject-centered as children are.[4]

The Learning Process

Need to Learn   Some employees will require training because they simply cannot do the work. Others come to training because it is a prestige assignment. Still others are there because they are "sent by their boss." Others simply do not like not knowing something. Since the need to learn varies from individual to individual, it is the job of the supervisor to help employees identify their particular needs. The difference between what they presently know and are able to do and what they need to know to perform adequately is known as the "development gap." It is this gap that training seeks to close.

Active Participation   It is important that adult learners share responsibility for planning and operating the training process. This can be done by allowing them to determine the objectives of the training. You can present the available options and show your trust in their judgment. By allowing employees to organize into project groups or to do independent study, you are respecting them and providing an opportunity for their active involvement.

Solve Real Problems A wise supervisor will make use of employees' experience. Let them share their experience through discussion, role playing, and case studies. Allow them to present the situations that are now causing them problems on the job such as workload issues. Do not be critical of their performance, but let them surface those things that really concern them and then direct the training to those real problems.

Feedback on Progress Adult learners need a sense of progress toward their personal goals. Let them set the criteria and methods of measuring progress. It need not be a written test in every case. Help them to find their own areas of weakness.

Learner-Controlled Instruction (LCI)

"Designers of learning systems for adults are constantly seeking new ways to utilize the unique 'adultness' of the learners."[5] LCI is a system that involves the learner in a number of key decisions about how learning will take place. Those decisions involve the sequence of learning steps, the pace of the learning, the methods and materials used, the objectives of the learning, and the evaluation of the learning.

LCI gives the learner a clearer statement of the objectives to be achieved, an explanation of the evaluation that will determine the achievement of those objectives, and materials, activities, and people available for reaching those objectives. The training room becomes a learning center with a very open climate. It is extremely important for the trainer and trainee to be committed to this approach as well as the trainees. Some learners do not operate well in this kind of atmosphere since they need more structure and organization or they feel threatened.

Each learner sets his or her own pace. This takes into consideration sight, hearing, and reaction differences due largely to age. The learners decide when to take the final exam. LCI is particularly effective when some trainees come to the training knowing some of the material already. Since the complexity of the material varies among learners, there is a need for a variety of materials. LCI makes the learner accountable for the learning. The role of the trainer is one of being a resource person to assist in the learning process. Andragogy (adult learning) is applied to the fullest in LCI.

Process Model

Malcolm Knowles says:

The andragogical model is a process model in contrast to the content models employed by most traditional educators. The difference is this: in traditional education, the teacher decides in advance what knowledge or skill needs to be transmitted, arranges this body of content into logical units, selects the most efficient means for transmitting this content and then develops a plan for presenting these content units in some sort of sequence. This is a content model. The andragogical teacher prepares in advance a set of procedures for involving the learners in a process involving these elements:

1. establishing a climate conducive to learning;
2. creating a mechanism for mutual planning;
3. diagnosing the needs for learning;
4. formulating the program objectives that will satisfy these needs;
5. designing a pattern of learning experiences;
6. conducting these learning experiences with suitable techniques and materials;
7. evaluating the learning outcomes and rediagnosing learning needs.

This is a process model.[6]

Trust Relationships

It is important that the trainer respect the individual and cultural differences among trainees. The psychological climate must be safe, caring, accepting, trusting, respectful, and understanding. A supportive interpersonal relationship between the trainer and trainees is important. Since such a relationship takes time to build, you should start immediately with new employees.

Trainees must feel free to express themselves in an environment of openness and low risk. Their positive behaviors should be rewarded. They should be given encouragement to voice their "hidden agendas" to satisfy their individual needs. Collaboration, meaning team activities, rather than competitiveness should be the watchword.

Informality

Trainees do not expect you to have all the answers. They will respect you more if you do not do all the telling (lecturing all the time). Present a problem and let the group solve it. Self-discovery can work wonders. Let group members decide when to take breaks and lunch and allow humor to enter into your training once in a while.

Individual Help

Remember that your employees will come to you with a variety of life experiences and with many differing levels of job skills. Their educational levels will also vary greatly. Your goal is to get all your employees to the same levels of high proficiency. This is often difficult to do in a typical classroom if you assume that all can learn at the same rate.

By planning a level of training for the middle of the audience, you may lose some slow learners and bore some fast learners. However, by planning to have individual study projects for the fast learner (or even letting them train others) and giving individual help to the slow learners, you can take care of the extremes.

PREPARING FOR TRAINING

Planning

You would be wise to turn down a training assignment if you lack knowledge or experience with the subject. You would also be wise to turn down an assignment if you are not given enough preparation time. Poor planning results in poor presentation, so you must have the time to plan well.

Mastering the subject matter is only half the job of preparing to give training to employees. The other half—equally important—is to plan the learning activities. You should plan each activity (lecture, question-and-answer period, practice, discussion, and so on) and specify the time expected for each. If you are a typical occasional trainer, it is likely that you will tend to *overprepare* the content and *underprepare* the design of the learning activities.

Setting Learning Objectives

Once you know the performance problems of your audience, you can determine the learning objectives. What do you want the employees to be able to do at the end of the training session? Write down what they need to know or do to reach those objectives. Be sure to let your trainees know your initial objectives in the first session. As mentioned previously, your initial objectives are the starting point as you encourage trainees to contribute to the final objectives.

Facilities and Materials

Consider the size of your audience when you arrange for a training room. Have you noticed that many training and conference rooms fall short of providing comfortable temperature, ventilation, lighting, seating, and freedom from distraction? The handy meeting room that serves adequately for short conferences may be deadly for a half-day training session. Generally, a "U" or "V" seating arrangement is best for encouraging discussion. Avoid putting desks or tables in rows, classroom style. If you are going to use audio-visual equipment, be sure it is reserved early; and when it arrives, check to see that it works. You may speak from a lectern or perhaps from a table in the front of the room. Is the chalkboard or flip chart adequate for the use you plan? Name cards at each place will allow trainees to get to know one another quickly and enable you to use their names when calling upon them. You will probably want to provide notepaper and pens or pencils. Distribute a roster unless you are certain that all persons involved know one another well. Any case studies, exercises, or handout materials must be planned and prepared before the class. Finally, plan the type of quizzes or testing you will do throughout your session. You will read more about session plans a little later.

Record Keeping

Planning should include determining what record keeping is needed for unit and organizational purposes. Training records may be essential for fair employment reasons. Information about training often goes to five destinations. First, as a supervisor, you will want a record of who was trained and what was learned. Second, employees who received training may want to know how well they did. Third, your firm's training department is likely to maintain records of employee training and may also want to know how well the training went. Fourth, the personnel department will want a record of training. Finally, higher management will want to know what training took place, how effective it was, and its cost.

Analysis of Training Needs

Job Standards The first step in determining the content of job training is to analyze the objectives of each job and the standards by which achievement is to be judged. This requires a task analysis, discussed in Chapter 5. To the extent that an employee fails to meet standards, there exists a "development gap." The task analysis should determine the knowledge, skills, and attitudes required and the degree of proficiency of each. This three-way categorization of needs (knowledge, skills, and attitudes) is more broadly useful, but it is especially valuable in organizing your thinking about development gaps.

Performance Discrepancy vs. Deficiency If a worker does not do the job up to the standards required or up to your expectations, there is a performance problem. It is very typical for supervisors to respond to such performance problems with the statement, "My employee just needs more training." But if a worker already knows what to do, further training is rarely the answer and may be a waste of time.

There is a difference between a performance discrepancy and a performance deficiency. A discrepancy only means that there is a difference, a lack of balance, between the actual and the desired. A deficiency means that a value judgment has been made about a discrepancy; and that the discrepancy is bad or in some other way unacceptable.[7]

Knowledge It is important to determine what event caused someone to conclude that a performance gap exists. The next question is whether or not the performance gap exists because the worker does not know how to do the job. A very simple question can be used at this point. If the worker's life depended on it, could he or she do the job? If the answer is yes, that is, the person is able to perform the job but does not want to, the deficiency is in execution or attitude, and training is not the answer. If the answer is no, that is, present knowledge and/or skills are inadequate for the desired performance, then the individual needs training.

Skill If there truly is a skill deficiency, the next step is to determine whether or not the individual was ever able to do the job. If the skill just is not used often enough, it may deteriorate. Perhaps simple practice will bring the skill back to the desired level. If you find a skill deficiency exists because the individual has never done the job, training is in order. Sometimes there are easier solutions than formal training, for example, checklists or on-the-job training.

Attitude If the performance problem is not a skill deficiency, training probably will not help. You should then ask whether proper performance punishes the worker. That is, if someone does a good job and because of this is given more of the same work to do (rather than given growth opportunities), he or she is being punished for doing a good job. If this is the case, simply remove the punishment.

In some cases, employees may not realize the significance of their poor performance. If it can lead to termination, make this clear. Sometimes there are obstacles to good performance such as noise, poor lighting, or poor procedures. If this is the case, the solution may be to remove those obstacles.

Establishing Learning Objectives

The performance discrepancy must be translated into a set of learning objectives. If you are planning training for a single employee, the learning objectives can be tailored to that individual. In a group training setting, the learning objectives must necessarily be more general.

Learning objectives should be expressed as "terminal behavior." This rather deathlike term is the educator's jargon for the behavior that the learner should be able to exhibit after the training has been completed. The usual statement is, "At the completion of this assignment, the employee should be able to...." This standard phrase is followed by a description of task performance in highly specific terms. For example, the employee may be expected to rate five policies without error, to list five exclusions found in a given policy, or to give the coinsurance formula. If properly stated, objectives leave little doubt as to what performance will be accepted as proof of learning. Learning objectives should, of course, be in writing and should be prominently featured in handouts and other study materials.

Some objectives are hard to put in writing. For instance, objectives that show a change in attitude are often difficult to state—but if that is the goal of training, it is best to say so.

One student of the subject has commented:

> Objectives, then, are useful in providing a sound basis (1) for the selection or designing of instructional content and procedures; (2) for evaluating or assessing the success of the instruction; and (3) for organizing the students' own efforts and activities for the accomplishment of the important instructional intent. In short, if you know where you are going you have a better chance of getting there.[8]

The sequence performance-conditions-criterion is usually followed in writing objectives. Here is an example:

1. Performance—Be able to rate a businessowner's policy.

2. Conditions—Given an application, Commercial Lines Manual, and a calculator, be able to rate a businessowner's policy.
3. Criterion—Given five applications, a Commercial Lines Manual, and a calculator, be able to rate five businessowner's policies with not more than one error within sixty minutes.

As you can see, this final objective statement includes all three components of a well-written, specific objective. Here is another example: "Given an oral description of the events involved in an accident, be able to fill in a standard accident report with not more than one error."

While it may seem that these objectives are wordy and difficult to prepare, they are essential for effective training. Remember, too, that you probably will need only a few objectives such as these for each session of instruction.

Session Plans

From beginning to end, each session should have a smoothly connected series of ideas, facts, details, exercises, and a variety of mentally stimulating activities. To reach your objectives and maintain time control, a thorough session plan is essential. The session plan also helps to contribute to your confidence by telling you where you are, what you should be doing, and what aids should be used.

Format There are three basic formats for session plans. The first is called the topic outline. It contains the main and subpoints stated in brief phrases or single words. This format is best used by experienced trainers. The second is the sentence outline. This format uses complete sentences. Third is the scripted, or manuscript, format. This is much more detailed, and it includes everything that is to be done—sometimes even jokes to tell when interest lags! The sentence outline is best for experienced trainers while the manuscript, or scripted, format is best for persons not experienced as trainers.

The amount of detail necessary for the session plan should vary by your skill as trainer, the complexity of the material, and the level of the audience. The extent of detail in your session plan should reflect your judgment of these factors and will probably vary from one training situation to the next.

Content Some prefer to have a session plan for each hour of instruction while others prefer to have one session plan for each block of instruction, which might run several hours. In either case, your session plan should follow the format similar to the Sample Meeting Outline shown in Exhibit 3-1.

Another example of an insurance supervisor's session format is given in Exhibit 3-2. This supervisor believes that each session plan should contain four parts—introduction, procedure, practice, and wrap-up, in that order. The introduction sets the stage for the entire session. The procedure is the "guts" of the entire session plan, the explanation, and examples. The practice segment reminds you to include time for employee involvement. Finally, the wrap-up concludes the training by giving employees a fresh, clear, and meaningful impression of what has taken place. Quizzes and question-and-answer sessions

Exhibit 3-1
Sample Meeting Outline

Subject:	First Quality Circle Meeting
Objective:	1. To understand the purpose, rationale, and processes involved in quality circles.
Materials:	Two overhead slides; projector; screen; two handouts.

Method	Outline

Lecture
Show slide
	I. Introduction
	  a. Welcome
	  b. Explain objectives
	  c. Meeting details
	  d. Background — firm's desire to involve employees in decision making

Lecture
 	
Show slide
 	
Handout
Discussion
Exercise
	II. Body
	  a. Define quality circle and its voluntary nature
	  b. State ground rules and areas of involvement
	  c. Describe role of steering committee, supervisor, facilitator, and members
	  d. Tell how circle can provide members a chance to be recognized as experts, two-way communication, and an opportunity to improve the quality of work
	  e. Introduce facilitator who explains problem-solving process
	  f. Facilitator explains brainstorming technique
	  g. Use brainstorming to choose a name for the group.

Handout
	III. Close
	  a. Summarize key points based on objectives
	  b. Announce next meeting
	  c. Meeting evaluation
	  d. Thank audience for attending

are good wrap-up activities. Think of the session plan as your road map to success.

Ideally, application of learning is never left to chance; and, as each new task, procedure, or concept is learned, it is applied in a real situation. This may require you to develop a variety of realistic illustrations. You are urged to ask employees to suggest applications and illustrations—involvement and realism should both rise. However, you should also have applications and illustrations to provide should employees be unable to do so.

TRAINING SKILLS

Much of the success of your training rests with you. The way you conduct

Exhibit 3-2
Training Session Format

Title:	Assigned Risk Auto Processing
Objectives:	1. Explain Auto Risk Processing 2. Practice Auto Risk Processing

Outline

I. Quiz on previous session

II. Review Answers

III. Recap Prior Session

IV. Introduction

Introduction	A. Explain what an assigned risk is and how we get it
	
	B. Explain why we handle assigned risks and the differences in this application
	
	C. Cover language: AR, statutory coverage; light, medium and heavy symbols
	
	   1. CA = light and medium
	   2. CB = heavy

V. Procedure

Procedure	A. Explain how the application is reviewed — give examples (handouts)
	
	   1. Determine surcharges, if any
	   2. Assign the necessary codes
	   3. Compute premium
	
	B. Show how to locate the above information and the listing of the necessary forms and codes

VI. Practice

Practice	A. Have analysts process a dummy new business and renewal; one sample for everyone

VII. Wrap-Up

Wrap-up	A. Hold question and answer period B. Review areas just covered and how performed C. Discuss importance of proper handling, proper rating, proper classification, and surcharging

Exhibit 3-3
Ten Characteristics of Good Trainers

Enthusiasm	— Make it obvious that what you have to say is worthwhile; training is not just a job, but a privilege and an opportunity; get excited about your subject.
Sincerity	— Believe in what you say and prove it.
Selection	— Don't tell all you know about the subject; select the most important parts from the trainee's standpoint; stick to 5 or 6 major points per hour.
Clarity	— Be clear in meaning and diction; organize your material well.
Patience	— There are no dumb questions, only dumb answers; people learn at different rates; never embarrass the questioner.
Examples	— Use plenty of them; make them personal; draw from your own experience; be sure they are pertinent.
Humor	— A great change of pace; keep it in good taste and appropriate.
Pace	— Vary your voice level, your position, and your presentation; take a break when interest lags.
Awareness	— Your trainees' actions will tell you how you're getting across; look for the frown, the wandering eye, and the intent concentration.
Empathy	— You were a trainee at one time yourself; put yourself in his or her place now; "the mind can absorb only what the seat can endure."

"TEACH THE PEOPLE, NOT THE MATERIAL"

your training sets the climate for learning. If you are enthusiastic and open, your behavior stimulates learning, growth, and development of employees.

Responsibility for Excellence

It is not the brilliance of your performance that is important, but rather the amount of learning that takes place. Brilliant lecturers may not be good trainers. The tricky part is to keep results in mind and overcome the natural tendency to judge your training as entertainment.

Your Personal Qualities

Your own attitudes will have a bearing on the learning that takes place. It is important that you know how others, especially the persons you supervise and train, perceive you.

In addition to a positive attitude, there are some other characteristics of good trainers, shown in Exhibit 3-3. If you lack any of these characteristics, it would be well to make a sincere effort to acquire them. Most important, though, is the realization that your job as a trainer is not to teach the material, but rather to teach the people.

Specific Skills·

There are a number of skills an effective trainer should possess. You should be able to resolve conflicts between yourself and trainees, as well as between trainees. Speak loudly and clearly, and periodically evaluate your pronunciation and enunciation. By varying your rate of speaking and by using strong gestures, you can keep your listeners' interest level high. Humor can be very effective as long as it is not at the expense of another person.

If you are training for the first time, you will probably be very nervous. This is normal, and even experienced supervisors and trainers report having "butterflies." Experience and rehearsal can reduce your nervousness. By being well prepared, you help your audience to relax as well. There is no need to apologize for anything if you are well prepared. Apologies may lower your audience's confidence in you.

Be conscious of your actions at all times. Seek feedback on any disturbing mannerisms or habits you have. Rehearse your use of visual aids so that you are comfortable with them. If you know your subject, you can devote your time to plans for communicating it to your audience.

Observing some basic business practices is also essential. Punctuality commands respect. Start on time and end on time, and schedule breaks where appropriate. Your assignments should be clear. Dress neatly to command respect. The objective, duration, and other dimensions of a training situation should determine what you wear. At times you may dress "up" to signify the seriousness of the occasion. In other training situations, you might deliberately dress casually to convey your desire for an informal atmosphere.

ON-THE-JOB TRAINING

Should training be done in the classroom with groups of employees or individually on-the-job? There is no one ideal way since both methods have advantages and disadvantages. Before making the decision consider the objectives, cost, time, amount of energy, and availability of instructors, among other things.[9] Giving the training yourself provides an opportunity to build closer relationships with employees. It allows you to communicate the level of performance you expect. On the other hand, poor learning may result if you are unskilled as a discussion leader or do not see your involvement as essential to success. Over the long run, of course, you will want to develop your training skills and should welcome opportunities for personal involvement in employee growth. Further, if you do the training, you will know immediately how well the employee has learned.

Advantages

On-the-job training is probably the most frequently used method. It often saves time, involves less travel, and no special facilities are usually needed. There is less interference with production when only one employee is involved at a time. Allowing the employee to train under operating conditions with the work that comes across the desk may be far more realistic than any classroom simulation.

Disadvantages

On-the-job training seems to take second place to production. It may be difficult for you to block interruptions. If the supervisor or trainer lacks skill as a trainer, the employee may not learn well. Sometimes employees resent being trained by their immediate supervisor for fear that the boss will see them at their worst or, perhaps, put too much pressure on them. On-the-job training often tends to become too informal and may seem poorly organized or loose.

Special Preparation Needs

In addition to the usual planning steps of determining if a training need exists and formulating the training objectives, there are some special steps you must take in preparing to do on-the-job training. One of these special steps is to break the total job down into each element or activity and prepare your plan to teach these elements in the sequence in which they are performed when the job is actually done. Secondly, you should prepare a timetable based upon your best estimate of how much the trainee can grasp within a given period of time. Finally, you should prepare the work area for training and assemble all needed equipment such as calculators, typewriters, files, and memo paper.

Steps

A five-step model is often used in conducting on-the-job training:

It is generally accepted that there are five basic steps to on-the-job training, and the first one is to prepare to instruct. This includes the preparation of a session plan, outline, or check list. Second, the trainee has to be prepared for instruction. He or she must know what objectives are to be reached. Thirdly, the operation has to be presented to the trainee. They need to see the job done correctly. Fourth, the trainee must perform each part of the operation as it is taught. Finally, follow-up is necessary, which includes the making of corrections and reinforcing areas of weakness.[10]

In short, on-the-job training involves much more than explaining how to do something. You should put the employee at ease and build confidence by praising small successes. Take an interest in the trainee and be patient. Make yourself available to answer questions. Reinforce the importance of the personal satisfaction to be gained by performing the job well. If you will do all of these things your on-the-job training should be effective and contribute to a positive supervisor-employee relationship.

CLASSROOM TRAINING

There are a number of advantages in classroom training: by taking the worker from the normal work setting, concentration should be high. Devoting full energy to the learning means that it should take place more quickly. Classroom training encourages greater use of audio-visual aids and generally allows for productive interaction among trainees. Employees may be more relaxed and fear mistakes less if the training is done in a group setting.

A chief disadvantage is that classroom training is usually quite costly. The cost of maintaining classroom training facilities may be high. But an even greater financial burden is the fact that the employee is away from normal productive activities, and this indirect cost of training, meaning the loss of productivity, can be substantial. Time may be (or seem to be) wasted for those who learn fast or who already know some of the session content. However, when large groups of employees have similar learning needs, the classroom is often the best and most economical solution.

Methods

The Lecture Supervisors who are proficient in their subject and who are comfortable before an audience find lecturing gratifying to the ego. This is because the trainer does most of the talking. Occasional questions to the audience may be allowed during the lecture, but generally there is little active participation by the audience. The trainer is in complete control, with the trainees in a passive role. There is little discussion or practice by the audience. The lecture method is not always effective. Its advantages are that a large amount of information can be presented to a large number of people in a relatively short period of time. It is frequently used to present new information.

The lecture has major disadvantages. Without audience participation, it is hard to evaluate just how much learning takes place. With the trainer in such strong control, it is important that the trainer be effective as a speaker. Unfortunately, some lecturers are just boring. Indeed, technical experts may be so caught up with the subject that they fail to communicate at the level of the audience. If you are a subject-matter expert, be on guard when you serve as trainer.

A question and answer or discussion period at the end of a lecture can increase its effectiveness. If the introduction is challenging and stimulating, the audience is likely to retain more from the lecture. Use of visual aids and handouts increases interest and provides written materials that supplement the lecture.

One commentator states:

> A trainer trains two things: subject matter and people. If the lecture method is to be used, some basic steps relating to people will help in preparing the material for a lecture:
> 1. *P*inpoint your exact purpose.
> 2. *E*xamine your audience.
> 3. *O*rient your talk to their knowledge and interests.
> 4. *P*artition your material into a few briefly worded ideas.
> 5. *L*imit your material to what your audience can take in mentally.
> 6. *E*xamples! Use lots of them illustrating every point.[11]

Discussion

While discussion takes more time than a lecture, it allows involvement which should result in greater learning. It is best used with small groups and can be especially useful in changing attitudes. The disadvantages include the fact that it works best with small groups and is time consuming. Moreover, there is a risk that the discussion will stray or even run counter to the training objectives.

Perhaps the most important role of the supervisor in a discussion is to keep the group on the subject. That requires subtle control. Sometimes it is best to be a "fellow learner" and not try to answer all the questions posed by the discussion. Courtesy rather than parliamentary rules should prevail, and conclusions should be reached by consensus. Some suggestions for a discussion leader appear in Exhibit 3-4.

Demonstrations

Demonstrations appeal to all senses and are best used with small groups. Demonstrations involve a "show and tell" by the trainer followed by individual practice by members of the class.

Role Playing

Role playing should be focused on a problem that is meaningful and important to the trainees. It is highly productive when the need for it arises spontaneously in the trainees. Usually, however, you will have to prepare the scenario and role descriptions in advance. It is a suitable method for gaining insight and skill into human relations problems and therefore needs an open, friendly atmosphere to work well.

The procedure is to describe a meaningful situation, ask for volunteers, and give the actors written instructions about their roles. Allow them time to prepare for their roles. Those not engaged in the role playing are asked to observe it and look for specific behaviors or themes. Following the role play, the actors are asked to tell why they behaved as they did and how they felt about their own and others' behavior. Then the observers are asked their opinions. Role playing should help the group to understand the importance of behavior in various situations and the subtleties involved in skillful behavior.

Case Studies

Case analysis is a good way to stimulate participation and discussion. Cases allow the application of new knowledge to real situations. They work best when they seem real. The case situations should be stated briefly and simply and should require the trainees to make decisions and take action. If not given as "pre-class work," cases require considerable time for digestion and analysis. Emphasis should be given to the steps taken to implement the solution.

Exhibit 3-4
Some Suggestions for a Discussion Leader

1. Prepare a discussion outline that suggests subjects and clearly states your objectives.

2. Start with a brief statement outlining the limits of the subject that sells employees on the need for the discussion and how they will benefit.

3. Select one point and ask "Who wants to speak on this?" If there is no response, ask "one who knows" and ask another to elaborate on it.

4. Watch that you do not talk too much. If you must contribute your ideas, do so as one of the group rather than as a leader.

5. You are not supposed to know all the answers. It may be better not to give all the answers you know.

6. Keep the discussion focused on the subject; see that each point gets the time it merits.

7. Encourage all to express ideas; try to get each member to contribute; keep check on who has participated.

8. Make sure that no one person does most of the talking; invite quieter persons to join in. Direct questions to specific individuals, occasionally.

9. Keep the discussion going by one of the following means:

   a. Ask questions that cannot be answered by yes or no.
   b. If a member asks a question, do not answer it, but refer it to another member.
   c. When you get no response to a general question, rephrase it and perhaps call on someone specifically.
   d. Use "why" and "how" questions frequently.
   e. Sometimes ask debatable questions.
   f. Ask a member to sum up the points made so far.

10. Never let anyone interrupt someone who is talking. If someone breaks in, say, "Just a minute, Bill has the floor," or "Your turn is next."

11. Keep control when arguments between members arise; after positions are clear, call on others to give their views.

12. Keep the meeting informal; establish courtesy rather than parliamentary rules.

13. Do not let the discussion die out. Stop it at its height and start summarizing. Reach conclusions on which all can agree or consensus is clear.

Notes and Handouts

Two other training aids have proven effective in training. The first is note taking. The act of writing down information helps the mind retain it. The best note takers spend 80 to 90 percent of their time listening for facts, ideas, and concepts, and the other 10 to 20 percent writing down the main ideas. Another classroom training aid is the "handout." Should the material be handed out before, during, or after the session? It depends on your objective. If an item is handed out first, give people time to review it and then refer to it as you progress through your session. If it is handed out at the end of the session, stress its use as a reference piece. Items distributed during a session are usually discussed or used immediately.

Getting Participation

Getting participation requires planning and hard work. Plan your sessions to get frequent employee responses. You can do this by asking well-thought-out questions rather than just making statements. Challenge your trainees with problem-solving exercises rather than simple applications that seem like busy work. You might stimulate involvement by assigning subjects to some employees for them to explain to other members of the class.

Part of your job is to control the group. Your trainees come with a wide variety of personalities, so be prepared to cope with them. One problem is the "know-it-all" who wants recognition. You can control the "loud-mouth" by asking him or her to summarize key points and then asking others to add their comments. The silent person may be uninterested or confused. Some people just want to listen. To get these people involved, you have to question them individually; but if they do not respond, do not press them. "Side trackers" usually want to avoid the topic. Either they lack confidence or do not know the objectives of the session. Ask these people to focus on the learning objectives.

The prime way to increase participation is through questions. Good questions will arouse interest, stimulate discussion, channel thinking, and give you an opportunity to determine if the employees understand the material. Distribute your questions equally so you cannot be accused of bias. The best questions are thought provoking. It is best to use open-ended questions that ask how and why, rather than questions that can be answered with a simple yes or no. Sometimes you will use general questions that are open to anyone for answers. At other times, you may wish to direct questions to specific individuals. Finally, when questions are directed to you, it may be well to re-direct them to other trainees. If the other trainees cannot respond or respond incorrectly, then it is time for you to answer. If you get a question you really cannot answer, admit it, and offer to get the answer and report back to the class.

Audio-Visual Aids

One author reminds us, "75% of what we learn is through sight and we forget 75% of what we hear within two days."[12] An audio-visual aid is any device for teaching and communicating that uses the senses of sight and hearing. The suggestions that follow may seem obvious but they are offered for the supervisor inexperienced as a standup trainer.

Audio-visual aids avoid misunderstandings that may be caused by words alone. They can serve as attention getters. They add a valuable change of pace to many sessions. The danger is relying too much on them. Because they are expensive and often slickly done, films or tapes may seem sufficient for learning to occur. Not so: employees usually need guidance in digesting them and distilling the main point. There should be a specific learning objective that governs the use of each audio-visual aid. They can be used to introduce, present, emphasize, reinforce, or illustrate your message.

Many classrooms have overhead projectors for showing transparencies. Transparencies are relatively easy to prepare on many photocopy machines. A blank transparency and a grease pencil can be used much like a chalkboard or flip chart to create your visual aid as you go along. They work best when the area around the screen is darkened somewhat. The most common misuse of the transparency is probably making them from typewritten copy. The original must normally be much larger than typewritten size for the transparency to be clearly visible in a typical meeting room.

There are many other types of audio-visual aids available today. Color slides and a slide projector can bring vivid photographs into the classroom. Motion picture films and video tape recordings are available on many insurance-related subjects. If your firm does not own the necessary equipment for playing them, equipment can be rented. Slides, films, and video tapes have the disadvantage of requiring a dark, or semi-dark room. Select your aids carefully and, when showing them, be sure they are introduced properly at the beginning and discussed thoroughly afterwards.

When preparing visual aids, be sure they are relevant to your subject. One aid per major point is a good rule. Keep them simple and add color if at all possible. Remember, they should supplement, not replace, your presentation. When using visual aids, talk to your audience, not to the visual aid. Practice their use before your session.

TRAINING EVALUATION

The most common reason for evaluation is to determine the effectiveness of the training so that future training can be improved. Evaluation can take many approaches. Each of them can be helpful as long as the objectives and limitations are understood. Most evaluation presupposes that the training was directed toward specific objectives, such as reduction of errors or ability to perform a task. The main factor to be evaluated is whether or not the learning objectives were met. Is the employee able to transfer what was learned to on-the-job performance? As a supervisor responsible for training, you are charged with evaluating its results—the real "pay-off." Evaluation devices should be simple to administer, use, and explain. Four different approaches will be discussed, with emphasis on testing to see that learning has taken place.

Reaction

The first thing to be evaluated is how well the trainees liked the training, which is called the *reaction*. It measures the feelings of the trainees, but does not include any measurement of the learning that has taken place. Because reaction is so easy to measure, almost all trainers do it. The following guidelines should be used to measure reaction:

1. Determine what you want to find out.

2. Use a written comment sheet covering those items determined in step one above.
3. Design the form so that the reactions can be quantified and tabulated easily.
4. Encourage trainees to add their comments.
5. You probably will get more honest reactions by making the forms anonymous.

A sample "reactionnaire" appears in Exhibit 3-5.

Learning

Even if reactions are enthusiastic, there is no guarantee that learning has taken place. It is important to determine objectively the amount of learning that has occurred. Learning can be defined as those principles, facts, and techniques that were understood and absorbed by the trainees. Learning in this sense does not refer to the on-the-job use of these principles, facts, and techniques. Here are some suggestions for measuring learning:

1. The learning of each trainee should be measured so that quantitative results can be determined.
2. If possible, a before-and-after approach should be used so that any learning can be related to the training received.
3. As far as possible, the learning should be measured objectively, that is, on the basis of data rather than on the basis of feelings and opinions.
4. Where possible, the evaluation results should be analyzed statistically so that learning can be proven in terms of correlation of level of confidence (a statistical concept).

Some of the methods for measuring learning are classroom performance and testing. Classroom activities such as demonstrations, discussions, and individual performance of the skill being taught can be used as evaluation techniques. Where principles and facts are taught rather than techniques, the most common method of evaluation is the paper and pencil test. Tests must be prepared carefully if they are to accomplish their purpose, and the manner in which they are given and used can affect the reaction to them. Adults like to know how they are doing, but tend to shy away from tests and grades if they are to be used for comparisons with others. After a test has been given and corrected, employees should be encouraged to review the material covered in it.

Job Behavior

An expert in the field of training writes: "There is often a big difference between knowing principles and techniques and using them on-the-job. The evaluation of training in terms of on-the-job behavior is more difficult than measuring reaction and learning."[13] A scientific approach is needed and many factors must be considered. Some guidelines for evaluating training in terms of behavioral changes are:

Exhibit 3-5
Standard Evaluation Form*

Course Title: _____ Date: _____

Location: _____ Instructors: _____

To guide us in planning future seminars and workshops, please answer the questions below. You need not sign the sheet unless you so desire.

How would you rate the following?

	Excellent	Satisfactory	Unsatisfactory
Quality of Presentation	_____	_____	_____
Adequacy of Course Content	_____	_____	_____
Length of Course	_____	_____	_____
Adequacy of Course Materials	_____	_____	_____
Conduct of Workshops	_____	_____	_____
Adequacy of Facilities	_____	_____	_____

If any factor is rated "unsatisfactory," please provide explanation:

_____

_____

_____

What was of most value to you in this seminar?

_____

_____

What was of least value to you in this seminar?

_____

_____

Additional comments would be appreciated.

_____

_____

_____

_____

_____

_____
Signature (optional)

* Reprinted with permission from *Evaluating Training Programs*, Donald L. Kirkpatrick (Madison, WI: American Society for Training and Development, Inc., 1973)

1. A systematic appraisal should be made of on-the-job performance on a before and after training basis.
2. The evaluation of performance should be made by one or more of the following (the more the better):
   a. The person receiving the training
   b. His or her supervisor
   c. His or her subordinates
   d. Peers or other people familiar with his or her performance.
3. The post-training evaluation should be made three months or more after the training so that the trainees have an opportunity to put into practice what they have learned. While evaluating behavior change is often a complicated procedure, it is worthwhile and necessary if your training programs are going to increase in effectiveness.

Job Performance and Results

Proving the results of training has always been difficult. It is hard to say that one particular training program was responsible for a reduction in expense ratio or loss ratio or an increase in sales. It is nearly as hard to say that specific training effort was the cause of error reduction or some other training objective. However, an effective supervisor or trainer will try to accumulate evidence that training has had an impact on job performance and on the overall results of the unit or firm. These benefits are difficult to prove, but if enough evidence can be shown, top management will support a vigorous training program. Top management usually shows three concerns:

1. Is training the best way to get desired results?
2. Are the dollars being spent on training producing the needed results?
3. What improvements can be made in training procedures to get a greater return on the investment?

You should be prepared to answer these questions and support your answers with evidence.

SUMMARY

Here is a list of the ten commandments of effective training. This list helps to recap the main points made in this chapter.
1. Determine your objectives. What should the trainee be able to do upon completion of the training that he or she cannot do now?
2. Analyze your audience. Consider their ages, educational levels, and previous experience.
3. Analyze your subject. Differentiate between "need-to- know" and "nice-to-know."
4. Prepare an outline. Every session should have an introduction, a body, and a conclusion.

5. Design your program. Determine what format, visual aids, and testing you will use.
6. Call on experts for assistance. No one knows everything.
7. Train with your student in mind. Consider the training environment and make your presentations clear and effective.
8. Maintain training records. Record who has completed what and how well.
9. Deliver your message with confidence and enthusiasm. Practice, practice, and practice!
10. Follow through on your training. Get feedback from both trainees and their supervisors after they are back on the job, and modify your program for future trainees.

Chapter Notes

1. Leonard Nadler, *Developing Human Resources* (Houston, TX: Gulf Publishing Co., 1970), p. 40.
2. Martin M. Broadwell and William F. Simpson, *The New Insurance Supervisor* (Reading, MA: Addison-Wesley Publishing Co., 1981), p. 107.
3. William McGehee and Paul W. Thayer, *Training in Business and Industry* (New York, NY: John Wiley & Sons, Inc., 1961), p. 47.
4. Malcolm S. Knowles, *The Adult Learner: A Neglected Species* (Houston, TX: Gulf Publishing Co., 1973), p. 55.
5. *Training and Development Handbook* (New York, NY: McGraw-Hill Book Co., 1976), p. 42-1.
6. Knowles, p. 108.
7. Robert F. Mager and Peter Pips, *Analyzing Performance Problems* (Belmont, CA: Fearon Pitman Publishers, Inc., 1970), p. 8.
8. Robert F. Mager, *Preparing Instructional Objectives* (Belmont, CA: Fearon Pitman Publishers, Inc., 1975), p. 6.
9. Martin M. Broadwell, *The Supervisor and On-The-Job Training* (Reading, MA: Addison-Wesley Publishing Co., 1975), p. 29.
10. *Effective Training* (Scranton, PA: International Correspondence Schools, 1969), p. 71.
11. Thomas F. Slaton, *How to Instruct Successfully* (New York, NY: McGraw-Hill Book Co., 1960), p. 71.
12. Martin M. Broadwell, *The Supervisor as an Instructor* (Reading, MA: Addison-Wesley Publishing Co., 1978), p. 85.
13. Donald L. Kirkpatrick, *Evaluating Training Programs* (Madison, WI: American Society for Training and Development, Inc., 1975), p. 10.

CHAPTER 4

Automation

INTRODUCTION

Computers were once the domain of the data processing staff. Programmers and DP analysts designed computer systems, and the only contact the supervisor had with computers was to receive printouts in funny looking type on paper with holes in both sides.

In recent years, the computer has come out of the climate-controlled room and into the general office area. Supervisors must now understand how to evaluate, select, and manage automated systems.

This chapter will define the basic components of an automated system and explain how each of these components fits into an office operation. It will then describe the various types of automated systems available in the insurance industry and how each can be used in a company or agency office.

You will learn the benefits of automated systems and how to evaluate which of these benefits apply to your department. You will be shown how to define your department's automation needs and work with software vendors and in-house programming staffs to design systems to meet these needs. You will then learn how to plan the installation of the system and the training of your staff, as well as how to manage your computer operation and provide for its security.

Moving from a manual to an automated environment can be a traumatic change for you and your staff. The final section of this chapter will explain the effects the change may have on your employees and how you can make the transition from the manual to the automated office as easy as possible for the people who work for you.

Definitions: Computer Terms

Automated Systems For the purposes of this chapter, we define automated systems as any office system utilizing electronic equipment which contains electronic commands (programs) stored in that equipment.

Components of a Computer System Automated systems are made up of hardware and software. Hardware is the equipment on which a system is run. Software is the instructions, usually stored on cards, tapes, or disks, which tell the hardware what to do. Software is "the brains of the outfit"; hardware is the brawn. Hardware and software, which together are called the system, can be further divided into four functions—input, output, auxiliary storage, and processing.

Input Input is used to get information from the manual environment (in the insurance industry, usually paper) into the system. Therefore, if an underwriter has accepted a risk, the information on this risk, such as exposures and limits, must be entered into the system. This is done through an input device.

Keyboards The most common input device used in the insurance industry is a typewriter-like keyboard in conjunction with a screen. This screen is also called a video display terminal (VDT) or cathode-ray tube (CRT). In our example of the new risk as input, an operator would enter the necessary data about the insured into the system by typing the information on the keyboard, verifying its accuracy on the screen, and using instruction keys on the keyboard, entering the data permanently into the system.

Optical Scanning Another type of input device is an optical scanning unit, which reads characters printed in specially treated ink. Banks use this type of input to read those odd numerals on the bottom of checks. The nine digit postal zip code is designed to allow use of optical scanning equipment to sort mail. You have probably seen bar code optical scanners used at supermarket checkout counters.

Electronic Input A third input device is electronic, with computers talking to computers. A computer in an insurance agency, for example, is able to communicate directly with a company system via a communications network. In this way, an agent will make the initial entry and the information will be fed directly to the company's computer.

Other Input Devices Direct input procedures are also available and under development. A "light pen" touched to the screen enters information into the computer. Policy applications, when completed with treated pens or typewriters, will directly enter data into the computer system without use of a keyboard.

Output Output enables the computer to exhibit information needed by system users. The common output methods used in the insurance industry are printers and the now familiar video display terminals or CRTs. Printers produce information on paper, somewhat like a typewriter, but at much faster speeds.

Computers can also output information via COM (computer-output microfilm). Printouts that used to fill hundreds of pages and scores of file cabinets, can now be put on transparent plastic sheets, called microfiche, and stored in a small section of a desk drawer. Insurance companies are making extensive use of this technology for long-term storage of data. Rating information in many states is presently made available to companies and agents on microfiche produced through COM systems.

Auxiliary Storage   Auxiliary (permanent) storage holds data in quantity. It is used to hold the kind of data you now have in the various files in your office, such as daily reports, accounting data, collection information on insureds, and claim reports. Auxiliary storage usually uses magnetic tape, small, flexible disks (diskettes or floppy disks), or larger, rigid fixed disks (hard disks). When looking at a computer system, you can often see the devices that constitute auxiliary storage. Sometimes a computer system grows by adding disks or disk drives.

Auxiliary storage also holds most of the programmed instructions (software) which tell the system what to do with the stored information. These programmed instructions might be compared to detailed procedures manuals. Just as procedures manuals tell your clerks what to do with the work in front of them, programs tell the computer what to do with the information in its memory.

Central Processing Unit   The central processing unit (CPU) is where the action takes place in a computer. The CPU consists of three parts: primary (temporary) storage, the arithmetic/logic unit, and the control unit.

Primary Storage   Primary (temporary) storage allows the system to take information it needs from permanent storage and process a transaction. For instance, policy information on all of an agency's or company's insureds may be stored in permanent storage. Temporary storage allows the computer to take one insured's policy data and extract just the information needed to issue a return premium endorsement and revise the policy data before returning it to permanent storage. This would resemble a clerk going to the file cabinet, pulling one daily report, and issuing an endorsement. Once the transaction is completed, policy information, including the endorsement, is returned to the file (in the manual system) or permanent storage (in the automated system).

Arithmetic/Logic   The arithmetic/logic unit allows the system to perform mathematical functions and to extract certain data from permanent storage. In our example of the endorsement transaction, the arithmetic/logic unit would calculate the return premium due the insured.

Definitions: Automated Equipment

The computer belongs to a larger class of devices called automated equipment. However, all automated devices are, in effect, computer systems.

Automated systems come in many sizes and shapes, from calculators that fit in your pocket to huge mainframe systems located behind locked doors in temperature-controlled rooms.

Electronic Calculator   The simplest type of automated system is the electronic calculator. It can be categorized as an automated system because it has all of the components: an input device (keys); output device (a small screen and possibly a tape); and central processing unit (CPU). The central processing unit usually has stored programs which allow easy calculation of such functions as square roots and reciprocals; and may have temporary storage to store calculations.

Programmable Calculator   The next step up the automation ladder is the programmable calculator. In a simple electronic calculator, the only programs that can be used are those that are built into the system. A programmable calculator allows the user to create simple programs and enter them into the system. The instructions for developing these programs come with the calculator and do not require knowledge of a programming language.

Programmable calculators are useful when there is a large number of repetitive calculations. Insurance rating provides a good example. The rates and calculation formula can be programmed into the calculator, allowing premiums to be developed with a minimum of input.

Intelligent Typewriters   So-called intelligent typewriters provide the ability to store and revise a small amount of text and make corrections simply by typing over what had already been keyed.

Word Processing Systems   Word processing provides for the manipulation of words in much the same way that data processing allows for the manipulation of numbers. For example, on a word processor, paragraphs can be moved, errors corrected, and columns adjusted with the tap of a button. In addition, forms can be executed and statistical reports produced in a fraction of the time taken by an electric typewriter.

Intelligent Copiers   Intelligent copiers integrate the entire text preparation, communication, and reproduction function into one system. Data can be entered into a system as it would be in word processing and then printed in selected type faces and output styles and transmitted to designated locations. For example, if ten people in different offices are to receive copies of a memo, it would be outputted on ten systems at the same time.

Mainframes, Minis, and Micros   What we usually refer to as computer systems are usually divided into three categories, mainframe systems, minicomputers and microcomputers. There are now no clear lines of differentiation among the three, since their capabilities keep changing.

At one time, you could have said that mainframe systems were large computers requiring their own climate-controlled locations and providing multi-terminal, multi-function operations. Minicomputers were stand-alone systems located in the general office area, providing multi-terminal and multi-function operations. Microcomputers were desk top systems, providing only one terminal and capable of doing one task at a time. Storage capacity also helped distinguish these systems. Mainframe systems had more storage and comput-

Exhibit 4-1
A Computer System

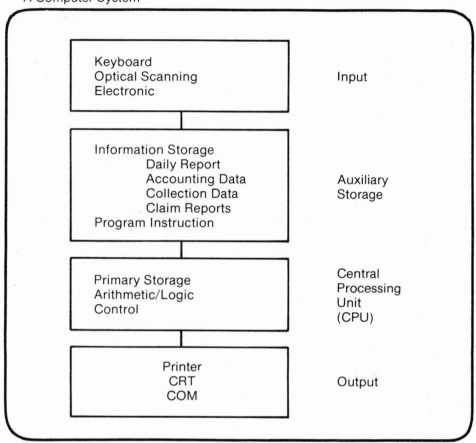

Keyboard Optical Scanning Electronic	Input
Information Storage 　　　Daily Report 　　　Accounting Data 　　　Collection Data 　　　Claim Reports Program Instruction	Auxiliary Storage
Primary Storage Arithmetic/Logic Control	Central Processing Unit (CPU)
Printer CRT COM	Output

ing capacity than did mini-computers, which in turn had larger storage and capacity than micro-computers. Price also served as a rough guide. A micro-computer might sell for $2,000, a mini-computer for $20,000, and a mainframe for $200,000.

The Control Unit If the CPU is where the action takes place in a computer, then the control unit is where the action takes place within the CPU. It controls the activities of the CPU and, therefore, the computer system as a whole. The control unit receives and interprets program instructions from primary storage. Based on the instructions, the control unit will issue commands to the appropriate part of the computer system. The control unit has been compared to a traffic cop at a busy intersection and might also be analogous to a supervisor who receives and interprets instructions from upper management and issues commands to the employees in his or her department.

To summarize, a system is made up of hardware and software, which consist of three parts, input, output, and processing. Data is entered into the system via input devices. Transactions are performed within the CPU and data is returned to the user on output devices.

These categories have been blurred in recent years as the smaller systems have become more powerful. For example, many microcomputers can now support multi-terminal and multi-task operations and the storage and computing capacity of many of these systems exceeds the power many mainframe systems had only five years ago.

The only distinction that we can make today is that mainframe refers to the largest systems available, minicomputers to the next largest, and microcomputers to the smallest.

Micrographics   Micrographics is a technology that has been around for many years and is now gaining wide usage. Many think of a microfilm system as roll or cartridge film that cannot be updated and is only useful for maintaining historical records. However, there are many micro-forms that lend themselves to the dynamic nature of file storage within the insurance industry.

Microfiche   Microfiche stores filmed images on transparent cards that can be read on an inexpensive microfiche viewer. An insured's complete file can be kept on one card. By using micro-thin jackets or updatable micro-fiche, new pieces of paper can be filmed and included in the file, making it possible to use such a system for active policyholder files.

Microfiche could prove valuable in a company branch office which expends a vast amount of time and space storing and maintaining policy files. Files which require large rooms for paper storage, for example, can now be placed in a single file cabinet.

Other Microfilm Systems   We have already mentioned computer-output microfilm (COM) as one output method from a computer system. There are now computer input microfilm systems which allow a computer to read specially treated microforms and enter data into its memory. A microfilm system with computer assisted retrieval can quickly locate specific information within a microfilm file.

There are many advantages to using microfilm as part of an automated system. It can provide increased file integrity. Once a piece of paper is filmed and part of the system, it cannot be lost as it might be in a paper file. In addition, copies can easily be made of microfiche allowing more than one person to view the file. Film is also more durable than paper and is, therefore, useful for long-term file storage.

In most jurisdictions, microfilm has the same legal standing as paper records. (Electronic storage has not yet gained this legal recognition primarily because of the ease by which automated records can be altered.)

An increasing use of computer output microfilm has been the output of inactive records from the computer to film. This reduces the amount of automated storage required. As files become inactive, they are output on film. For example, when a policy is renewed the new policy is placed in the electronic file and the expiring policy is output on film. This provides the required historical record without overburdening computer storage.

Facsimile Transmission Facsimile transmission of documents is another automated technology gaining increased popularity. It has been possible for many years to send printed material and photographs over telephone lines, using inexpensive facsimile transmissions systems. Unfortunately, it took as much as five minutes to send one piece of paper so it was impractical for sending the many documents that must be transmitted from one insurance office to another each day.

Recent improvements in facsimile technology have made it possible to send a piece of paper in seconds, rather than minutes, and make this technology more economical for our industry.

Imaging A technology related to facsimile is image processing, which provides electronic storage and transmission of actual documents rather than just alphabetic and numerical characters. This would allow storage of signatures or the diagrams often used in claim or engineering work; and the use of this stored data in computer operations.

AUTOMATION APPLICATIONS

There are innumerable applications of automated technologies within the insurance industry, and more are being developed every day. In this chapter we will cite only the most important applications.

Accounting

The most obvious application is in the accounting function. Most companies and many agencies have automated their billing, accounts payable, accounts receivable, general ledger, payroll, and other accounting operations. Automated systems maintain accounting records and provide data for the analysis of these records.

Forms Preparation

One of the most useful word processing applications for the insurance industry is the output of forms. Persons producing typed forms, such as declarations pages, spend more time lining up forms in the typewriter than they do keystroking. Word processing equipment can virtually eliminate alignment problems. Typists key in the necessary information and the system is programmed to output the data in the proper place on the forms being used. Similarly, statistical reports are far easier on word processing systems.

Standard Paragraphs

Word processing systems provide storage of standard paragraphs to be printed in letters and reports. For instance, a company engineering department may store standard introductory copy, explanations, and loss control recommendations. When the engineer completes his survey, he can tell the typist to insert paragraphs 1, 2, 4, 13, 26, and 42a in the recommendations to the insured. By pressing a few keys, the typist issues the report without requiring her to type the standard copy.

Standard Letters

Word processing systems can produce prepared letters and send them to a specific group of people. For example, collection letters can be developed and automatically sent to any insured whose payment is 5 days past due, 15 days past due, or any other criteria. The letters can be prepared, personalized, and mailed from the word processing system.

Marketing

When a company or agency has identified a segment of the insurance market to be pursued, automated systems can identify potential clients and the coverages and services they need. Sales solicitation letters can be developed and sent to these prospects.

Automated systems can also be used to update and add coverages for current insureds. Unless the company or agency writes the complete line for every account and every coverage is at full value, additional sales opportunities exist. An automated system can reveal what new lines or additional coverages can be offered to present insureds and then can develop the solicitation letters to offer these coverages.

Could the same thing be done without automation? Yes. But it is not likely to be done as thoroughly or as extensively as when done by automation. Can you imagine how long it would take to go manually through 3,000 files to check for the existence of personal umbrella coverage? In minutes, the computer can identify insureds who might want the coverage, and the word processing equipment can generate letters to these prospects.

Once a marketing program has been instituted, results must be analyzed. Automated systems can be used to track a marketing program and determine how well objectives are being met and perhaps identify where improvements can be made.

Underwriting

Many insurance companies are using computers in the underwriting functions. Computers can be programmed to accept risks that the company clearly wants, and reject those that are well outside of the carrier's underwriting guidelines. Questionable risks are referred to the underwriter. This frees the underwriter from having to review every risk, including those on which acceptance or rejection is pre-determined by company guidelines.

In addition to assisting the underwriter with the selection process, automated systems can help with the classification of risks. Besides saving time and eliminating paperwork, automated classification significantly reduces classification errors and provides increased consistency. Computers can also rate, develop the proper premiums, and generate the policy.

The use of automated systems in the underwriting functions will eventually mean an almost instant transaction, from the input of the application in the agent's office through the issuance of the policy. The industry has long sought the elimination of the time consuming multi-step procedure now being used to submit and underwrite a risk and produce a policy.

Customer Service

Once a risk is "on the books" it must be serviced. Automated systems can be used extensively to calculate and issue endorsements, premium adjustments, and the like. We can expect that insurance people will cling to the term "on the books" long after the policy is really "in the computer."

Daily Report Maintenance

The "daily" is probably the single most important document in the insurance business. The age-old name "daily" refers to a time when field men were required to make a report every day, hence a "daily report", on all new lines written. This report was then, and still is, the original agreement to insure. It provides data used by a number of agency and company people: agents, accountants, underwriters, auditors, and others. Automation allows simultaneous access to the daily and ends the frustration of waiting for this vital record to make the rounds.

Accuracy of records is greatly improved by automation when a system provides on-line inquiry. All employees who require information about an insured can get it simultaneously from the central processing unit. When a file is updated, the revised information is available as soon as it is inputted. People who need data can get it without depriving others of access to the files. Accuracy is usually improved because data is entered once and retrieved for many uses, not entered again and again on different records by different people. The only problem is the obvious one: an error originally entered reappears whenever the file is used until someone discovers it and corrects it.

Training

The computer will also be helpful in staff training. Programs are available to teach new employees specific jobs within the insurance industry. Whether it is the steps necessary to rate an automobile policy or how to adjust a workers compensation claim, an employee can be trained at his or her own pace. The system can monitor progress, only allowing the person to move on to a more complicated procedure when the preceding one has been mastered. Computer Assisted Education (CAE) will free you, as supervisor, from routine training and allow you to concentrate on difficult training problems which require innovative solutions.

This completes our discussion of how automated technologies are used in insurance operations. Your unit may not be able to utilize all of the technologies discussed. However, you have an ever growing range of choices when you "go shopping" for better ways to get the work done.

AUTOMATION BENEFITS

In order to identify problems to be solved and opportunities to be developed, you must know the benefits that your department can gain from automation.

Labor Saving

Your first thought may be the reduction of person-hours required to do the unit's work. Automated systems often allow operations to be conducted in a fraction of the time the work once took. Therefore, overtime and use of office temporaries can be curtailed; and often staff can be reduced. Another aspect of reduced labor is the ability to perform additional work without adding to staff or increasing the hours worked.

Uniformity

Automated systems help ensure uniformity of work among your staff. With manual procedures it is not uncommon for employees to do the same job differently, even though they were trained to follow the same procedures. This usually means that only one of them is using the correct procedures and some may be doing the job quite inefficiently.

By nature, automated systems demand uniformity. If an employee attempts to deviate from the approved procedure, the computer may refuse to accept the input. More sophisticated systems will tell the operator that he's made an error and show him what he must do to correct it.

Error Reduction

Automated systems help to reduce errors. For example, rating errors will be reduced if rate tables are stored in the system. If accurate exposure information is entered, proper premium will be outputted. Many systems contain error-checking functions that notify the operator whenever pre-specified types of mistakes are made. For instance, the system might stop processing operations to notify an operator that the zip code that was entered does not correspond to the state indicated. One or the other must be wrong. This error-checking function is called *editing*.

Appearance

Work appearance should also improve. In addition to the reduction of errors, output will be free of erasures, forms will be lined up, and appearance should be of a high, uniform quality.

Work Quality

Many users find that the ease of changing information in a computer system is a blessing. It enables them to be more demanding of their work than they might be if it were done manually. When preparing final copies of reports or proposals, the preparer might make an error which he would "live with" in the manual environment because of the difficulty of making the change. With most automated systems, the change is easily made and the error corrected.

Quality of reports can be enhanced by graphs and charts made possible by computer graphics software available for systems of all sizes including small personal computers.

Decision Aid

Most of a decision maker's time is spent collecting and manipulating information. Relatively little time is spent in actually making the decision.

As an example, consider the underwriter. An underwriter spends a good deal of time collecting information about a prospective insured from the agent, loss control engineer, credit bureau, and other sources. The underwriter then must take all of this data and arrange it so that it adequately describes the risk. Only then can the underwriter make the decision.

With automation, the data can be entered into the system, arranged, and results outputted so the underwriter can view the full scope of the risk and make the decision. In a sense this means that more time is available for the decision itself. Much of the data entry will be performed by clerical employees, or by the originating agency, making a further saving of the underwriter's time.

Reports Management

In large organizations each level of supervision and management gathers, analyzes, and consolidates data and reports to the next higher level. Automation usually simplifies multi-level reporting. Systems can be programmed to direct information to various levels of management in the format each needs, or to report only when a figure falls outside of a predetermined range.

Simplification of reporting among organizations within our industry can bring great benefits. For example, an independent adjuster will prepare a report for his files and send a copy to the insurance company, which may then prepare a similar report for the agent and insured. With the development of an automated industry network, it may be possible for the adjuster's report to be received by all interested parties at once without rehandling.

Our discussion of the benefits of automation should conclude with the optimistic note that we expect even greater benefits in the years ahead. Technological improvements, declining automation costs, and insurance industry network arrangements paint a promising future. By combining your knowledge of the uses of automation with the benefits, you will be able to identify specific automation opportunities. We turn now to the process of automation.

THE PROCESS OF AUTOMATION

When discussing the process of automation, we will concentrate on the development and installation of computer systems, since they are the most complex of the automated systems we've discussed. This same process, however, applies to smaller systems such as programmable calculators and intelligent typewriters. The difference is the detail that goes into the process. It will be simpler to speak as if you were automating an operation that is now performed manually. This makes the explanation easier but please remember that these ideas apply to any change involving automation, including system upgrades or interfacing with other systems.

Some supervisors will direct this process of automation by themselves, while others will have extensive help from a data processing staff. Whether you do it yourself or have help, it is your responsibility to ensure that each step is carefully followed since you are responsible for the performance of your unit.

Operations Analysis

The first step in the process of automating your department is to analyze current operations thoroughly. It is an accepted fact that if you automate inefficient systems, you are going to get inefficient automated systems. Therefore, step one in the process of automating your department is to follow the procedures outlined in Chapter 5 on improving operating procedures and maximizing productivity. A department is not ready for automation until manual systems are as efficient as possible.

Automation Applications

The second step is to develop a list of potential automation applications within your department, identifying the uses you will make of automation, the benefits you anticipate and the technologies you expect to use.

Whenever possible, benefits should be translated into dollars. For example, improved collection activities should reduce nonpay cancellations and increase investment income. It should not be difficult to determine the company's or agency's increased income due to these improvements. Similarly, improved quality of output and the ability to conduct direct mail marketing programs should increase sales. An estimate should be made of this increase.

Since automation may allow the firm to do new things, estimates of the benefits should be made despite the difficulties of quantifying new activities.

Establishing Priorities

Once you have identified potential applications and benefits, you should prioritize these items. Rarely can a system give you everything you want at an acceptable cost. When establishing priorities, look at the goals of the organization as well as the needs of your own department. For example, if the organization is planning an aggressive marketing program, automation applications that support this program would have a high priority. If the firm plans to open additional offices, systems that facilitate communications might come first.

System Specifications

Once priorities have been set, the next step is to develop detailed system specifications. In stating specifications, the insurance and the technical begin to merge. Specifications describe the functions the system must perform and the input, output, and processing that will be required.

Specifications should list, in as much detail as possible, each of the functions needed in a system and how they will operate. For example, an agent who wants a system that includes the accounting function might state the system must issue monthly statements to all insureds. These statements must be sorted by producer and must include pre-billed as well as current items. This information, along with a copy of the statement, itself, will tell the vendor or system designer what the user requires from the system.

Locating Software

Once specifications have been developed, there is usually an examination of off-the-shelf software that might meet the needs. There is a danger that purchased software may not meet all of your current specifications and may lack the flexibility to meet needs as they evolve. However, insurance organizations have been able to make use of much standard software, and that designed expressly for use in the insurance industry. Off-the-shelf software is usually less expensive than custom software and usually requires less time and effort to implement. You will have to decide whether your automation requirements can be satisified by off-the-shelf software or require a system developed to meet your specific needs.

Request for a Proposal (RFP)

To request assistance from a vendor, it is now customary to prepare a *Request for a Proposal* (RFP). In the RFP, explain to the vendor exactly what you want and include the detailed specifications discussed above. The RFP should include a request that the vendor describe how the system will meet your specifications.

You should also tell the vendor what information you need in order to make your decision.

System Expandability   Ask about the expandability of the system. Can additional memory and peripheral devices be added and at what expense? What percentage of the system's memory and capabilities will be utilized with the department's current workload?

A good rule of thumb is that a computer should be expanded when it has reached 75 percent to 80 percent capacity. If a proposed system is at or near the 80 percent level, you should consider a larger system.

Back Up   Determine the procedures and time involved with backing up the system. Data in an automated system exists on magnetic media and can therefore be copied fairly easily. It can also be erased easily. It is recommended that the data on a system be copied (backed up) at least weekly, and often more frequently. This ensures that if something happens to the data, it can be easily reconstructed.

Some systems can be backed up fairly easily, but others require more complex input and time. Before you accept any system, you should know what will be required to back it up and how often it must be done.

Response Time   You should also evaluate the system's response time. This is the number of seconds between the operator's depressing an instruction key and the system's execution of that instruction. More sophisticated, and therefore more expensive, systems usually have shorter response times.

Vendor Financial Responsibility   You are going to be dependent on the vendor for the life of the system. Changes and updates to the system are likely and you want to be sure the vendor will be around to do this work.

Vendor Staff   You will want to know what insurance experience and expertise the vendor's staff has. This may not be as important if you are buying a system that is not specifically designed for an insurance operation, such as a standard word processor. However, if the system will rate and issue commercial lines policies, you should evaluate the expertise of the people who have developed that system.

Training and Installation Support   Determine what support the vendor will give you with the training of your staff and the installation of the system. If automation is new to you, you are going to need a good deal of vendor support. Even if you are already using automated systems and are familiar with their use, you will need training on the specific system to be installed.

System Cost   You will want to know *all* of the cost you will incur when you buy the system. Ask the vendor to list all hardware costs, including peripherals, and all software costs. In addition, you will want to know the monthly maintenance costs for both the hardware and software.

Operating Manuals   The vendor should provide an operating manual for the system as part of the initial proposal. The operating manual gives a detailed explanation of how the system works, and would complement the procedures manuals that must be developed.

Screen Design The RFP should specify the location of data on the screen as it relates to input forms. For example, if the first bit of information on the entry form is the policy number and it is in the upper left hand side of the application, the screen should request that information first and place it on the upper left hand side of the screen. The type font as well as the word and number display format should be specified in the RFP to ensure that they are easily readable. (Screen design can be enhanced by the proper use of color. It has been shown that green and buff backgrounds are easier on the eyes than red, orange, yellow, or black backgrounds.)

References You will want the names, addresses, and telephone numbers of organizations that are using the system the vendor is proposing. You will want to talk to them to ensure that the system is performing as promised and as desired.

Receipt of the Proposals You will receive proposals from vendors or system design plans from the systems design unit of your firm. In either case, determine if the system being proposed meets your specifications. The vendor or systems design department should be required to respond to each of your specifications, even if their recommendation is not to automate some aspect of your operations. A vendor's system may not be able to meet one of your specifications, or the system design staff may feel that meeting one of your requirements will be too expensive. However, each of your specifications must be discussed in their proposal.

Planning for the Automated Environment

At the same time that you are preparing the RFP and evaluating systems, you should determine how your operations will change when automated. Some changes may be required by the system, while others become possible in the automated environment and may help your unit reach full productivity.

For example, a statistical report, which is now being completed in pen or pencil may be produced by the new system. This will require that the people who are doing the job be trained to use a keyboard. This is an operations change that is required when installing an automated system.

An automated system is often most productive when data is spooled (held for printing after all input is completed) and outputted at one time, often at the end of the day. For example, an employee may now type an invoice, remove it from the typewriter and put it in an envelope before typing another invoice. Using an automated system, all invoices would be inputted into the system before any are printed. Continuous feed forms would be used to print out all invoices at the end of the day. Someone would then stuff them into envelopes and place them in the mail. This is an example of an operations change that is not required. An invoice could still be mailed immediately after it is typed. However, efficiency would be enhanced by spooling the invoices and outputting them all at one time.

New Forms and Supplies New forms are often required when an activity is automated. In the example of invoice issuance above, full utilization of the system would require buying continuous feed forms. As supervisor you must determine if these forms are now available or must be designed and what they will cost. Time should be allowed for securing any necessary approval and for interdepartmental coordination.

Floorplan and Furniture You should also determine what floorplan and furniture changes will be necessary, if any. An automated system often requires its own furniture for the system, itself, and for the comfort of the employee using it. Computer keyboards are most comfortable to use when at a height lower than a standard desk. For that reason, the keyboard should not be placed on an employee's desk when it's going to be used for long periods of time.

Screens must be placed in a position that is comfortable for the user. Space is needed for raw data documents, for form storage, for printouts and data to be entered, as well as for other non-system work that an employee must do.

When ordering furniture, you will have to look not only at the automated work stations, but also at other furniture that may be needed. For example, you may require special cabinets to store disks or microfiche files.

The physical layout of the office may require relocating electrical cable and possibly adding to the electrical power your department receives.

Changing a department floorplan and getting delivery of furniture can take a good deal of time and should be considered when planning the system's installation. It does little good to have a new computer delivered in two months if it will take three months to get the furniture and electrical cabling needed for its proper use. It is easy to underestimate the time needed to go through channels in a large organization. What might seem to you to be a minor facilities modification may turn out to be a major change in building or utilities.

Lighting Lighting may have to be changed and furniture moved to prevent glare on screens and provide proper illumination for operators. Before automation, the most sought after desk was usually one by a window. This is a poor location for someone using a terminal since glare from sunlight often makes the screen unreadable. Soft, indirect light is usually best for automated systems.

Printer Location Automated system printers are often substantially louder than the standard electric typewriter and placing them in an open office area may disturb people. You should determine if printers should be in partitioned areas or protected with sound surpressing devices.

Downtime Contingency plans for system breakdown situations will require careful thought. "Downtime" will be a new phenomenon to you if you have not worked in automated activities before. Even the best computer systems will not be operational for at least a few hours a few days a year. Depending on the complexity of the problem and the distance that repair persons must travel, your system may be down for a day or more at a time.

What will happen to your department's work when your system goes down? Can you tell the people who use your services that the system is down without creating problems or ill will? How essential is it that you give at least emergency service?

Whatever contingency plans you use, arrangement should be made before the system arrives.

The most obvious contingency plan is to revert to a manual system. This solution is not as easy as it sounds. As time goes on, there will be fewer and fewer people who know the manual procedures. After a few years, your staff may consist mainly of new employees who have never worked with the former system, and a few senior employees who may not remember it. A contingency plan to revert to the old system would require that staff members be trained on manual operations that are no longer being used. In addition, you would have to maintain the records and manuals needed for the manual system. For example, if you are to revert to a manual rating system, you would have to maintain up-to-date rate manuals. Can you imagine a less exciting job than maintaining records to be used if the system goes down?

A more practical solution would be to find another organization using the same system and arrange a reciprocal agreement that would allow each of you to use the other's system when one system is down. The other organization might be another unit in your company, or another agency or company. This will allow you to continue to operate while your system is being repaired. When making these reciprocal arrangements, be sure to verify hardware and software compatibility, to ensure that the operations of both organizations are completely identical. Obviously, these reciprocal agreements are simplified in a large organization with many operating systems which have been developed by the same inhouse staff.

Plans should also be made for catastrophic contingencies, such as fires, in which all data is destroyed. Back-up disks are the best solution to this problem. Periodically, copies of disks are made and filed off premises, sometimes in a vault or in someone's home.

Position Guides You must also analyze your department's position guides and job descriptions and update them to reflect new employee duties. The updating of position guides should also include a review of job grades and salary levels. Employees experienced in operating automated systems may be in high demand. There is a danger of losing an employee to a competitor because you ignored the fact that new skills with an automated system made the employee more valuable to your organization and to other employers as well.

Performance Standards Performance standards should also be reviewed. Automated systems may increase the number of items an employee can handle and reduce the expected error rate. This ability to do more work of improved quality is one of the justifications for increasing salary and should be reflected in performance standards.

New performance standards will probably be needed. For example, if you are installing a microfiche system for active files, you may have to develop standards for loading or copying a jacket.

Staff Training and Orientation   Plans must also be made for the training and orientation of your staff. Training on a new system is a vital element in the system's success. Training includes use of the system itself, and the new operating procedures that have been developed around it.

Training should recognize the staff's present knowledge of and feelings about automation. It is wise to expect resistance to change—any work change—but extra caution is called for with first-time automation. The strangeness of the system may make employees hesitant at first, and training may have to be done in small steps.

The first step in orientation is usually focused on the hardware. Employees should sit down at the terminal and be allowed to "play" with it for a few hours. They must be given the opportunity to get a feel for the keyboard and see how their actions cause entries on the screen. Practice, and practice alone, may be needed to reassure employees that keyboard mistakes will not cause data loss, system malfunction, or other imagined disasters.

One of the best ways to let employees get acquainted with the terminal is through the use of video games (that's right, video games)! Many of the video games designed for home systems and arcades are available on business computers. Although some may say playing video games in a business office is a waste of time, the use of these games can reduce the fear some employees have of computer terminals.

Once employees have the feel of the terminal, they should be shown the operation of the overall system, without necessarily talking about specific job functions. This initial explanation should pay particular attention to showing them the failsafe features built into the system to prevent catastrophic erasure of vast amounts of data. Some employees are afraid to work at a terminal because they think that by hitting one wrong button they may destroy some valuable file. Most systems are programmed to prevent such an occurrence.

You should begin training on the automation of specific job functions only after employees feel comfortable with this new entity in the office. If the installation is your department's first automated system, you will find that training time is lengthened because employees have to learn not only a new job, but new technologies as well. In addition to training on the computer system, you must instruct your people on any new manual procedures that have been developed.

All employees whose jobs will be affected by the system should be given orientation. For example, if you're installing a word processing system in a transcribing department, everyone who uses that department's services should be shown what the system can do and how they can use it. If an invoicing system is being installed, employees in the collection department should receive orientation, since their copy of an invoice may be in a different format than they have been used to. A word of caution—resist the temptation to include too many details in the orientations. You may find it wise to prepare a number of briefings, each tailored to the knowledge needs of participants.

Conversion   A good deal of effort should go into planning the conversion of manual records to an automated system. There are two ways to convert to the new system. You can use a crash conversion program, or you can convert over an extended period of time.

A crash program requires that you convert all of your records to the new system as quickly as possible. For instanee, you might start with all policies whose last three numbers are 001 and work until all 999s have been converted.

The advantage of a crash conversion is that the new system is in place in a short period of time, and parallel operations are unnecessary. Crash programs, however, can be very expensive, since people often have to work overtime, office temporaries may be required, or records sent out to a service bureau for conversion. In addition, crash programs can create confusion during the conversion period, since large numbers of files are unavailable at any given time.

If converting files over a period of time, you have less of the short-term confusion and expense but you must operate two systems, the manual and the automated, during the conversion. For example, one common conversion method in the insurance industry is to place new business, renewals, and annual installments on the new system, but not convert existing policies. This means that, for a period of one year, a policyholder's records may be on either or both systems, and both have to be kept operational until all policyholder files have been converted. You should perform a detailed analysis of both conversion methods to determine which is best for your department.

Realizing System Benefits

Many supervisors have a misconception that they will gain all of the benefits anticipated from a new system within a few months after installation. In fact, you will have to go through the entire conversion and training process before you realize these benefits. Automated systems must be looked at as investments. Time and money must be spent when a system is purchased or developed, but benefits will accrue only over a period of time. In the first year after the system's installation, the initial expense could be substantially higher than the benefits derived. Dividends will come only after the system is fully operational and people become productive.

Testing

Plans must also be made to test the system when it arrives. A representative sample of department work should be run to ensure that the system does everything the vendor or data processing staff promised. The test material should include the most complex work that the system is expected to handle.

This testing plan, along with the actual testing of the system after it is delivered, is especially important when buying systems from outside vendors. Warranty periods may be limited. If you wait too long to discover system flaws, you may have difficulties getting the vendor to make the necessary changes.

Control

Plans must also be made for the control of the system. Once it is installed and fully operational, you will want to keep a log of all problems so you can identify trends and make corrections. You will also want to compare actual benefits with those that were anticipated.

System Installation

Once you have ordered a system and planned for its installation all that remains is to follow your installation plan. Make adjustments to the plan where necessary.

SYSTEM SECURITY

Once the system is installed you must be concerned with its security. In any business operation, whether it be manual or automated, data can be destroyed, stolen, or misused; and you share in the managerial responsibility to prevent this from happening. The breach of security is made easier by automation because vital data is concentrated in a small space. There may be no visual signs that someone has tampered with the system and that data has been altered or destroyed.

Physical Risks

The physical risks faced by automated systems are similar to those faced by other pieces of office equipment. These are fire, flood, water, lightning, windstorm, and smoke. The fire, flood, water, and lightning risks are complicated by the possibility of the system being destroyed by direct damage or by damage to electrical circuitry leading to the system.

A physical risk that is unique to many automated systems is demagnetization. Data is stored and processed by electrical impulses. These impulses can be destroyed with many magnetic fields. For example, a telephone placed on top of a floppy disk can alter the data or program stored on the disk when the telephone bell rings.

Food and beverages can cause trouble in the automated office. Office equipment can be damaged by spilled coffee and even by crumbs lodged in the equipment. Coffee or doughnut crumbs can harm the delicate circuitry of an automated system and cause substantial amounts of data to be lost.

Losses Caused by Employees

System security can also be breached by acts of employees. The most common problem is probably loss due to human error. Employees may input incorrect data and it may be quite difficult and time consuming to correct these errors when they are discovered.

Employees may also erase files in error. Although many systems are programmed to make improper erasures difficult, no system is absolutely foolproof.

Deliberate criminal acts may also breach the security of a system. Staff members may divert company funds to their own accounts. Although this type of embezzlement is also possible in a manual system, it is often made easier by automation.

Employees may steal operating data and offer it to competitors. In a manual system, a good deal of time and effort would be necessary for an agency employee to make a list of expiration dates and sell them to another agency. In an automated environment, this data can be obtained quickly and often copied in electronic form, so that no paper record ever leaves the office.

Employees can also sell the software, itself. It may have cost hundreds of thousands of dollars to conceive, write, and debug a program; yet it can be copied electronically and stolen in minutes. Although many systems have built-in programming to prevent this, no system is foolproof.

A disgruntled employee can deliberately sabotage a system. An unhappy staff member may erase data and input incorrect information.

Losses Caused by Outsiders

The final threat to a system's security comes from those outside of the organization. This could include people who want to steal data for their own gain, or those who are angry at your organization or the insurance industry in general and simply want to get back at the establishment. In addition, some people have made breaking the security of large computer systems a game. "Crash clubs" exist for the sole purpose of breaking into computer systems just for the fun of it.

The most obvious way for an outsider to steal data is in collusion with employees. The employee has access to the data and the outsider may know how to sell it. An outsider can also break into your premises after hours and gain access to your system.

Outsiders may pose as repair people, making a "routine" check of the system. This is often done at the end of the work day, in the hope that your staff will leave at the normal time and give the "repairman" free access to the system.

Systems that communicate with other systems outside of your organization open the possibility of data being stolen during transmission. Computers communicate with other computers via standard telephone lines, making wire tapping possible.

In addition, persons at either end of the transmission could exceed their authority and breach a system's security. For example, when an agent is transmitting data to one company, an employee of that company could obtain information about clients the agent has insured with another company.

Preventing Breach of Security

There are a number of precautions you can take to prevent a breach of security.

Reducing Physical Risk   The best protection against physical damage is to back up all magnetic media regularly. This involves making a copy of all programs and stored data and keeping these backup disks off premises. If the original disk is destroyed, you are able to use the copy to continue operations.

The growth of automated systems has spawned many computer service centers, whose function is to provide data processing services to organizations which cannot justify their own computers or who have small systems but need some of the power of larger, more expensive computers. These service organizations may be willing to establish emergency back-up facilities for you.

You should also store a supply of computer generated forms off premises. You cannot continue your operations on someone else's computer or through a service bureau, if forms are not available. If your forms have been destroyed, by fire for example, you'll need an immediate supply to continue operations.

Naturally, you will want to take the standard precautions against such hazards as fire and flood as well as to take such common sense precautions as requesting that employees not bring food and beverages near the computer or place discs near telephones.

Reducing Losses Caused by Employees   Training must be thorough. Training disks, not "live" data, should be used until an employee becomes competent. You can make copies of an actual working disk for use in training. This provides instruction on current work without jeopardizing the working disk itself.

The accounting profession has developed procedures for preventing embezzlement on both manual and automated systems. Your organization's accounting staff should review the system to ensure that it provides all recommended accounting checks and balances.

Access codes are usually used so that only authorized employees can enter the system or reach data. Sensitive data should only be accessible to employees having a need to use that data. Furthermore, it is possible to give employees, through their computer passwords, the right to see a file but not to erase or alter it.

Companies should establish a policy that employees suspected of crimes involving computer operations will be prosecuted to the full extent of the law.

When an employee who has access to an automated system is fired, he or she must be asked to leave immediately, and not be allowed back at the computer. If given even a few minutes at the terminal, the employee can cause enormous damage.

A computer system can be programmed to produce a transaction record. This is a list of all transactions that have been processed through the system, and the name of the employee who did the processing. You should review this record periodically, to look for signs of questionable transactions. For example, an employee embezzling money would have to have checks issued or funds transferred electronically. A transaction record may also help catch an employee who sells data to an outsider. Questionable entries or extra copies of disks or data should trigger further investigation.

Traditionally, detailed background checks are done on higher level employees and those having direct access to cash. However, only limited reference checking is usually done on members of the general office staff. Automation may prompt a change in this procedure, requiring background checks on any employees who have access to sensitive data.

An employee's personal problems may lead to unexpected or irrational behavior. For example, an employee who is heavily in debt or facing serious personal pressures at home may exhibit changes in behavior. If an employee's personal life may tempt him or her to damage the computer system, or attempt to benefit from its use, you have a responsibility to protect the company. As a supervisor, you cannot afford to ignore signs that an employee is experiencing great personal stress. (See Chapter 5, "Understanding Others," *Essentials of Supervision*, for a discussion of emotional behavior.)

Reducing Losses Caused by Outsiders   To prevent collusion between outsiders and someone within your organization, follow the suggestions in the previous discussion on preventing abuse by employees.

Repair people should be thoroughly screened before they are given access to your system. You should require them to make appointments before coming to your office. They should not expect to be given access to your system simply because they "show up." Verify with the vendor that a repair person was sent and check the identification of anyone not known to you. If repair people have to work after hours or on weekends, security requirements may warrant the presence of an employee. Repair people should not be allowed to take any software or printed material out of the office unless you know in advance why it is needed and are convinced that it will not be misused.

Check the security of your office against burglary. Your office might not warrant special security provisions before automation. Once automated, the equipment value and data risk may justify the installation of burglar alarms and other security provisions.

There are a number of steps organizations should take to prevent abuse by employees of the organization at the other end of a data communications line. Access codes are essential. All parties should be given access only to the material they are entitled to use.

When possible, programs should be written so that data being transmitted is taken off line, making it impossible for either party to access unauthorized information. For example, data to be transmitted can be copied onto a floppy disk and placed in the communications system. In this way, only the data being transmitted can be accessed by the receiver. Also, transmission lines should not be kept open after transmissions are completed. The telephone should be "hung up" and the connection broken once the data exchange is complete.

Where the amount of transmissions and potential losses warrant it, data can be scrambled or encripted. The message is then unscrambled at the receiving end.

These precautions against abuse in communications can be provided by the system designer. They are not free, of course, and the designer is not likely to incorporate them unless you request them.

Insurance   One of the best security measures against all types of loss is to purchase computer insurance. Like the shoemaker's children who have no shoes, insurance organizations often forget to purchase insurance to protect their own assets and business operations. Many insurance companies have developed policies that cover losses resulting from the exposures we have discussed. Supervisors should investigate these policies and recommend their purchase, where applicable.

MANAGING CHANGE

Automation means change in the way you operate your department. This change can be revolutionary, as well as evolutionary. It often happens quickly rather than over long periods of time. Disruption and anxiety are often part of the automation picture.

Our society is changing very quickly. In prior generations, society was fairly stable and change came slowly. People were able to cope with change. Now, however, change in all areas of our society is coming rapidly and people often have difficulty adjusting to it.

The rapid change from the manual to automated environment in insurance can cause many problems for you and your staff. Employees often resist change; and you have to deal with this resistance as you get in touch with and overcome your own fears of automation.

Resistance to change is usually expressed in subtle and indirect ways. Indeed, persons who loudly welcome automation may unknowingly retard its progress as they cling to the old ways.

Loss of Job Competence

There are many reasons why your staff may resist the installation of automated systems. Employees, especially senior employees, are comfortable in their jobs and confident in their ability to do them. They have been successful for many years and received praise for their work and salary increases based on their performance. Automation introduces a new method of doing their work. There have been operational changes before. But prior changes were usually from one manual method to another and quite easy to learn. This new monster, the computer, is another problem altogether. The change is major and employees can hardly be sure that they can handle everything as well as before. They fear, not without justification, that they will not be as competent as before, or that their competence will not be needed.

Threat to Job Security

The fear of the loss of job competence often leads to a fear for job security.

Your staff may have heard stories of people being laid off when computer systems were installed. Whether there is any truth to these stories is irrelevant. People believe them. Assurances that this will not happen do little good if employees do not believe them. Many people will be afraid that, as soon as the computer is rolled in, they, and many of their friends, will be fired.

Changed Social Environment

The computer also changes the social environment of the office. Within any office operation, friendships develop. In addition, a status system evolves. For example, a commercial lines rater may take a good deal of pride in her job and be shown a certain respect by her peers because of the complexity of work that she does. When the computer takes over part of her job, both her self image and the way she is seen by others may change. The job changes brought about by automation, real and imagined, disrupt the social life in the office. The person who sits next to you now may not be there when the computer arrives.

Failure to See Relevance

Employees often resist change because they don't see the relevance to them in personal terms. Detailed studies can demonstrate that automated systems will cut cost and improve service. But what does this mean to an employee? Often very little.

In many organizations employees receive salary increases or promotions based on individual performance rather than unit results. It follows that saving money, improving service and increasing company profits may mean little to the employee. Employees are more concerned that, with the new system, their performance may no longer earn a good rating and raise.

This resistance to change is often the cause of the complaints of physical distress we sometimes hear associated with automated systems. Earlier in this chapter we noted the importance of designing terminals, work stations, and the office environment to provide for employee comfort. Even when we do this, however, we often still hear people complaining of eye strain, backaches, muscle aches, and other ailments. These physical symptoms may sometimes be psychosomatic illnesses, caused not by the new system, but by the fear of the new system.

Acceptance of Change

There are four levels of acceptance of change:

1. Maintain Status Quo An employee at this level wants to maintain the status quo. He or she resists any attempt to change the job. He or she will find many reasons why the system will not work, and takes an inordinate amount of time to learn new operations. The employee points out what is wrong with the system while ignoring its benefits.

2. Coping with Change The employee at this level is learning to cope with change. He or she has accepted that the new system will be installed, does not like it, but goes along with it. He or she takes a long time to learn and points out system problems, but settles in, accepts the inevitable, but has no intention of doing anything to bring about the complete conversion any sooner than is necessary.

3. Acceptance At this level the employee readily accepts change and is learning as quickly as possible. He or she shows the belief that the new system will work and be worthwhile.

4. Innovation At the fourth, and highest, level is the employee who is the innovator. In addition to accepting the change that is already being brought about, he or she sees the value of automation and is looking for new uses for the system.

It is your responsbility to bring employees to as high a level of acceptance as possible. Although not all unit members will become innovators, your objective should be to get all staff members to level three, acceptance, and as many as possible to level four.

Employee Participation

The most important step in gaining acceptance is to make as many employees as possible part of the planning process. As soon as you decide to consider automated systems, the employee whose job will be affected should be made part of the team that will follow the automation process. In this way, the employee will be part of the decision-making process and understand the changes from the beginning.

There is often a tendency to include only management and technical people in the planning process and ignore the office staff. This is a misktake. If you are considering a system that will change your file operation, make the file clerk part of the planning group.

Proper Training

Thorough training is always important when introducing something new into the office. It is especially important when introducing an automated system. A well planned, thorough training program will go a long way to bringing people to the third and fourth levels of acceptance.

Before training begins, employees should be told that errors are to be expected during the training period and that, in fact, making errors is often the best way to learn. This should help employees relax and overcome the normal tendency we all have of wanting to do things right and being embarrassed when we fail.

An employee may become apprehensive if an appraisal or salary review is due in a time when he or she is learning new procedures and may be making many mistakes. The employee's work output may actually decline during this period. Reassurance from you about trial period performance expectations takes on great importance.

Recognition

Once employees have learned the system, new skills and competence should be recognized. We have already discussed the importance of reviewing position guides and performance standards to reflect properly job changes. An employee who has learned to operate an automated system should be bringing about the benefits that caused the company to buy the system in the first place. These benefits should, directly or indirectly, save the firm money or increase sales; in either case, profits should increase. Should some of this increased profit be put into the salaries of the employees who operate the system? In the eyes of many, the gains should be shared with the people who help create them. In a sense, automation makes employees more valuable to the company. We could put it another way: not sharing the gains could be asking for problems in morale and motivation. As a supervisor, you must conform to the organization's salary guidelines. Nonetheless, you should take action to find and eliminate salary inequities that result from automation.

This completes our discussion of the supervision of an automated system. As you can see, the introduction of an automated system adds a major new dimension to your responsibilities. You must understand how your own job will change in the automated environment and prepare to change yourself while leading your staff members through an extensive process of change.

CHAPTER 5

Work Management
and Performance Standards

INTRODUCTION

Supervisors must have systems to control department operations. The overall control process should include work measurement coupled with performance standards for each employee. This chapter will explain the steps you should take to develop operations and performance standards.

You will be shown how to document and analyze your department's operations to ensure that your systems and procedures are as efficient as possible. You will then learn how to develop quantity and quality standards for each of the tasks performed in your department and to integrate these standards into an ongoing measurement program. You will also see how the results of this measurement program can be incorporated into the development of performance standards for your department.

A thread that runs through this entire chapter is the importance of employee participation when developing a measurement program. For a work measurement/standards program to work, employees must be part of its development.

Throughout this chapter we use the word *task* to define a complete activity and *step* to define part of a task. For example, "rating a commercial auto policy" is a *task;* and "looking up the comprehensive rate" is a *step* within that task.

WORK MANAGEMENT

If you are to control your unit, you must establish standards that indicate the quantity and quality of output you expect. In addition, you must develop procedures to measure the work produced. It is necessary for you and your unit members to work together to determine how department operations are to be performed, what standards of performance are expected, and how you, as supervisor, will determine if work is being performed properly and standards are being met.

Purposes of Work Standards and Measurement

Standards are essential if you are to determine the person hours needed to operate the department and to schedule employees to meet these person hour needs.

Staffing In order to ensure that your department's work is completed, you have to know how many person hours will be required to do the work and when these person hours will be necessary. You'll want to be sure that you have people available to accomplish work on a timely basis without having too many employees scheduled. You also want to ensure that people are available just when the work has to be done. For example, an accounting department has a particularly heavy load when monthly, quarterly, and other periodic statements are due. Without work standards, you have only crude ways of knowing the number of hours needed to complete a task or the staff needed for the next peak workload period. Decisions on overtime, borrowing employees from other departments, or hiring office temporaries are enhanced by sound data.

Employee Performance You also need standards to evaluate the individual productivity and work quality of each employee. Standards serve as goals. They allow you to pinpoint your performance expectations, and they give the employee "something to shoot for." Like par to a golfer, employees accept standards as a target or, if not a target, a measuring rod.

Unit Performance In addition to measuring the individual productivity and work quality of each employee, you want to know the overall results of your unit or department. Is the department properly utilizing the personnel hours for which the firm is paying and does the work quality meet standards?

Work Flow Work measurement also provides for the balancing of work both within and among departments. You always want to be sure that each of your employees has enough work to do, without being overburdened. The fluidity of our business often changes the amount of work coming to one employee's desk and, without standards and a measurement program, you may not see a change.

Quality When discussing measurement of work, we often immediately think of work quantity, forgetting that quality and timeliness are just as important. When establishing standards, we want to determine the quality of work we require and the total time the work should be in the department before it's completed. For example, in addition to saying that a billing clerk should be able to complete an average of eight invoices an hour, we might also say that no more than 2 percent of those invoices should contain errors and that all invoices should be issued within forty-eight hours after receipt in the billing department. By looking at the total picture of work quantity, quality, and timeliness, we can properly balance our need to have a productive staff that is giving proper service to agents and insureds.

Coordination   A problem that often arises in many large organizations is friction among departments through which work flows. The issuance of a policy, for example, involves underwriting, rating, policy typing, data processing, accounting, and records departments. The ability of each of these departments to do its job is dependent on the preceding department forwarding accurate work on a timely basis. If inaccurate work is received or if work is received late or unevenly, problems are created for the receiving department.

Without standards and a measurement program, the supervisor of the receiving department often has a difficult time trying to resolve problems with the supervisor of the sending department. However, if the receiving supervisor can show, for example, that 10 percent of the work coming into the department was received with errors, or that a given number or percentage of items were received late and had to be rushed through to meet timeliness standards, it will be easier for the two supervisors to attack the problem. Work measurement will not eliminate workflow peaks and valleys, but will help you plan for them and collaborate with other unit supervisors in responding to them. It is easier to solve problems with objective data.

Long-Range Planning   Work standards and a measurement program also help you plan for future staffing needs. One of the most frustrating problems you face is having an increasing workload and not enough staff to handle the work. This means that people have to be hired and trained at exactly the time when you and your senior employees have the least amount of time to train newcomers.

A program of standards and work measurement will show you when work volume is increasing and allow you to project when additional staff will be necessary. If your firm is planning a marketing program to increase writing in the property lines and you are the property rating supervisor, you can see that your current staff would have difficulty with a significant increase in work. You also know that it takes from three to six months to train a property rater. You may consider hiring an additional rater immediately so he or she will be trained by the time the marketing program begins to show results. Similarly, you can plan staff reductions in anticipation of falling work volume, automation, or methods improvement.

Elements Measured

There are five elements that are measured and controlled in a work measurement program.

Time   The time it should take to perform each individual task is the first element to be measured and controlled. For example, in a commercial lines rating unit, you would want to determine how long it should take to rate an *average* Commercial Property or SMP policy or an *average* endorsement. Depending on the complexity of the work, standards may be needed for major subcategories of tasks. We can develop a standard for rating an average commercial property policy with one location, two to five locations, and six to ten locations. (When we discuss specific measurement techniques, we'll explain how to handle jumbo and nonaverage types of work.) Determining the average time is not tricky. The time period must be long enough, perhaps a month or two, to include the full variety of tasks about as often as handled through the year.

Units Per Employee Since the measurement program we will describe will convert work units to hours, we can determine the number of hours an employee works and calculate the number of work units that relate to those hours.

Total Units The number of work units the entire department should complete in a given time should be measured and controlled. This is no more than totaling each employee's work units.

Quality In insurance, quality relates to the accuracy of work processed.

Timeliness Timeliness of work refers to the time that elapses from the entry of work into the department or position until its completion. Timeliness standards may figure in company-wide service improvement programs. If not, you may want to set department goals for improvements in timeliness. Is this important? It would be hard to find an insurance company or agency that did not have "better service" as a stated objective.

DEVELOPING A WORK MEASUREMENT PROGRAM

It is your responsibility to ensure that the necessary standards are developed and a program to monitor these standards is implemented in your department. In a large organization, an in-house staff of specialists may do the technical elements. In smaller companies and agencies, you will probably be on your own.

Employee Involvement

The first step you must take in the implementation of a measurement program is to get your staff totally involved. The development of standards and a measurement system should not be performed by the supervisor and in-house work measurement department, and then handed to the employees. Those whose work is going to be measured and monitored must help with the development of the standards and implementation of the program. If a work measurement program is to work, you must have the complete cooperation and commitment of your staff. Of equal importance is the fact that some of the best ideas come from the people who do the work. If your unit is small and has few identical jobs, you will probably want all employees to participate. In large departments and where jobs are identical, a few employees can take an active role and speak for the others.

Phases

There are four phases of a work measurement program:

1. *Work Description*—The first step is to document all of the tasks performed in your department. In this way you are sure that you know every task being performed by every employee and exactly how it is done.
2. *Procedures Analysis*—Once the tasks have been documented, review each of them to determine if they can be simplified. You may find tasks that can be eliminated or that some of the steps now being followed to complete a given task can be eliminated or consolidated without affecting the work output.
3. *Standards Development*—When you are satisfied that your procedures are as streamlined as possible, you then develop the quantity, quality, and timeliness standards for each task in your department.
4. *Monitoring*—Once standards have been developed, you must determine how your department's output compares to the standards. This monitoring program should not only measure the work, but it should also help you make necessary adjustments in your operation to improve results.

Work Description and Analysis

Task List The first step in the development of a work measurement program is to document the work presently being performed in your department. The best way to start is to have each of your staff members complete a *Task List* (see Exhibit 5-1). On this form employees list the various tasks they perform and estimate the average number of hours each week they spend on each task. If work volume varies, the averages may be for longer periods of time. An employee may have a "miscellaneous" category, but that should be for no more than 10 percent of total time.

When you review each employee's Task List, compare what is listed with current job descriptions and procedures manuals as well as your own knowledge of the work done in the department. In addition, be sure that employees who are doing the same type of work describe tasks in the same way. You will also want to be sure that administrative functions, such as supervision and training, are included if an employee regularly does this work. The purpose of the Task List is to document all of the work being performed in the department and get a rough estimate of the time spent on each task.

Task Analysis Chart Once each employee has prepared a task list and you are satisfied that they all are complete, you should prepare a "Task Analysis Chart" (see Exhibit 5-2).

On the left-hand side of this chart, you list all of the tasks your department has identified. Along the top of the form, you list each employee, the tasks to be performed and the number of hours estimated to be spent on each task. You

Exhibit 5-1
Task List for Work Distribution Chart

NAME: Joe Wilson		POSITION: Commerical Lines Rater	
DEPARTMENT: Commercial Lines Rating		SECTION: ————	
SUPERVISOR: Smith	PREPARED BY: A. Smith	DATE: 6/11/85	
TASK			HR. PER WEEK
Rate commercial lines property policy			10
Rate commerical lines property endorsement			4
Rate commercial lines property renewal			12
Rate commercial lines property cancellation			3
Rate commercial lines property reporting form			7
Total			36

then total the hours spent on each task and determine the estimated number of hours your department spends each week on each task.

When you have completed the Task Analysis Chart, you are ready to begin your first analysis of your department's operation to see where improvements can be made.

Task Improvement Look first at the tasks themselves and determine if every one of them is necessary and if a proper amount of time is spent on a particular task. It is not uncommon for a supervisor to be unaware of a task an employee is performing. A change in procedure in another job or in another unit might modify a task in some unrecognized way. A change in the physical

Exhibit 5-2
Task Analysis Chart

TASK	Percent of Total	Hours/Week	Name: J. Wilson / Position: / Task	Hours/Week	Name: M. Jones / Position: / Task	Hours/Week	Name: / Position: / Task	Hours/Week	Name: / Position: / Task	Hours/Week	Name: / Position / Task
Rate policy				10		7					
Rate endorsement				4		8					
Rate renewal				12		10					
Rate cancellation				3		6					
Rate reporting form				7		8					
TOTALS				36		36					

Department: Commercial Lines Rating — Prepared By: A. Smith — Date: 6/14/85 — Page 1 of 1

environment and equipment may similarly alter the way a task is performed and the time required to perform a given task.

You may learn a great deal as you examine the time required for tasks. Your department may create a monthly report which takes ten hours to prepare. You may question whether the report is worth the ten hours it takes to complete it. Any task that can be eliminated or simplified will add to your department's productivity.

Next, take a look at the number of tasks each employee does and whether his or her skills are being properly utilized.

If an employee is responsible for a large number of tasks, possibly as many as ten or twelve, productivity may suffer. Going from one task to another means a need to "put away" the old work and "set up" the new. This "put away" and "set up" time is unproductive. The other side of the coin is the employee who has too few tasks. This employee may find the work monotonous, and quality may suffer.

Where possible, employees should have between four and six tasks as their regular assignment. This gives the job diversification necessary for job enrichment without creating the inefficiencies of performing too many tasks.

You should also study the Task Analysis Chart to ensure that employee skills are being properly used. Is a trained typist spending a significant amount of time on nontyping work? Is a technical employee spending time on clerical tasks?

The Task Analysis Chart will also help you evaluate staff strength. Review the chart to determine if there are any tasks that only one person performs regularly. If so, you should train someone else in that task as a backup.

Finally, you may want to determine which tasks account for the bulk of your department's work. You will often find that two or three tasks require as much as 70 percent of your department's person hours. This information about the activities that are the most time consuming becomes important in the next phase of the work measurement program, procedures analysis.

Procedures Analysis

Once you have completed the review of the Task Analysis Chart, you are ready to look at each of the tasks in your department. Each task consists of many steps. Looking up the rate for a given piece of property in a manual or on a microfiche viewer would be one step in the task of rating a commerical property policy.

When you prepared the Task Analysis Chart, you probably found that two or three tasks accounted for as much as 70 percent of your department's work. Give them the most careful attention. Efficiencies that can be brought about in these major tasks will provide the greatest return.

Flowcharting The key to procedures analysis is the process flowchart. This is a graphic representation of the sequence of all operations. It documents all steps required to complete a job, from the time it comes into the department until it is completed, filed, and sent to the next processing unit.

You will want to develop flowcharts for all of the tasks in your department or at least the major tasks. (A sample flowchart appears in Exhibit 5-4.)

One way to get your employees involved in this work measurement program is to teach them how to develop flowcharts and ask them to prepare charts for the tasks they do. You can then collect and review them. You will want to be sure that employees who are doing the same work describe the same steps. If different employees are using different steps, you will want to find out why.

In addition, you'll want to ensure that transportation steps connect. In an agency, for example, if the Customer Service Representative indicates that endorsements are sent to the bookkeeper, you will want to verify that the bookkeeper's flowcharts indicate receiving that endorsement.

You will also want to verify that each task starts with the receipt of the work and ends with a description of where it is sent. Flowcharts should assume a blank desk before the job starts and after it's completed. The first step on the flowchart should show where work comes from. For example:

"Receive endorsement from the mail clerk."

Exhibit 5-3
Flowchart Symbols

Symbol	Classification	Action
◯	Operation	Produces or accomplishes
▷	Transportation	Moves
▽	Storage	Keeps
☐	Inspection	Verifies
◖	Delay	Interferes

These five basic symbols are augmented by expanding the operation and storage symbols to provide a more explicit graphic.

Operation	◯	Operation
Symbols	⊙	Operation generating a new document
	Ⓢ	Sorting operation
Storage	▽ᵀ	Temporary storage
Symbols	▽ᴾ	Permanent storage
	▽ˣ	Destruction

Some flowcharts require the use of some specialized symbols.

◇	Decision
⬡	Predefined process
▱	Document
⬠	Off-page connecter to connect two flows on different pages

The symbols, combined with an annotation of process steps, form the composite parts of the flowchart.

Exhibit 5-4
Flowchart

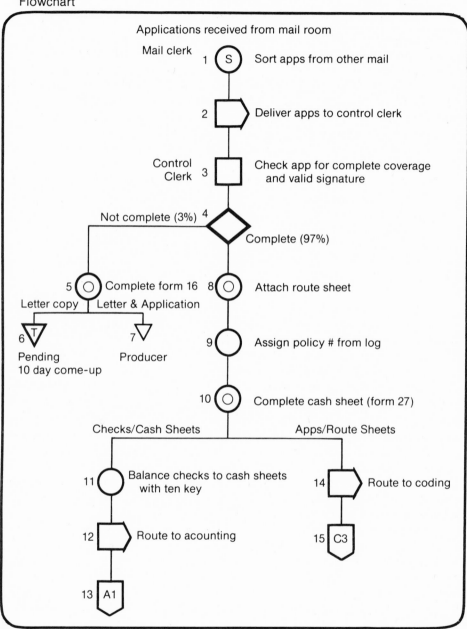

The last step should show where the work goes. For example:

"Send endorsement to billing clerk."

Analysis of Flowcharts Once the flowcharts have been completed, they must be analyzed to determine where improvements in procedures can be made. Every member of your staff should take part in this analysis. Each should review not only his or her own flowcharts but also those of others in the department. You might divide the staff into teams of two, with each team reviewing the flowcharts of the members' tasks and determining where improvements can be made.

The first question to ask when analyzing flowcharts is whether a particular task must be performed at all. You asked this question when analyzing the task analysis chart, and you should ask it again. What would happen if this task were eliminated completely? Could the department still meet its objectives? Would agents or insureds still be properly served? If sufficient reasons cannot be found for performing a task, it should be eliminated.

You may think that a given task is unnecessary but believe that some level of management would not permit eliminating it. If you think this is the case, you should show management how much time the task is taking and ask if it can be eliminated. You may be surprised at the answer.

For those tasks that cannot be eliminated, look at each step represented by a symbol in the flowchart and ask if it is necessary. Frequently, a lengthy procedure covering many pages of flowchart can be simplified, allowing the task to be completed but requiring only half the steps.

An inefficient procedure often found in the insurance industry is the copying of an item of information on many forms. A good deal of clerical time is often spent copying the insured's name, address, policy number, and other information on multiple forms within a task. If this is happening, see if forms can be combined, allowing the recording of common information only once.

Determine if exceptions can be eliminated. Whenever there is an exception, someone must make a decision, and the possibility of error exists. Often the reasons that originally necessitated exceptions have long disappeared but exception processing still continues. "Temporary procedures" die hard. Verify why each exception is necessary and eliminate all you can.

You will also want to determine if the task is being performed in the proper location in the office. A task may require frequent reference to files or manuals, and this reference material may be on the other side of the room or in another room in the office. If you find this to be the case, consider moving the task or the reference material.

You should also ask whether the employee's work station is properly designed to do the job. For example, if a task requires frequent reference to files or manuals, room should be provided on the employee's desk for these items. Calculators and computers should be evaluated: are they fast enough? Is the work area quiet enough for the work that is done there?

You should question whether each step is performed in the proper sequence. Should steps be performed earlier or later in the work flow? For example, it may take a week for an underwriter to receive a motor vehicle report. The report should be ordered early in the procedure, and other aspects of the task of underwriting an automobile risk can be done while waiting for it to arrive.

You also want to ask if each task is being performed by the person and department best suited for that task. We live in an age of specialization. Specialization increases as organizations grow. You should be asking if each task could be more efficiently performed by someone specifically trained for that task.

You should also attempt to delegate work to the lowest job level at which it can be performed. Clerical work should be removed from those holding technical positions, and more routine clerical functions, such as filing, should not be done by skilled employees such as raters and typists.

Analyze the procedures used to bring work to each employee. It is not uncommon for processing delays to be caused by work sitting in outbaskets waiting for transfer to the next work station. Work in process should be moved between work stations as quickly as possible.

As you can see, flowchart analysis is a creative process and is limited only by the imagination of those doing the analysis. By involving your entire staff, you will not only gain their support for this program but will tap their creativity in streamlining the work flow.

Employee Meetings   Once employees have been trained in flowchart analysis and have had the opportunity to analyze their charts, either individually or in teams, you should schedule one or more meetings to discuss proposed changes. The results of these meetings will give you the final input you need to decide which recommendations to implement. All recommendations and new procedures should be documented and made part of the work measurement file.

Developing Clerical Standards

Once you have implemented all of the new procedures, you are ready to begin developing standards. It is essential that your employees become an integral part of the standards development process. Employees may resist being measured. They may be upset by any implication that they are working on an assembly line and are expected to handle so many items per hour. Some may fear that standards will be set so high that no one will be able to reach them. Many fear that failure to meet standards will result in loss of promotions and salary increases. Employee fear and resistance are *normal* responses to measurement and standards. Making employees part of the standards development process is essential if they are to accept the standards and the measurement program that goes with it.

The standards should measure the time it should take a well-trained employee to complete a task working at a normal pace under existing office conditions. Therefore all trained employees performing their jobs properly should be able to meet standards. It is vital that department members believe that average workers, not superstars, were studied.

Measurement Techniques   In order to determine the amount of time each job takes, you can use one of four methods.

Observation.   Either you or a member of your staff can observe someone doing a job and determine the average time it should take to complete one item. This is done by timing an employee completing a number of batches of work, determining how long each batch took, and dividing by the number of items processed in each batch and averaging the results. This gives the average time it takes to process one item.

This technique can be used when work is completed in batches and when the job is started and finished without interruption. For example, typing of invoices could be measured this way. However, you could not measure the clerical work involved in processing a claim since there are many interruptions. Processing has to be set aside pending the next development in the claim procedure.

Ideally, observation should be used only with employees who are comfortable when being observed. Some people get quite nervous when being timed. They may work faster, slower, or with abnormal caution. It may be necessary to observe a number of batches before employees relax and do their work as they normally do.

Batches of work should be observed at different times during the day and on different days of the week. Most people are more alert earlier in the day and become fatigued as the afternoon wears on. Since our standards should reflect the time it takes to do a task under normal working conditions we want to be sure to do some timing later in the day when people often work more slowly. Similarly, people may become more fatigued as the week wears on.

It is usually not a good idea to do time observations if people work overtime during the week or on Saturday. At these times employees are usually not subject to the normal distractions in an office so they are not working under normal conditions.

Observations must include a good sample of the normal workload. Samples should include some very difficult items, some easy work, and many average items.

When you have completed your observations, calculate the average time for each task.

Time Ladders.   Time ladders (see Exhibit 5-5) allow individuals to measure their own work. You and the employee determine what tasks are to be measured and assign a letter to each task. The employee then completes the time ladder for a period of two weeks, indicating the number of items processed and the time taken.

Since time ladders should account for every minute of the work day, there must be symbols for personal time such as lunch or breaks (P), waiting for work (W), and miscellaneous (M), which accounts for all other activities.

Time ladders are most useful with employees who would be nervous with observations or who have a large number of tasks to perform. Time ladders also take less time than time observations, since only one person is involved rather than two.

Exhibit 5-5
Time Ladder

Dept._____ Section_____ Position_____ Name_____ Date_____

TIME	CODE	VOL	TIME	CODE	VOL	TIME	CODE	VOL	TIME	CODE	VOL	TIME	CODE	VOL	TIME	CODE	VOL
8:00			9:30			11:00			12:30			2:00			3:30		
2			32			2			32			2			32		
4			34			4	M		34			4			34		
6			36			6			36			6			36		
8			38			8			38			8			38		
10			40			10			40			10			40		
12			42			12			42			12			42		
14			44			14			44	M		14			44		
16			46			16			46			16			46		
18			48			18			48			18			48		
20			50			20			50			20			50		
22			52			22			52			22			52		
24			54			24			54			24			54		
26			56			26			56			26			56		
28			58	A	2	28			58			28			58		
8:30	B	5	10:00			11:30			1:00			2:30	8	D	4:00	A	4
32			2			32			2			32			2		
34			4			34			4			34			4		
36			6			36			6			36			6		
38			8			38	C	2	8			38			8		
40			10			40			10			40			10		
42			12			42			12			42			12		
44			14			44			14			44			14		
46			16			46			16			46			16		
48			18			48			18			48			18		
50			20			50			20			50			20		
52			22			52			22			52			22		
54			24			54			24			54			24		
56			26			56			26			56			26		
58			28			58			28			58			28		
9:00			10:30			12:00			1:30	E	8	3:00			4:30		
2			32			2			32			2			32		
4			34			4			34			4			34		
6			36			6			36			6			36		
8			38			8			38			8			38		
10			40			10			40			10			40		
12	D	3	42	M		12	M		42			12			42		
14			44			14			44			14			44		
16			46			16			46			16			46		
18			48			18			48			18			48		
20			50			20			50			20			50		
22			52			22			52			22			52		
24			54			24			54			24			54		
26			56			26			56			26			56		
28			58			28			58			28			58		
9:30			11:00			12:30			2:00			3:30			5:00		

INSTRUCTIONS:
1. When you stop doing one task and start another, draw a line across the column.
2. Enter the proper code designation and the volume of work completed in the columns indicated.

WORK CODE	DESCRIPTION	ITEM TO BE COUNTED
A Policy	Policy	Policy
B Endorsement	Endorsement	Endorsement
C Renewal	Renewal	Renewal
D Cancellation	Cancellation	Cancellation
E Reporting Form	Reporting Form	Reporting Form

M= Misc

Exhibit 5-6
Time Log

Date	Item	Number	Start	Stop	Total
6/11	A	4	8:20	9:45	85
	C	8	10:04	11:24	80
	E	2	2:30	2:50	20

NOTE: Between 9:45 and 10:04 and between 11:24 and 2:30 work other than the item other than those listed on the log was done.

A= Policy
B= Endorsement
C= Renewal
D= Cancellation
E= Reporting Form

When all time ladders have been completed, the average times for each task should be calculated.

Time Logs. The use of time logs (see Exhibit 5-6) is similar to time ladders except that they do not measure every task performed. You ask the employee to keep a log of the time spent on one or more tasks. Time logs are used when you are able to develop standards on most of an employee's jobs using a more accurate method, such as observations, but must ask the employee to keep logs for one or two tasks. For example, you might ask an employee to keep a log only for rating personal umbrella policies even though that employee also rates auto and homeowners policies. You may have decided to use time observations for auto and homeowners policies but prefer a log for umbrella policies because they occur less frequently.

Case Study Technique. The case study technique is a self-measurement method used when work is not normally completed without interruption and delay. For example, the work involved with processing a claim is often spread over a period of time. The initial claim report is received and a file is set up. That file may be put in a pending drawer until various documents are received or the adjuster has made an inspection. Each time work is done on the account, the file is pulled, tasks completed, and recorded, and the folder is refiled until the claim is closed. In this situation, you could not use time observations or ladders to determine the amount of time needed for a claim, but you could use the case study procedure.

A *Case Study* form (see Exhibit 5-7) is inserted in the file when it is created. It lists all of the steps to be followed. The form stays with the file until

Exhibit 5-7
Case Study

Description of Step	Start	Stop	Total
Rate Commercial Property policy			
Get rating manual from shelf	10:50	10:54	4
Look up rate in manual	10:54	10:55	1
Calculate premium	1:02	1:30	28
Put manual back on shelf	1:30	1:32	2

NOTE: Rater was interrupted at 10:55 to do some other work and didn't get back rating this policy until 1:02

the claim is closed. Every time a task is performed, the person doing the work logs the time spent. When the claim is closed, you remove the form from the file and use it to calculate the time it took to do the complete task.

Time ladders, time logs, and case studies are all self-measurement techniques. They offer a way of getting employees involved in the measurement program. The standards that are eventually developed are not seen as something imposed from the outside, but rather as standards they helped to develop.

Self measurement does have its drawbacks, however. Staff members may misinterpret instructions so that employees doing the same job may be keeping records differently. For example, one employee may deduct the time spent on a short interruption, such as a telephone call, while another may include it as part of the existing office conditions. Unless each employee uses the same recordkeeping criteria, the data will not be accurate. Employees may also forget to keep the records and, rather than admit this, they may well invent results at the end of the day.

Time Estimates. Time estimates, although the least scientific method of developing standards, are used when you have no other way of developing a standard or when you have insufficient time for a more accurate study.

To develop a standard using time estimates, simply list all of the tasks you want to measure and ask the employees doing the job how long each item takes. Be sure to determine the time to do normal work and not the very easy or difficult items.

If more than one person in your department does a job, ask each one individually to estimate the time it takes to complete it. Barring conclusion, if they give you similar times, you can have confidence in the figures. Naturally, you will want to add your own experience to develop these figures. If you have recently done the tasks whose times are being estimated, you have some idea how long it takes to complete an item.

Exhibit 5-8
Measurement Planning Form

Task	Measurement Method				
	OBS	LAD	LOG	CASE	EST
Rate commercial property policy	X				
Rate commercial property endorsement	X				
Rate commercial property renewal				X	
Rate commercial property cancellation			X		
Rate commercial property reporting form					X

NOTE: OBS= Observation
      LAD= Time Ladder
      LOG= Time Log
      AVE= Average Case Study
      EST= Time Estimate

Measurement Planning Now that you know the various methods of measuring clerical tasks, you are ready to begin developing standards.

The first step is to complete a "Measurement Planning Form" (see Exhibit 5-8). On this form, you list all of the tasks you plan to measure and which measurement method you plan to use for each. You should develop standards for tasks that account for at least 90 percent of the working time in your department. Some complex tasks may be unmeasurable. For example, an agent may decide not to measure the time it takes to reconcile company accounts current. The time this task takes may vary from a few minutes to a few hours, depending on which company's statement is being reviewed and the complexity of the problems found. Other tasks are done so infrequently that they are not worth measuring. However, when you are finished, 90 percent of your department's time should be covered in your productivity program.

Explain to your employees how measurement is done and allow them to do some practice measurement that will not be included in the study. It is difficult to say how many items have to be measured to constitute an accurate measurement. You want to be sure that enough measurement has been taken to fairly represent the workload. When additional measurements have an insignificant effect on averages, you can conclude that you have enough data.

When developing the sample, exclude that small number of "jumbo" items. For example, if it takes approximately five minutes to prepare an invoice, but you have one account that gets a quarterly invoice that may take an hour and a half to put together, that one large invoice should be considered "unmeasured." You do not want it in your sample.

Calculate Average Times Once measurement has been completed, average all the figures that have been developed to calculate the average time it takes to do each task. Apply your own judgment to decide if the average should

Exhibit 5-9
Department Standards Form

| Department: _____ Prepared By: _____ |
| Section/Unit: _____ Date: _____ |

Task	Standard	Item Measured
Rate commercial property policy	39 min. (.6513)	Policy
Rate commercial property endorsement	12 min. (.2004)	Endorsement
Rate commercial property renewal	35 min. (.5845)	Renewal
Rate commercial property cancellation	10 min. (.168)	Cancellation
Rate commercial property reporting form	8 min. (.1336)	Reporting form

be the standard. For example, if there is only one person to measure and that employee is new at performing the task, you will want to adjust the average to reflect the time it should take a well-trained employee. Therefore, if the person being timed took an average of ten minutes to do the job, you may want to set the standard at, say, eight minutes. Similarly, the average of a particularly fast employee would be adjusted upward.

The employee doing the job should be given the opportunity to review the standard in keeping with the pattern of employee participation followed throughout the work measurement program.

Department Standards Form When you have developed all of your standards, list them on a "Department Standards Form" (see Exhibit 5-9). This lists each task along with its standard in terms of the average time required to do the task.

You will note that we have listed each standard in minutes as well as in percentage of hours. This is done by multiplying the number of minutes by .0167 (1/60 = .0167). Therefore, the standard for a task taking one minute would be .0167, and the standard for a task taking thirty minutes would be .501 (30 × .0167). You will see the significance of this conversion from minutes to a percentage of an hour as we develop the control program.

Once you have developed standards you will want to continually monitor your operations to determine if standards are being met and, if not, what action must be taken to improve results.

Controlling Human Resources

Supervisors in the insurance industry may not think of themselves as controlling resources. Supervisors (foremen) in factories often have responsibility for hundreds of thousands of dollars' worth of equipment and materials. This gives visibility to their responsibility for resources. We in the insurance industry may need reminders of our obligation to control our central resource, human talent.

If an employee earns $9 per hour, and works a 35-hour week, that employee is earning $16,380 per year. To that should be added the cost of employment benefits, perhaps one third of the salary. If you have a department of ten people being paid $12 per hour (including benefits) you may be responsible for $120 every hour of every workday of the year or over $200,000 per year. If your employees are, say, only 80 percent effective, it is costing your company over $40,000 per year.

You will be able to use this control program to evaluate alternative plans of action and new procedures. For example, when deciding if you want to install an automated system, you have to be able to weigh the hours saved by the system against the cost of the system. The results from your measurement program in person hours saved, translated to dollars saved, can be compared with the dollars spent on systems.

Task Tally Sheet   Each of your staff members should be given a task tally sheet (Exhibit 5-10) on which you have listed the tasks performed.

The employee is asked to "stroke tally" each task accomplished. This process of keeping track of completed work may seem cumbersome and irritating at the beginning; but after a while it becomes just another step in getting the job done.

In addition to keeping track of the amount of measured work done, each employee will indicate the time spent in activities other than measured work. These items are listed at the bottom of the sheet. Unmeasured work would be any work for which standards have not been developed or those "jumbo" items that were not included in the time surveys.

You will take these individual sheets and transfer the figures to the Weekly Reporting Form.

Weekly Reporting Form   The key to your control program is the weekly reporting form (Exhibit 5-11). In the space labeled "Task," list all of the tasks for which you have developed standards, along with the standard hours (minutes $\times$ .0167) for each task.

Once you have totaled the items processed for each task in the department, multiply that figure by the standard and get the total standard hours for each task. Add these figures to get the standard hours for your department for the week.

The standard hours in Exhibit 5-11 represent the number of person hours it should have taken to process your department's work. By completing the right side of the Weekly Reporting Form, you will record the number of hours actually worked and be able to analyze the results.

The Hourly Allocation section records the number of hours available in the department. Scheduled Hours are the number of hours each employee is scheduled to work. For example, if there are ten full-time employees in your

Exhibit 5-10
Task Tally Sheet

| Department: _____ Prepared By: _____ |
| Date: _____ |

Task	Item Measured	No. of Units
Property policy	Policy	JHT JHT JHT
Property endorsement	Endorsement	JHT JHT JHT JHT JHT I
Property renewal	Renewal	JHT JHT JHT JHT JHT JHT JHT III
Property cancellation	Cancellation	JHT JHT JHT III
Reporting form	Reporting form	JHT JHT JHT JHT JHT

Unmeasured Activities		Actual Hours
Overtime (Specify)		
Vacation		
Absence		
Loaned		
Supervision		
Training (Specify)		
Unmeasured (Specify)	Clark Account	2:35

department, and you work a 35-hour week, scheduled hours is 350 hours. Add in the scheduled hours of any part-time employees. Overtime, time borrowed from or loaned to another department, vacation, and absences are recorded where indicated on the form.

You will next calculate the time spent on supervision and administration and time used to process work not covered by standards. What remains is the number of hours available to process measured work.

Once you have completed these calculations, determine the key indices on the bottom right-hand side of the form. These figures give you the basis for evaluating the work being performed by the department. (You can now see why we had to multiply our standards by .0167 to convert minutes to a percentage of hours. If we had not done this we would be calculating minutes on the left-hand side of the Weekly Reporting Form and hours on the right-hand side. By making the conversion, both the left- and right-hand sides of this form reflect hours.)

The first of these indices, "Personnel Utilization," compares standard hours with hours available to process the department's work. "Nonstandard time" is the number of hours spent doing work for which no standard has been developed. "Administration" represents the time spent on supervision and training; and "Absence" includes illness and personal time taken by employees.

Exhibit 5-11
Weekly Reporting Form

Department: _____

Period Ending _____ By_____

WORK ACTIVITY

Task	Standard Time (Hours)	Number of Units	Standard Hours
Rate commercial property policy	.6513	45	29.309
Rate commercial property endorsement	.2004	128	25.651
Rate commercial property renewal	.5845	122	71.309
Rate commercial property cancellation	.1670	14	2.338
Rate commercial property reporting form	.1336	77	10.287
			Total 138.895

Backlog Task	Work On Hand	Standard	Hours Of Work	Remarks

MANHOUR UTILIZATION

_____ Hours/ _____ _____ Equivalent Personnel	Totals
1. Hourly Allocation:	
A. Scheduled	326.25
B. Overtime (+)	
C. Borrowed time (+)	
D. Vacation (−)	
E. Absence (−)	72.50
F. Loaned (−)	
G. Net hours available	253.75
2. Less Administrative Time:	
A. Supervision/administration	36.25
B. Training	
C. Total administrative time	36.25

3. Adjusted net hours Available for work (1G-2C)	217.50
4. Non-standard time Unmeasured work	34.25
5. Total hours available for work covered by standards (3-4C)	183.25
6. Standard hours	138.95

KEY INDICES

Personnel utilization (6÷5)	79.79
Non-Standard time (4C÷1A)	10.50
Administration (2C÷1A)	11.11
Absenteeism (1E÷1A)	22.22

Analysis of Department Performance

Once the weekly reporting form is completed, you are ready to analyze your department's performance. The following is a sampling of the questions you should ask when reviewing performance. As part of the development of your measurement program, you should add to this list questions that pertain specifically to your operation. The development of the questions and the analysis, itself, constitute an excellent department project.

You should also compare trends over a period of time as well as look at each week's or month's results individually. For example, 80 percent utilization would be a good result if it was at 65 percent three months ago, and has been steadily climbing. That same 80 percent figure is a red flag if 90 percent is normal for your department.

Measurement Analysis

Scheduled Hours

Increasing, decreasing or remaining constant?

If increasing, are open requisitions being filled or is staff being increased?

If staff is being increased, is work load increasing?

If decreasing, is work load decreasing?

Is staff being adjusted due to previous overstaffing?

Is staffing proper for workload?

Does personnel utilization indicate that staffing is at the correct level, high, low?

Overtime

Is overtime necessary?

Is it used to fill in for peak work periods or is it constant?

Is it due to open requisitions?

It is being used to fill in for absenses?

Could borrowed time be used?

If no overtime is ever shown, are you staffed for peak workloads rather than average?

If overtime is regular, are employees stretching work to earn overtime?

Borrowed Time

Is utilization being affected by borrowing untrained staff?

Is it being used to save overtime whenever possible?

What jobs are easy enough to permit "quick" training of borrowed staff?

Vacations

Are vacations scheduled to fit the workload?

How many employees, and which ones, can be on vacation at the same time without adversely affecting work scheduling?

Has utilization been affected by key employees being on vacation?

Is everyone else "pitching in" to get work done during vacation periods?

Has cross training been done to fill in for vacations?

Absence

Are valid reasons given for absence?

Are some individuals habitually absent?

Are there reasons for absence other than the ones given? i.e., job dissatisfaction, lack of enthusiasm, lack of work, too much work, poor training.

What is being done to control absences?

Loaned

Is time being loaned when your work is light?

Is there proper coordination between units when scheduling borrowed and loaned time?

Are there continuous excessive amounts of loaned time which may indicate overstaffing?

Supervision/Administration

What is being done in supervision/administrative time?

Are hours shown adequate for the needs of the unit?

How much time are supervisory personnel spending on processing the department's work?

What kinds of work are supervisors doing?

Are supervisory problems unresolved because supervisors are too busy processing work?

Training

Who is doing the training?

Is enough time being spent on training and cross training?

Is turnover affecting the time spent on training?

Is the time spent on training showing the desired results?

Is there regularly scheduled training and cross training?

How long does it take to train a new employee? Can it be reduced?

Unmeasured Work

Is unmeasured work increasing or decreasing?

Should standards be developed for tasks that are now unmeasured?

Have there been procedures changes in work that was previously measured that make the standards inapplicable?

Is unmeasured work planned to fill in during slack periods?

Standard Hours

If measured work is increasing:

Is this increase permanent or temporary?

What training and work reorganization are necessary?

Should you consider adding to staff?

Should you consider borrowing or overtime?

If work is decreasing:
Is the decrease permanent or temporary?
Should work reorganization be considered?
Should staff reduction be considered?

Personnel Utilization
Increasing or decreasing? Why?
If below 80 percent
Can person hours be reduced?
Can staff be reduced?
Will work load increase in the near future?
Can people be loaned to another department?
Can excess person hours be used to cross-train your staff?
If above 90 percent
Is heavy work load permanent?
Should you add full-time or part-time employees to staff.
Should you schedule overtime?
Should you borrow people?

Nonstandard Time
Is it above 10 percent?
Should additional standards be developed?
Is all nonstandard work necessary?

Administration
If below 10 percent
Is the supervisor spending enough time on administrative duties?
Is enough training and cross-training being done?
If above 10 percent
Is too much time being spent on administration?
Could the supervisor process some of the department's work?

Absenteeism
What is causing absenteeism?

Backlog
Is work on hand acceptable?
Should overtime be scheduled?
Should you borrow people from another department?
Should you use office temporaries?

Your analysis should also review the relationships between various figures. For example, if utilization is low, are you increasing training to take advantage of the work slowdown? If a heavy backlog exists, is absenteeism high because of employee frustration? If utilization is low and backlog is high, your staff should be able to process the work without an increase in work hours. If utilization is high and backlog is increasing, an increase in person hours should be scheduled to accomplish the work.

Documentation

Once you and your department have completed the analysis, you should prepare a report in which you document the findings and describe steps you will be taking to improve operations. This may be no more than a report to yourself and your department to ensure that everyone understands what is to be done and who has responsibility for which assignments. The report can help develop the spirit of teamwork that is necessary for a department to improve productivity.

Remedial Action

The results of your analysis should also be used in reporting to your manager and in requesting action from other departments. For example, if you determine that you must add to staff or schedule overtime, your analysis report can be used to justify the expense. If you find that work is being delivered to you from another department unevenly, the data you have developed will aid you when talking to the other unit's supervisor. Similarly, action plans to remedy problems (e.g., reduce backlog) should be communicated to other supervisors whose departments will be affected.

Periodic Review of Standards

As part of your evaluation, you will want to review the standards periodically to ensure their accuracy. During the first few months of the measurement program, you may find that some standards are not correct and want to adjust them. In addition, when tasks change, the standards will often change. Constant monitoring is necessary to maintain accuracy of your program.

QUALITY CONTROL

The work measurement program establishes how much work an individual or department should perform. Quality control refers to how well work should be done. There are two main measures in a quality control program: error percentage; and timeliness. Error percentage tells how much of the work was processed incorrectly. Timeliness measures the number of hours or days it took to complete the task.

Clerical Quality Control

The first step in the development of a clerical quality control program is to determine exactly what you are going to measure. Look at the tasks you have defined in the work measurement program. For each of these tasks decide how you will measure work quality. For example, in a policy typing department, you might look at the number of policies on which mistakes appear on the insured's copy. You will need to stipulate how errors will be counted. For instance, does a policy with three errors in the property description count as one error or three? You will also need to specify the work flow points at which errors are determined. Will you examine work for mistakes or wait for errors to be reported by subsequent users?

Acceptable Error Ratio

The next step is to determine the error percentage that is acceptable to you, your management, and your staff. Although you might like to believe that no errors leave your department, human beings are not perfect and some mistakes are inevitable. Double checking all work to eliminate errors may be possible, but rarely is it worth the cost. The question is simply how many mistakes are acceptable.

In order to make this determination, you must analyze the consequences of each mistake. The more critical the consequences, the lower the acceptable error ratio. For example, spelling the insured's street incorrectly on a policy is not as critical as charging $100 premium instead of $1,000. Therefore, you might establish as a standard that you will allow a 5 percent error rate on a typist's spelling errors, but only 1 percent rate where incorrect premium is involved. You therefore would have a dual standard program, one for major errors and one for minor errors.

Timeliness Standards

Once you have established your quality criteria, you will want to develop standards for timeliness, that is, the time each item is in your department. When establishing timeliness standards, you should first prioritize your department's work. For example, you might determine that quotes and new lines have the highest priority, followed by endorsements and current month renewals. The lowest priority would be future month entries such as renewals and installments. Your objective would be to process high priority items as quickly as possible, with lower priority items not requiring such fast service. If quotes and new lines are high priority, the standard might be to have 90 percent of these items processed within twenty-four hours after receipt in the department. A lower priority item, such as an endorsement, might have a standard of 90 percent processed within three working days; and the lowest priority tasks might have a standard of five working days.

An alternate method of setting a standard is to state that a specified task should be accomplished a given number of days prior to a specific event. A renewal should be issued no less than fifteen days prior to the renewal date. A January first renewal might be received in the policy typing department in November, but does not have to be out until December 15. It could be held in the department for over a month and still meet standards.

You will note that timeliness standards have two components—the standard, itself, and the percentage of items that must meet the standard. Ideally, you want all work to meet standards; but, realistically, you recognize that some items will be delayed. By setting a percentage figure indicating the number that should meet standards, you recognize that a small amount of late work is acceptable.

As we have stressed, coordination among departments affects standards of timeliness. You want work to enter your department at regular intervals and in enough time to process it by the timeliness standard. Obviously, standards contingent on incoming work will have to be set in conjunction with the departments that feed these items to you. Improvement in one department should affect results in related units.

Just as with work measurement standards, quality and timeliness standards should be set with the cooperation of the employees in your department. Where possible, they should establish the standards and you should approve them.

Once standards have been established, they must be documented. Documentation can be no more than a simple list of all the measured tasks in the department, indicating the quantity, quality, and timeliness standards that have been established.

Comparing Results to Standards

Once quality and timeliness standards have been developed, you must establish the procedures that compare actual results with the standards.

Review All Work   One method is to review all work after it has been processed and determine if it meets standards. In our example of the policywriting department, you or someone on your staff would examine each policy after it was completed. You would determine if it met the timeliness standard by comparing the incoming date stamp with the date of processing. (If a date stamping procedure is not being used in the department, it should be instituted as part of the measurement program.)

You will then review the work itself to search for errors you have defined. You would stroke-tally the number of items checked, whether it met the timeliness standard, and the major or minor errors detected. At the end of the measurement cycle (usually one month) you determine the percentage of work that met each standard.

Sampling   You may decide to review only a sample of the work rather than every item that is processed. If an average of one hundred endorsements is processed in your department each month, you might want to review twenty and use that sample to determine if standards have been met. If quality seems to be a problem, you might examine a larger sample, or all endorsements until you are meeting standards, at which time you can reduce the sample size. Statistics texts provide quidance in determining sample size. However, you might follow your own judgment on sample size if you are not ready to adopt a fully scientific approach.

When sampling, be sure to include a representative of different types of work with varying degrees of difficulty. In addition, you may decide to review a larger sample of more critical items or of tasks being handled by inexperienced people. Therefore, you might only check 10 percent of the standard endorsements being processed but 100 percent of the commercial lines quotes. You might also decide that a senior employee would have less work checked than a trainee.

Quality control does not necessarily have to be done immediately after the work is processed. You may decide to do all quality control at a specific time during the week, such as on Friday afternoon when the workload is light. Work that has been processed can be held for review at that time. The copies of the work going outside of the department need not be held up. Instead, the internal copy can be placed in a pending file awaiting review.

INDIVIDUAL PERFORMANCE STANDARDS

The measurement program just described will tell you how well *your department* is doing, but must be refined to reflect how well each employee is doing. Position guides and procedures manuals tell your staff members *what* their job is. Performance standards tell them *how well* they are supposed to do it to be considered as performing at an acceptable level. Performance standards should complete the sentence, "You have done a good job when...."

Standards differ from objectives in that objectives change over time, while standards change only when the job changes. Objectives usually have a stipulated time frame, while standards do not. For example, the standard might be that a policy typist must process 90 percent of new policies within twenty-four hours after they are received. This standard applies to all typists and is constant over time.

A trainee may be processing only 60 percent of the policies within twenty-four hours, and this may be acceptable due to inexperience. This typist may have a three-month *objective* of processing 80 percent of the work within twenty-four hours; and meeting the 90 percent standard within six months.

A senior employee may be meeting the standard but may set an objective of processing 95 percent of the work within twenty-four hours. Remember that standards express the performance expected of the well-trained employee. Senior people, who usually receive more money and higher benefits, can be expected to regularly exceed standards.

Performance standards help the employee as much as they help you. The employee wants to know what is expected of him or her in the most concrete terms. The employee needs to know how actual job performance compares to the standards, and what must be done to improve. As supervisor you need objective criteria by which to appraise staff members. In the delicate process of performance appraisal (discussed elsewhere in this text) you will be grateful that your evaluation is based on clear standards and measured results.

You will also be able to use performance standards in determining rewards, corrective action, and discipline for employees. For example, the fact that the senior employee described above reaches the 95 percent objective will carry much weight when reviewing his or her salary. Similarly, if an employee is not meeting standards, corrective action, such as training and coaching, should be implemented and, if necessary, disciplinary action taken.

MEASURING TECHNICAL WORK

Just as we can develop standards and a measurement program for file clerks and policy typists, we can also develop them for the technical positions in our industry, such as underwriters and claim adjusters. There are two methods for measuring technical work, the *Standard Method* and the *Account Load Method*.

Standard Method

The standard method uses the techniques described above but develops standards for steps in a process rather than for complete tasks. When you have developed the standards for each step in a task, you add the standards together to determine the standard for the task. For example, underwriting a piece of new business may involve such steps as reviewing an application, ordering an inspection, reviewing the inspection when it arrives, and rating the policy. You develop standards for each of these steps and add them together to determine the standard for underwriting a piece of new business.

Technical jobs involve such activities as "Meeting Time," "Telephone Time," and "Decision Making Time;" and these processes must be taken into consideration when developing standards. The "Case Study" measurement technique is likely to be the main one used in examining technical positions.

Account Load Method

As you can see, the standard method may become difficult to apply to technical positions, especially those working with complex commercial lines where telephone time, meeting time, and decision making time can vary so widely.

The account load method breaks each of the accounts handled by a technical employee, such as an underwriter, into three categories: those that require very little work throughout the year; those that require an average amount of work; and those that require a significant amount of work.

A workers' compensation policy on a small service business might be an example of an account requiring very little work. After the policy is issued, it will probably be filed and not worked on again until the renewal. Most personal lines policies would also be in this category. A policy with monthly reporting forms, or multiple changes throughout the policy year, would be an example of an account that required significant work. Standard commercial lines policies would fall into the category of policies that require an "average" amount of processing during the year.

When a measurement program is instituted in a technical unit, the supervisor should sit down with each member and review each of the existing accounts. Those requiring very little work during the year should be given a point value of "1"; those requiring average processing, a value of "5"; and those with a significant amount of processing should be given a value of "10." The supervisor and employee should then determine what a normal "account load" should be for the well-trained technician. For example, it might be decided that an underwriter should be able to handle an "account load" of 100 points. This could consist of 100 personal lines policies, 10 accounts with a significant amount of work, 20 average accounts or any combination totaling 100.

The underwriter has the ongoing responsibility for servicing accounts and meeting quality and timeliness standards. (We will discuss quality control for technical tasks later in this chapter.) When a new account is written, you and the person who will be handling the account will assign it a point value based on your knowledge of the amount of work required on similar accounts. Periodically, you should review accounts and evaluate the point values assigned to them. Point value adjustments should be made where appropriate.

Comparing actual results to standards is, of course, your control function. If an underwriter who works on accounts with a point value of 100 (full load) is backlogged, you should question why and expect the employee to get current. However, if the same employee had an account load of 120, the backlog would be understandable and you would want to do what you could to help him or her catch up.

You will also be able to use the account load method to balance your department's workload. By periodically reviewing the account value handled by each member of your staff, you can see if there is a work imbalance. For example, many company underwriting departments assign an underwriter to a group of agents. If one of those agents begins to place significantly more business with the company, the underwriter handling that agency will have a heavier workload.

You can also use the account load method to determine account assignments to new employees as well as senior staff. If an account load of 100 is the norm, a new employee might be required to handle a load of 75, slowly building up to the 100 level as experience is gained. Similarly, senior people, who have more experience and are probably earning higher salaries, might handle a load of, say, 120 or 125.

Quality Control for Technical Tasks

Many of the techniques for technical job quality control are the same as those used for clerical work. Underwriters must complete an application properly and must do it within a fixed amount of time after the request is received from the agent. In such situations, the same standards and measurement techniques can be used as for clerical positions.

If you are supervising a technical unit, you will also want to evaluate the subjective decision making of your employees. For example, did the underwriter accept risks that should have been accepted and reject those that should have been rejected? Did the claim adjuster obtain and consider all of the facts before making his decision? Where possible, objective criteria should be used in the evaluation of technical quality.

Technical supervisors must also apply judgment when evaluating performance. If an agency underwriter submitted a risk to the wrong company in your judgment, you may conclude that an error was made. Naturally, you will want to discuss this submission with the underwriter and explain why you think it was handled poorly.

SUMMARY

Despite the complexity of insurance jobs, many insurance tasks can be measured and performance standards set. Employees and supervisors may resist on the ground that there is more variability than uniformity in the work flow. It is an understandable human tendency to perceive one's job as unique, unpredictable, and beyond measurement. Supervisors may *assume* that their employees would fight the establishment of measures and standards. This assumption may not prove true. Against such reluctance must be posed the idea that employees want and need to know how they are doing and what you expect of them. Work measurement and performance standards are tools for improving your department's performance and the rewards of your staff members.

CHAPTER 6

Performance Appraisal

If your job as supervisor ever causes you to lose sleep, chances are that it will be when you have to appraise the performance of subordinates. Is there anything in supervision more delicate or scary? Can any supervisory duty create more anxiety than gearing up to tell someone that his or her work is poor—or just average? If you are a typical supervisor, you will feel less than sure of yourself when appraisal time arrives. To you it may be a dreaded ordeal.

Performance appraisal asks you to "play God" over employees. That telling phrase has been part of the management vocabulary since Douglas McGregor used it in a classic 1957 article on performance appraisal.[1] Managers and supervisors feel uncomfortable about having the power to control the careers and even the work satisfaction of other persons. They do not feel right about "inspecting" employees and sending them back for "rework" (coaching and development). They shrink, probably unknowingly, from judging the worth of human beings.

Organizations have tried a great many techniques of performance appraisal in the search for a system that does not ask the manager or supervisor to play supreme being. Organizations have tried and discarded a surprisingly large array of techniques in the quest for a technically sound evaluation system. In recent years, appraisal systems have also been revamped for another reason: to conform to fair employment guidelines.

In this chapter we will examine a number of performance appraisal techniques. It is doubtful that your organization uses more than a few of them. Nonetheless, this review should prove valuable since it sheds light on the difficulties of evaluating performance and suggests how far we have gone in trying to come up with a better way.

If performance appraisal is a murky area, then the appraisal interview is the most frightening part. If you lack confidence in your ability to discuss performance with an employee, your uneasiness is likely to result in a biased evaluation. If you are afraid to tell someone of poor performance, the unconscious, easy way out is to raise the evaluation. Accordingly, this chapter will take a close look at that crucial confrontation, the performance appraisal interview.

THE APPRAISAL PROCESS

As supervisor, you are responsible for developing human resources within your unit. You must identify and observe critical job behavior and results. You must measure the degree to which a person's performance meets expectations. You must stimulate and encourage performance improvement by giving feedback in a nonthreatening way. You do these things as a continuous process, often quite informally and often in a minute or two. This ongoing informal appraisal is usually supplemented, at least in large organizations, with some sort of formal performance appraisal procedure. That more formal, deliberately designed, periodic appraisal—the official appraisal—is the subject of this chapter.

Benefits of Performance Appraisal

What are the benefits of a formal performance evaluation process? Since the most obvious answers to that question may obscure others, let's take time to review the benefits.

To the Organization An effective appraisal system aligns employee efforts with organizational and unit objectives. It serves as a major vehicle for the control process discussed in Chapter 2. Messages delivered during formal appraisal may well be the loudest messages that employees ever hear.

To the Supervisor Your firm's formal appraisal procedure gives you a framework on which to hang the many scattered bits of information you have about employees. It organizes the way you present your evaluations to the employees and to your manager. If you are a typical supervisor, formal appraisal requirements force you to be more detailed and more objective than you otherwise would be in assessing performance and its results. Lastly, the documentation of performance is absolutely essential if you are to comply with the letter and spirit of fair employment requirements.

To the Employee People have a natural need to know how well they are doing. They seek the sense of security and the feeling of self-worth that come from knowing that they are contributing to the success of the unit. Employees need to know what is expected of them in the most specific terms possible. They want to improve: for most people, doing better than before is a source of deep satisfaction. The appraisal system provides the structure and the timetable under which employees meet these universal needs for feedback and improvement.

PURPOSES OF PERFORMANCE APPRAISAL

With so many benefits from a performance appraisal system, there is an odd danger: the system may be asked to do too much at once. Let's consider the major purposes or goals that enter into the design of performance appraisal systems.

Evaluation Goals

Performance appraisal systems are designed to measure employee performance. Sometimes the evaluation is relative—that is, employees are compared with one another. Sometimes the appraisal is meant to be absolute, and performance is weighed against standards of some kind. The evaluation results are put to a host of uses, including:

- Salary decisions
- Promotions
- Job reassignments
- Bonuses, profit sharing, or other special compensation
- Prizes or other special awards
- Staff planning, including succession planning and human resource inventories
- Identifying training or other unit needs

Development Goals

Employee evaluation is not the only purpose of most performance appraisal systems. The goal of improving performance often stands on equal footing as an overall system objective. In fact, some systems are designed to foster performance improvement as their primary goal, with measurement as a secondary interest. Such systems reflect the belief that the greatest payoff to the organization comes from spurring employees toward higher achievement. Consider the potential return if every employee is challenged—and helped—to make the very most of his or her talents. Just imagine the results within your organization if every employee increased productivity by 10 percent this year and sought similar gains year after year.

The general goals of employee development include:

- better performance on the present job,
- increased knowledge,
- new or improved skills,
- increased problem-solving ability,
- cross-training in other jobs,
- becoming qualified for promotion, and
- becoming qualified for special or additional duties.

With so many possible applications, clearly performance appraisal is a potent device. Its potency, like that of a patent medicine, can be harmful if we assume that performance appraisal can cure all of our organizational ailments.

LEGAL REQUIREMENTS

Fair employment requirements were discussed in detail in Chapters 8 and 9 of *Essentials of Supervision*. They are of such overriding importance in performance appraisal that a brief summary is appropriate. Here are seven key legal considerations affecting performance appraisal.

1. The courts have ruled that any and all decision-making processes, including background checks and supervisory performance ratings that affect an employee's status, are tests and thus subject to scrutiny for negative impact.

2. An employee who files action under Title VII has the burden of establishing that discrimination exists on the surface of a prima-facie case. Once a prima-facie case is established, then the organization has the burden of proving that decisions regarding appraisals were nondiscriminatory.

3. Once a violation of Title VII is established, it is not necessary to prove that the defendant "intentionally" discriminated against anyone. The motivation or intent becomes unimportant, as the real issue is the impact or result of the discriminatory action.

4. The courts have looked unfavorably upon appraisal techniques based on subjective supervisory judgments. Also, trait scales have been found to lend themselves to biased evaluation. Trait scales include such ambiguous terms as commitment, initiative, and aggressiveness.

5. A validated measurement instrument includes a proper job analysis. Job analysis defines the knowledge, skills, and behavior required on the job and forces the appraisal to become job-related.

6. Performance standards must be presented to employees. (However obvious it may seem, companies may neglect to communicate performance standards to employees. A simple case illustrates this point: a dismissed employee won a complaint against the company because she was never shown her own job description.)

7. Any company would be wise to model a performance appraisal system after the Uniform Guidelines of the 1978 Civil Service Reform Act. This Act requires that employees participate in identifying the critical elements of their jobs, be evaluated solely on the extent to which they satisfy the requirements of the position, that any reward be tied to performance, that appraisal be conducted at least once a year, and that the individual should have an opportunity to respond orally and in writing.

In reviewing landmark legal decisions one message is clear—make sure that performance appraisals deal only with important elements of job performance and the tested traits or factors identified as essential to job success. If problems do arise, it is the employer's responsibility to prove that employment decisions are based on job-related criteria.

WHO SHOULD EVALUATE?

In most instances, supervisors and managers have the responsibility for appraising the performance of their subordinates. Any other appraisal procedure would seem to weaken the position of the superior. Nonetheless, organizations have tried a variety of other approaches in the search for better appraisal systems. Some other-than-supervisor appraisals may have been tried as an antidote to possible bias by the supervisor. Other approaches were probably born of a belief that the superior may not always have full information about employee behavior and performance. (For example, a claims supervisor can rarely observe the adjuster's skill in communicating with claimants.) Some approaches may have been born of desperation and the hope that a drastically different approach will do away with the flaws in conventional appraisal.

There are six possible answers to the question, "Who should perform the evaluation?"

1. Supervisor
2. Employee
3. Peers of the employee
4. Subordinates
5. Persons outside the employee's unit
6. A combination of the above

We can look at these arrangements with some criteria in mind. The appraiser must have an understanding of the objectives, the employee's job, and all circumstances leading to the successful accomplishment of the job. The appraiser must be able to observe the employee in the performance of the job frequently and be able to recognize when the job is performed to established standards.

Appraisal by the Supervisor

Advantages   Most appraisals are conducted by the employee's immediate supervisor. Appraising subordinates is simply assumed to be the obligation and right of a supervisor or manager. Only a few organizations break from this pattern. The superior usually controls the rewards and punishments available. It is taken for granted that the immediate supervisor is the one person who is in the best position to observe an employee's performance and behavior, assess the employee's strengths and weaknesses, and judge overall results as they affect the department. For most employees, the only person to satisfy is the supervisor.

Sources of Error   Are there weaknesses in a supervisor appraisal? Biases can subvert any appraisal method, but what particular biases are present when evaluation is done by the employee's supervisor?

Stereotypes. It is common for stereotyping to seep into and contaminate a supervisor's review. Stereotyping means to slot people into broad categories. We all find that stereotyping is an easy way to classify people and form opinions about them. For example, "He hangs around with Charlie's group, so he is as conscientious as they are."

Friendship. As work relationships develop, it is natural for friendships also to evolve. A supervisor may become too closely involved in an employee's private life (e.g., by knowing of marital or economic problems) to see the person in a clear and unprejudiced light. It is tempting for a supervisor to become involved in the social side of the work environment, but a proper distance must be kept if appraisal is to be objective.

Playing God. The supervisor may feel uncomfortable in the role of the appraiser. This role requires the supervisor to "play God" and render verdicts both positive and negative. The majority of untrained supervisors are uneasy in this new role, especially if the supervisor is promoted from within and must now manage former peers and friends.

Unit Results. Compare two baseball pitchers. One wins twenty-five games for the team that wins the league pennant. The other wins eighteen games for the team that finishes at the bottom of the standings. Who is the better pitcher? Obviously, the performance of the entire unit colors the evaluation of individual performance. It is difficult to rate individuals objectively when the unit is outstandingly good or bad.

The Peer Appraisal

Research has demonstrated that peer appraisal can be an effective method of performance analysis in some situations. Peers see an employee performing the work task and interacting with peers and lower and upper level personnel. The employee naturally behaves differently in different circumstances. For example, he or she may demonstrate to a supervisor one style of behavior and reveal a different personality when out of view and performing the job. Is it the peer who sees a more "total" employee and is in a better position to evaluate?

In order for a peer appraisal method to succeed, the conditions must be right. There must exist a reward system that does not lead to competition for promotion or raises; and information about and results of work performance must be available to peers. For example, members of a word processing unit may be required to proofread one another's work. They may know more about the quality and quantity of an employee's work than the supervisor knows.

Peer appraisal can be a workable alternative to supervisory evaluation when the supervisor is unable to observe behavior on a regular basis. This may occur in field assignments. Peer evaluations may be valuable in training programs: fellow students may be better judges than instructors in some cases.

Peer appraisal has pitfalls. Competition between employees may result in biased and unrealistic evaluations. It is tempting to make someone else look bad in order for the evaluator to look good. In rating someone else, you are likely to emphasize the importance of the things that you also do well. A negative or favorable evaluation of a peer could be given for ulterior motives.

In general, the peer appraisal has a place only in unusual circumstances or as part of a broader process of observation and evaluation.

Self-Appraisal

Self-appraisal appears to be valuable in organizations where goal-setting and analysis of successes and failures is realistic and an integral part of the organization. Self-appraisal is based on the assumption that the employee is in the best position to know the job and judge his or her own performance.

Self-appraisal has both positive and negative aspects. Research in organizations with self-appraisal procedures indicates these advantages: (1) more satisfying and constructive appraisal interviews, (2) superior job performance, (3) the process forces the employee to focus on the expectation of the job, (4) supervisors get a clear picture about how employees view their jobs, and (5) the process is valuable in encouraging employee self-development.

Negative aspects of self-appraisal occur with employees who are relatively inexperienced in performance reviews. In particular, new employees may need a more traditional atmosphere with greater structure and closer supervision.

In general, employees are very realistic in evaluating their own strengths. However, supervisors must be able to handle the occasional instance of an employee whose self-image is excessively high.

Self-appraisals appear to be effective in encouraging employee development. Even if your organization's performance appraisal system does not provide for self-appraisals, you might consider adopting them within your unit. You might ask employees to evaluate their performance on the same form that you use. Self appraisals bring to the surface the employee's perception of job standards as well as their assessment of present effectiveness. They uncover the aspirations and blind spots of employees. They help you to plan the appraisal interviews with an awareness of the personal needs and views of individual employees.

Appraisal by Subordinates

This appraisal procedure is rare, and rightly so. Appraisal by subordinates tends to dilute the power of the supervisor's position. In most cases subordinates lack a clear picture of what is expected of a supervisor. The results can be biased as an employee is less likely to record a negative review for fear of retaliation. Employees naturally tend to give favorable reviews to supervisors they feel close to or think of as friends, even if that supervisor's results are poor. Easygoing and undemanding supervisors may get the highest ratings.

The possibilities for unreliable and biased reviewing are great enough to discourage the use of appraisal by subordinates.

Appraisal by Outsiders

Organizations may use "outside" people to help in the appraisal process. For example, if an employee has just received specific training in a particular skill or service, the trainer may serve as appraiser.

In one variation of appraisal-by-outsiders, a representative of the personnel department visits units to interview managers and supervisors about the performance of the employee. A report is written and sent to the supervisor who makes any changes and then approves the report. An advantage is consistency and, if the personnel representative is skilled at questioning, greater objectivity. This method takes the process out of the hands of the supervisor and thereby eliminates one vital responsibility of a supervisor. It may be a cold and one-sided process since the reviewer does not observe the employee at work.

The Who-Should-Appraise Issue

There is no question that appraising subordinate performance is essential to the role of the supervisor. However, even appraisal-by-the-boss is subject to bias, and there may be wide differences in standards set by individual supervisors. From time to time, organizations seek to make appraisal more objective by getting other people involved. These other-than-the-boss appraisals might play a role in some situations (probably unusual ones). In general, appraising employee performance is the job of the supervisor. As a supervisor, you may not find performance appraisal the most pleasant of your tasks. Nonetheless, it is at the center of your supervisory role.

METHODS OF PERFORMANCE APPRAISAL

The chances that you will develop your own appraisal form are slim. In all probability you will have to use a form provided by your organization. As we will see, there are advantages and drawbacks to the various formats in common use.

Checklists

The checklist technique is a popular method for evaluating employee performance. A list of general traits, behaviors, results, or job characteristics is usually provided. Checklists assume that excellence in the tasks or behaviors specified means excellence in overall job results.

The Simple Checklist This is one of the easiest instruments to use in rating performance. Behavior or performance traits are listed. The rater reviews the list and checks the statements that best illustrate the employee's performance. Items can be traits, behavioral descriptions, or descriptions of job results. Items might include quality of work, dependability, initiative, job knowledge, meeting deadlines, or following underwriting guidelines.

The rater reviews the employee's performance on each item while using an established scale such as:

Outstanding   Superior   Above Average   Average
Below Average   Unsatisfactory

Space is often provided for the rater to include comments.

The simple checklist is easy to use. In some firms, all employees are rated on the same factors and the checklist makes no attempt to reflect specific job characteristics. For example, a receptionist may be rated on the same general traits as an administrative assistant. This type of checklist may be appropriate for low-level positions where it is difficult to set individual goals and performance objectives. It is suggested that a separate and more relevant checklist should be developed for positions in which performance objectives can be set.

Weighted Checklist   The weighted checklist adds a numerical weight or value to each item. Sometimes the form is administered and returned to the corporate headquarters where someone trained in testing and evaluation or psychology analyzes the review. The rater may not know the value of the weight assigned to each item. In general this method is impersonal and can miss the daily characteristics or skills required to perform a given job to standards. Like the simple checklist, it tends to remove the supervisor from the responsibility of being a manager of individuals.

Forced-Choice Checklist   This is a more complicated checklist method. The forced-choice checklist presents groups containing two to five statements. There may be as many as sixty groups. The statements are structured so that each group appears to contain statements of similar value. Here is an example:

Check two statements that best describe the employee:

     a. Handles work assignments in a timely manner
     b. Handles work assignments confidently
     c. Meets deadlines
     d. Accepts assignments without fuss

Note that all four items are favorable. Another group might contain four unfavorable descriptions.

All four selections may be of value, but perhaps a and b have been identified as characteristic of a productive employee. The checklist would contain many such examples of traits (ideally, identified by research) that the organization considers characteristic of a productive employee.

The statements may appear confusing, but the intent of the forced-choice checklist is to allow the rater to be as specific, accurate, and unbiased as possible. The supervisor is now the recorder of behavior and is no longer in the role of judge. In fact, the supervisor does not know how good a rating he has given an employee. The reviews must be sent to a trained scorer for analysis.

The objective of a force-choice checklist is to minimize the rater's bias. The rater has little way of knowing which statements are the important ones and would have a difficult time slanting the review.

The forced-choice method has drawbacks. The forced-choice method does not usually allow specific comments by the rater and keeps the rater in the dark as to the overall evaluation given an employee. The process may seem more like a psychological test than a review of job performance.

The Essay Method

The essay approach does away with the ease of a checklist and requires the reviewer instead to write a narrative or description of the employee's performance, perhaps within designated categories. For example the review would comment on (a) a general impression of the employee's performance, (b) the specific strengths and weaknesses of the employee, (c) the readiness of the employee to move up to a better job, and (d) training and development required to improve or expand skills. The essay method can be used as an appraisal instrument alone, or as part of a larger one.

For the busy supervisor, the essay method may prove to be a problem. The effectiveness of the method is limited to the ability of the reviewer to write clearly and analytically. Many supervisors would rather use the simple checklist as it requires little thought and writing time. Some jobs are so highly structured and routine that an essay appraisal is inappropriate.

If used in a controlled way, the essay method can provide the supervisor with the opportunity to be highly specific in identifying skills, successes, and shortcomings.

In the hands of a supervisor who is comfortable in expressing observations and thoughts on paper, and who takes the time, the essay method can be of great value. More than any other appraisal method, the essay elicits the supervisor's perception of each employee—it gets out the supervisor's picture of the employee with as few restrictions as possible. The essay may be the best appraisal method for fostering open exchange between supervisor and employee over their views of job requirements.

The Critical Incident Method

The Critical Incident Method requires the supervisor to make diary-type notes about the effectiveness or ineffectiveness in handling tasks.

An example of a positive critical incident:

5/19

John demonstrated great composure and professionalism in handling an irate call about the status of a claim. The employee dealt with the heart of the matter in a clear and understanding way.

An example of a negative critical incident:

5/19

John demonstrated poor judgment in passively taking a call

from an irate policyholder and not telling the caller what we do to serve his interest.

At formal appraisal time, the supervisor is supposed to pull the critical incident notes from the employee's file, review them, and thus see the high (and low) points of the employee's work for the entire rating period.

At first look, the critical method seems to go far to offset rater subjectivity and prejudice. It was thought that by connecting concrete behavior to acceptable standards of performance, the employee would develop a clear understanding of what is expected and respond accordingly. Clearly the critical incident method does stress facts (observed behavior or work performance) over subjective global impressions.

What about drawbacks? The Critical Incident Method is time consuming, costly, and requires that the rater be trained to use this method for the best interests of all. The supervisor is put in the role of constant judge and could spend the entire day as observer and recorder. The method is open to inconsistency, as note-taking may reflect the daily attitude of the reviewer. It is possible that some acts could be blown out of proportion or a favorite employee's poor performance overlooked.

Because of physical closeness or interrelated work, the supervisor may be in a position to make frequent notes about some employees but may rarely see the behavior of others. There is also a tendency to see the bad incidents and not notice the good ones.

A supervisor who has the opportunity to observe behavior, and is willing to analyze and record it, may find this method very worthwhile. If well done, the resulting picture of the employee's performance is commendably specific and thus easily received by the employee. Even if not used as an appraisal method, there is clear value in recording important events and referring to them when making a formal performance appraisal.

There are a number of other methods, or combinations of methods, used to appraise employee performance. This brief look at some common ones should make it clear that each method has advantages and drawbacks. In some organizations, appraisal forms rarely last more than a few years. The drawbacks of whatever method is used lead to the creation of a new form or approach. That, in turn, has a limited life span and it, too, gives way to something newer.

Special Purpose Appraisals

Organizations may conduct special appraisals for specific purposes. A separate appraisal of employee potential might be made apart from the appraisal of job performance. A special appraisal might be performed as a firm prepares for a reduction in staff or the closing of an office. Employees being considered for termination might be given special evaluations.

The organization's regular appraisal method might be used or another method chosen for such special purpose evaluations. Their success seems to rest heavily on how clearly raters understand the purpose. It is not easy to keep them distinct from the regular appraisals. Sometimes the results seem hard to explain. For example, a low promotability evaluation might be given to a person whose job performance is excellent.

The fact that organizations resort to special purpose appraisals adds support to our argument that a firm's performance appraisal process is likely to have shortcomings that go along with its strengths.

COMMON RATING PROBLEMS AND HOW TO AVOID THEM

We have all seen football plays in which the instant replay shows us one thing while the referee saw something quite different. Even the best performance appraisal system, like the best referee, is not perfect.

When we talk about "rating errors" we mean the difference between one person's perception and reality. Human perception is never perfect; some error is normal. When we praise a person for having good judgment, we underscore how difficult it is to control one's preferences and dislikes when assessing human events.

No matter how hard one tries, it is impossible to eliminate all bias. However, it is possible to minimize rating errors if they are called to our attention. The most common rating errors include the halo/horns effect, first impression, central tendency, positive and negative leniency, contrast effects, and similar/dissimilar effects.

Halo and Horns Effects

The *halo effect* refers to the activity of making generalizations about a person's performance based on how he or she accomplishes one task or displays one exceptional skill.

For example, an employee who is superior in one area may be inaccurately rated as superior in other activities. Naturally the converse is true (the *horns effect.*) The rater's impression of one area carries through to all other areas of the appraisal.

To guard against the halo or horns effect, the supervisor must consider each item or category independently. One technique for doing this is to rate an employee, wait a few days, and re-evaluate the employee by filling in the evaluation form in reverse order. Discrepancies between the two evaluations may bring bias errors to light.

First Impression Effects

The *first impression* effect refers to the mental process of allowing one's first opinion (either favorable or unfavorable) to color later perceptions of the employee's work performance. For example, during the first few weeks on the job an employee does an excellent job or shows creativity in handling problems.

The next few months the employee does work that is only average. The supervisor's evaluation may be overly influenced by the fine initial performance. The converse may be true as well. An employee who experiences initial problems on the job, and corrects them, may be in for a negatively biased review.

The supervisor may only remember the beginning ratings and not notice improvement. The process is a normal one: we tend to see things that confirm what we already know. We tend not to see things that would cause us to reorganize or change our views. The remarkable thing about this mechanism is that the person actually does not see evidence that runs mildly counter to a strong first impression.

Central Tendency

The *central tendency* bias occurs when a rater takes the easy road and rates everyone as average in performance. Managers and supervisors sometimes use this device to protect themselves. If an employee does well, the manager can feel confident that the rating was fair. If the reverse occurs and the employee fails, then the supervisor can still feel comfortable with the rating. The tendency to rate all employees as average goes beyond protective behavior by raters. The simple fact is that some people tend to see most employees as average.

Negative and Positive Leniency

Negative and positive leniency problems occur when the supervisor rates all employees either too hard or too easy. Negative leniency or tough rating may discourage employees and lead them to perform to minimal standards because exceptional performance goes unrewarded. Positive leniency, or rating on a loose and less critical basis, may create false expectations for the employee.

Are central tendency and positive and negative leniency equally common? We cannot be sure, but suggest that positive leniency is the most common practice and constitutes the greatest problem. Supervisors and managers tend to give high ratings because it makes the appraisal interview more pleasant. Indeed, this can be so pronounced that some appraisal systems are made worthless as everyone is rated above average.

Contrast Effects

The *contrast effect* occurs when the manager rates employees against other employees and not against the specific job requirements. The rating should be on the exact requirements the employee is paid to perform.

Similar/Dissimilar Effects

The *similar/dissimilar* effect occurs when the supervisor judges more positively those employees who are like him or her. The closer the employee resembles the supervisor, the more favorable the rating will be. Similarities can be of many kinds, including attitudes, background, interests, pastimes, and values.

Information Errors

Problems arise when raters have incomplete or wrong information about employee performance. This may occur when employees work outside of the office, when an employee has worked under the supervisor for only a short time, and in many other situations. A supervisor has difficulty saying "I don't know" on the rating form. It is tempting to base ratings on conjecture and limited data.

Criteria Differences

To one supervisor, quality of work is all-important. To another supervisor, good performance means getting the work done on time. To still another supervisor, the most important thing is teamwork in helping the unit to achieve its goals. The employee may have still another concept of what constitutes excellent performance, perhaps a picture that includes personal growth. The need, then, is for employee and supervisor to understand each other's notion of effectiveness and to resolve the differences as much as possible. The differences are subtle. They exist not so much in the criteria used to judge performance as in the relative importance of each criterion.

Neither the job description nor a list of performance targets may fully convey these shadings of priority and importance. It follows that, as a supervisor, you must make explicit the criteria, and their relative importance, that you will use to judge the work of each employee.

Lack of Organizational Support

An effective performance appraisal procedure may be fruitless if not supported by the organization. The best appraisal form and procedure may be undermined if the organization demonstrates little commitment to employee development, offers minimal training in appraisal, and ignores the results of horror stories in making promotion and salary decisions. For instance, one organization gave salary change announcements two weeks before appraisals were to be done.

Inflexibility

Another problem with performance appraisal systems is that the job description is rather rigid and may not accurately describe the daily reality of getting the job done. Tasks, methods, goals, responsibilities, and skill requirements change while the revision of a document always lags behind.

The appraisal format itself is usually a standard one meant to cover a wide

The Appraisal Dilemma

There is no such thing as a perfect performance appraisal system...or even a system that could be called excellent. We hope that you remember this when you find yourself struggling to operate within the restrictions imposed by whatever system your organization uses.

At the heart of the problem is this: we ask too much of an appraisal system. We want it to evaluate employees — to measure their contributions with yardstick accuracy or better. We want it to identify potential — to pick out the dancing stars of tomorrow from the chorus line of today. We want it to be a nourishing meal that helps its recipients to grow. We often want it to do other things as well, such as parceling out salary increases or selecting the unlucky ones at staff reduction time.

We might design an appraisal system that does any one of these things to virtual perfection. The problems come as we try to do too much with a single appraisal system.

If we have to boil it down, we can reduce the mixture to the two major purposes of an appraisal process — evaluation and development. These goals clash in many respects. The goal of accurate evaluation calls for a system that is objective, impartial, consistent, precise, and cold-blooded. The goal of employee development asks for a system that is flexible, understanding, sympathetic, and treats each employee as an individual. In short, it is uniform *versus* individualized treatment. In this sense, performance appraisal poses a dilemma.

What can you, as a supervisor, do about this appraisal dilemma? For one thing, you can demand that your organization be clear about the purposes to be served by its appraisal procedures. You can stress these goals to your employees, and be explicit when you address other goals. You can ask — again and again if need be — that employees tell you what feedback they want from you. You can take your organization's appraisal system as the necessary but incomplete framework, adding to it your commitment to use yourself to help others grow.

range of jobs. (The essay format is an exception.) We can offer two bits of advice for dealing with an overly inflexible system. First, ask the employee to give you an update on the job as he or she sees it before you begin appraising performance.

Second, consider adding comments on the form or supplementing it with a memorandum when necessary to give an accurate picture of a person's performance. You may recall the suggestion given earlier that employees be asked to appraise their own performance as an early step in the formal supervisory appraisal. While you must operate within the framework of your organization's forms and procedures, you should be able to find ways to make a performance appraisal flexible and responsive to the needs of the individual employee.

Because of the importance of accurate performance evaluations, many firms have instituted training workshops for supervisors and managers. Our discussion of biases should make you interested in attending any such training.

If training is not available to you, you may still want to discuss your appraisals with your manager in a conscious attempt to identify the biases that creep into your perception of employee behavior and performance.

IDEAS FOR IMPROVING PERFORMANCE APPRAISAL

Job Analysis

A *job analysis* seems essential for any appraisal system to succeed and to prevent illegal discrimination. The four federal agencies responsible for enforcing fair employment (the Equal Employment Opportunity Commission, the Civil Service Commission, the Department of Labor, and the Department of Justice) published a set of *uniform guidelines* for employee selection procedures. The guidelines state that there shall be a job analysis which includes an analysis of the important work behaviors required for successful performance.

Job analysis requires a systematic collection of job-connected information for each job. More specifically, it is concerned with what is to be done, how it is to be done, and why it is to be done. In cases in which job analysis has not been done, the courts have rejected claims that appraisal instruments were valid.

Since job requirements, procedures, and resources tend to change gradually, you must be watchful that job analyses have not become out of date.

The Critical Incident Method

Earlier we discussed the critical incident technique as one of the basic methods of performance appraisal. It also serves as a technique that enhances appraisal under other methods. The recording of critical incidents can also improve job analysis.

In many organizations, the standard appraisal period is a year. Reviewing a year's file of critical incidents is likely to prompt a number of "I forgot that" reactions. It seems particularly easy to forget when some events happened and to be unsure if they should be included within the appraisal period. Often the recording of a critical incident involves no more than making a photocopy of a document to serve as a reminder of some event.

Clearly, the routine recording of critical incidents is a practice of far-reaching value. It is the best antidote to the halo/horns effect and an unrivaled memory jogger.

Publicizing the Appraisal Program

Are employees fully informed of the appraisal system and their rights within it? We suspect that a touch of secrecy still infects the appraisal process in many organizations. There is—or can be—unpleasantness involved, and human beings are ingenious in avoiding unpleasantness. It is easy to put appraisal out of mind while concentrating on doing or supervising the job. An unrecognized desire to get it over with quickly may be the reason some supervisors skimp on explaining the appraisal procedure to employees. You are safe in assuming that employees do not fully understand your organization's performance appraisal mechanisms.

In making the appraisal process less of a mystery to employees, you should address two needs. First, employees need to know the details of the appraisal procedure. Second, they need to know the standards by which they are to be judged.

Your communication effort should begin with your own preparation. You should study the forms and guidelines for their use. Special attention should be given to the employee's right to see the evaluation and to appeal it. Organizations differ, of course, in giving explicit rights to employees within the appraisal system. One specific point to determine: does the employee's signature on the appraisal form signify that he or she agrees with the appraisal or merely has seen it?

It is recommended that you conduct a staff meeting, perhaps annually, to explain the appraisal program, its objectives, steps, and paperwork. You might also want to explain the job analysis procedure. You should be prepared to receive a range of feelings about being appraised and about the accuracy of the yardsticks you will use.

After such a unit meeting, you might meet with groups of employees who perform similar jobs. At these meetings you can detail the criteria you will use to judge their performance. Copies of the appraisal form should be distributed. You should "walk through" a typical appraisal and discuss the development of a performance improvement plan. Employees want to know more than the mechanics of the appraisal procedure. They want to know your thinking about applying that procedure to them.

Employee Participation in Appraisal

To what extent should employees participate in the appraisal of their performance? Organizations differ sharply in their willingness to give employees a voice in the design of the appraisal system or in the evaluation of performance.

Through meetings such as the unit meeting recommended above, employees are often given opportunities to express their views about appraisal. Quite possibly, such expressions could influence the criteria, relative importance, and standards you apply when appraising performance. On a larger scale, firms often respond to feedback in the search for an appraisal system that works. Also, employees often participate directly in job analysis.

When an organization follows *management by objectives*, employees have a direct role in defining the performance expectations for their jobs. Under MBO, the comparison of actual results against previously agreed-upon goals becomes the central focus of performance appraisal.

You should ask employees to provide any information they wish you to consider before evaluating their performance. This step is particularly beneficial when your information is incomplete. Sometimes relevant performance data is not reported to you routinely but can be assembled when needed. Progress on long-term projects serves as an illustration. Even if there are no special circumstances, you should ask employees to submit anything they want you to see before evaluating their work.

Self-Appraisal

Should employees rate themselves as part of the appraisal process? Opinion seems divided on this issue.

Many supervisors see vast benefits in self-appraisal as a preliminary to the appraisal interview. Self-appraisal usually means that the employee is given a copy of the appraisal form, fills it in, and either returns it to the supervisor in advance or brings it to the interview. Self-appraisal brings out the employee's perception of the position requirements as well as of his or her own accomplishments. This can be invaluable: change begins from where the employee is, not from where you think the employee is. Self-appraisal makes it glaringly obvious when an employee has a totally unrealistic self-image. Self-appraisal can give shape to the appraisal interview. It removes the need to dwell on elements on which you agree. It directs attention to the points on which perceptions differ and suggests how much disagreement exists.

Some arguments have been raised against self-appraisal. There is a fear that the employee's self-rating will distort the supervisor's rating and the final evaluation become a compromise. There is also a possibility that the appraisal interview becomes little more than a side-by-side comparison of the two evaluations.

Making Feedback Effective

It is a cliché to say that supervisors must give performance feedback to employees on a constant basis. Its importance cannot be stressed too emphatically. Feedback given in the annual or semiannual formal appraisal should complement the day-in and day-out performance feedback given employees. Allowing one to dominate the other is unwise. The red flags are thinking that there is nothing left to say at appraisal time or, just the reverse, saving everything for the periodic appraisal.

Here are some guidelines for making feedback effective.

Frequency Within limits, the more frequently feedback is provided, the more likely behavior will change. Feedback given too often, however, can be destructive and sensitivity to its impact is needed.

Timeliness There should be as little time as possible between the performance and the feedback. Take care of problems immediately and do not allow them to pile up only to be dumped on the employees. Fast feedback usually works better than large doses.

Objectivity Feedback should be expressed in terms of observed specifics of work behavior and job performance. For you it means curbing the tendency to generalize ("You cannot meet deadlines") and sticking to the facts at hand

("You are late with this report"). You may recall the old saying, "punish the act, not the person." Giving feedback should mean giving descriptive information, not attacking the person. You may have noted the paradox in preferring descriptive to evaluative feedback: the way to get your evaluation across is not to make evaluative statements.

Positive Tone Any feedback should convey a positive regard for the individual and end with an expression of your confidence in the individual.

Essentials of Supervision, the companion volume to this text, gives many guidelines for understanding others and improving communications. We urge you to review them and apply them to performance appraisal. We will not repeat them here, but we will give additional guidelines specific to the performance appraisal interview.

THE APPRAISAL INTERVIEW

In many organizations, the appraisal paperwork is but a prelude to the interview. Nonetheless, the interview—or anxiety over it—strongly influences the appraisal and the very perception of performance. One may not "see" poor performance when seeing it means having to confront the employee with pain-inducing news. Conversely, confidence in your ability to conduct the appraisal interview enables you to perceive performance more accurately and to give more helpful feedback to employees.

Despite wholehearted attempts to confine the interview to performance, the employee's personality seems exposed. If you are too harsh, or overload the employee, defensive reactions occur and the employee may stop hearing you. Yet you want to be honest in giving feedback. You can see the challenge posed by poor performers. The appraisal interview thrusts you into the dilemma we have seen before—the goal of accurate evaluation must be tempered by the goal of encouraging improvement.

Planning the Interview

Planning is critical to the success of most ventures, and the appraisal interview is no different. You should prepare for the content of the interview, the method of presentation, and the coaching strategy.

Recommendations from Experts Many helpful suggestions appear in the vast literature about appraisal. We will pass along some of these suggestions.

Kirkpatrick identifies five key objectives that must be accomplished for an appraisal interview to be successful.

1. To reach agreement on the performance of the employee
2. To identify strengths
3. To identify performance areas that need to be improved
4. To agree on a performance improvement plan for one area needing improvement

5. To agree on what is expected, for example, standards, or behavior changes, for the next appraisal period[2]

Bernardin and Beatty identified five critical elements that a supervisor must understand in preparing for the interview:

1. A thorough knowledge of the rating scales, of how ratings are derived, and how specific behaviors relate to numbers on forms
2. An understanding of the goal-setting approach to motivation
3. A thorough knowledge of each employee's performance
4. An understanding of the purposes for the interview and the parameters that affect their accomplishments
5. An ability to give negative feedback[3]

We cannot over-emphasize the importance and productive opportunity a well-prepared and structured performance interview affords. Parnes believes that two types of preparation must be done: preparation of the content of the interview and preparation of the process. Content planning deals with what will be discussed.

Determine the Sequence of Ideas   In planning content, you should be concerned with gathering appropriate data, the analysis of it, and establishing a logical and reasonable sequence of ideas. You would do well to organize your major points in an outline format. Each should be supported by facts and behavioral observation. Your "homework" might include challenging your ideas and preparing for possible responses to them.

You may want to go so far as to plan the opening of personal remarks to put the employee at ease. Plan any scene-setting remarks and anything you want to say about the appraisal procedure. Plan the ending—what you can say that will be honest yet end the session as positively as possible.

Advance Notification to the Employees   At least two weeks prior to the interview date, you should meet with the employee for a preparation and planning session. This should be a brief meeting to ensure that the employee knows how the appraisal is to be conducted. The objective of the interview should be discussed. If not done before, the employee should be asked to provide any data he or she wishes to have considered. A copy of the appraisal form should be given to the employee. In most systems, the employee can be asked or encouraged to conduct a self-evaluation as preparation for the interview.

Preparation Checklist

Before the interview, you should be concerned with:

- *Time and Place.* The right time is when both parties are free from other concerns and can sit in a private room without interruption. You should consider the employee's work flow as well as yours. The first thing in the morning might be ideal for you but a poor time for the employee. If the appraisal system requires that you appraise all unit members at once, scheduling the interviews can be difficult. We suggest that you schedule no more than three interviews per day to avoid emotional overload, physical fatigue, and blunted sensitivity.

- *Employee Information.* Help the employee to obtain job descriptions, past appraisals, and any other documents of relevance.
- *Facilities.* The room should be arranged in an informal manner. Instead of sitting at a cluttered desk, you should sit next to the employee or across a table. It is important to create an atmosphere of warmth and concern rather than an adversary situation. Telephone calls should be intercepted and a *Do Not Disturb* sign hung on the door. No one should be able to see into the room or overhear the conversation.
- *The Opening.* It is important to put the employee at ease as soon as possible. You should not trust your ability to ad lib but should plan remarks appropriate for each interview. However, the opening statement you plan may be discarded in favor of spontaneous comments about sports, current events, or something else that reflects the employee's interests.
- *The Interview.* The employee, once past the general opening statements, will expect to get right to the business at hand. You must respect this desire and start with a discussion of why the meeting is taking place, the ground rules of the interview, and what role each person will assume.
- Discuss the job description.
- Review the performance appraisal instrument and procedure. Indicate what happens to the documents after they leave your hands.
- Present the employee with copies of all appraisal instruments.
- Ask for the employee's self-evaluation if one has been completed and not yet been received. It is not recommended that you discuss it in total. Your interview plan should provide the framework.
- Report your appraisal to the employee and discuss it item by item. If a self-appraisal was done, next compare the two and thoroughly discuss the major differences.
- Keep an open mind—be willing to change an evaluation when the employee presents evidence that justifies change. Be willing to hold fast when the employee cannot present convincing data or argument. Avoid slipping into a bargaining or compromise mentality.
- Summarize the evaluation.
- Direct discussion to the future and urge the employee to formulate specific growth objectives soon. It is not recommended that you go into any detail on plans for improvement. Doing so dilutes the attention given to performance.

THE DEVELOPMENT INTERVIEW AND PLAN

The appraisal interview should be confined to a discussion of performance. It should not contain an announcement of salary change. Doing so only detracts from or contradicts the evaluation of performance. Similarly, we recommend that the appraisal interview not serve as an employee development interview. It is hard to look backwards and forwards at the same time. Instead, employee development should be the subject of a separate conference. The development interview is often held about two weeks after the appraisal interview. It addresses any needs identified in the appraisal interview but is not limited to them.

You might think of the development interview as having two focuses: performance improvement and development itself. In this sense performance improvement refers to correcting any deficiencies in doing the present job. Most performance improvement goals are based on the results of the formal appraisal process. Beyond performance improvement lies personal development in a broader sense. This sense embraces efforts to enrich one's job, to qualify for higher positions, and to acquire knowledge and skills of life-long value. There is no strict division between the two. Acquiring a particular skill may have both performance improvement and development value.

Some firms have elaborate employee development systems. These usually require a development interview and accompanying paperwork. Other firms have yet to establish formal procedures in this regard. Even if your organization does not require you to conduct a development interview, you may wish to do so. Here is a checklist to assist you.

Development Interview Checklist

 I. Preparation for the Interview
  A. Review your mutual understanding of job duties, standards, objectives, assignments, and work priorities.
  B. Review the employee's background.
   • Education
   • Training
   • Experience
  C. Review the employee's past jobs and job performance.
  D. Review the strengths and development needs discussed in previous development interviews.
  E. Review resources:
   • Your organization's training, education, and educational assistance programs
   • Community programs
   • Resources within your departments
   Plan to make a few critical points. Decide in advance which skills are most important for the employee to develop. Plan to allow the employee to direct attention to skills or needs that he or she considers important.
 II. Conducting the Interview
  A. Beginning the discussion
   • Set the stage. Informality and a friendly atmosphere are important. Be sincere. Be yourself.

- Explain the purpose of the discussion.
- Make it clear that the discussion is a two-way conversation—a mutual problem-solving and goal-setting exchange.

B. Body of the discussion
- Summarize the employee's recent performance appraisal (employee strengths and improvement needs) against objectives set during last review.
- Ask the employee to summarize his or her recent development activities and development needs.
- Talk about strong points.
- Encourage the employee to examine development alternatives.
- Before discussing the suggestions you may have, let the employee tell you what development plans he or she may have. Add your thoughts after the employee indicates a readiness to hear them.
- Help the employee set personal targets. The goals should come from the employee, not from you. Otherwise, commitment and drive will falter.
- Reach agreement on development plans with the employee. Plans should spell out what you are going to do and what the employee intends to do.

C. Ending the discussion
- Summarize what has been discussed—make it positive and show enthusiasm for the plans you and the employee have made.
- Give the employee an opportunity to make additional suggestions.
- Close discussion on a friendly, harmonious note.

III. Post-Interview Activity
A. Make a record of:
- Plans you and the employee have made (give a copy to the employee).
- Points requiring follow-up.
- Commitments you have made for action on your part.

B. Evaluate how you handled the discussion.
- What did you do well?
- What did you do poorly? How would you do it differently?
- What did you learn about the employee? About your job?

C. Resolve to do an even better job next time!

Development Plan Checklist

A development plan should conform to the following criteria:

A. Practicality: the plan should relate directly to job performance required for improvement.
B. Time-Specific: deadlines for action must be realistic and agreed upon.

    C. Content-Specific: the plan must clearly discuss what is to be accomplished, avoiding generalization.

    D. Require Commitment: the supervisor and employee both must express genuine belief that the plan will work and agree that it was developed mutually.

SUMMARY

Performance appraisal is, in a word, tricky. Nonetheless, it is so essential in managing people that most organizations of any size have some sort of formal appraisal process. This process usually embodies trade-offs among objectives, approaches, and methods.

One dominant goal of performance evaluation systems is to measure the human resources of the organization. Another goal of critical importance is the promotion of better performance. Other goals may relate to salary administration, identifying people for promotion, or other organizational requirements. The organization's formal appraisal system necessarily represents priorities or compromises among such goals.

Appraising subordinates is a core supervisory function. From time to time organizations seek to offset weaknesses in supervisory appraisals by involving others. These measures are of limited value and popularity, but their occasional use helps us understand the forces that make supervisory appraisals imperfect.

Appraisal formats vary with objectives and other considerations. An essay format may be the most flexible and sensitive to individual circumstances. However, the essay does not serve as much of a measurement device, and comparisons among employees are all but impossible. Many other formats exist; they must be judged against the objectives of the appraisal system.

As a supervisor, you should be interested in the design of the appraisal system as a framework for your efforts to help employees to change and develop greater competency. Within the limits imposed by the system, you provide all-important performance feedback to employees and help them reach out for personal and job-related growth. In doing this, much depends on your skill in conducting that delicate process called the appraisal interview. The tensions that surround performance appraisal bear witness to its central importance in your leadership role.

Chapter Notes

1. Douglas McGregor, "An Uneasy Look at Performance Appraisal,"*Harvard Business Review,* May–June 1957.
2. Donald Kirkpatrick, *How to Improve Performance through Appraisal and Coaching* (New York: Amacom, 1982), p. 51.
3. John Bernardin, and Richard Beatty, *Performance Appraisal: Assessing Human Behavior at Work* (Boston: Kent Publishing Company, 1984), p. 278.

CHAPTER 7

Cases: Problems and Opportunities

INTRODUCTION

This chapter is unlike the others in this book. Its purpose is to provide you with opportunities to solve supervisory problems. The text material it contains is brief and, in some respects, summarizes ideas you have studied before. The unique value of this section is its presentation as an action checklist.

The heart of this chapter is a series of cases. Each describes a situation and series of events that confront an insurance supervisor. You are to put yourself in the position of the supervisor. Basically, you must decide what the problem is (a diagnosis phase) and how it should be handled. Note that we do *not* ask how the problem should have been avoided or prevented. Redesigning the past does not solve a problem. To prepare for the problem-solving exercises, let us first summarize the recommended approach you should take in handling performance problems. We begin by contrasting performance problems and discipline problems.

PERFORMANCE PROBLEMS VS. DISCIPLINE PROBLEMS

Lois comes in late all the time, but she does more work and better work than anyone else you have.

Charlie is always in before anyone else, and he is sometimes the last to leave. However, he is slow and makes more than the average number of errors. He has been with you for over fifteen years—a trusted, loyal employee.

Jerry is doing a good job as a marketing representative calling on his present agents, but he is not turning up any new ones. He is just not prospecting.

Kim is your company's goodwill ambassador and super sales-type on the telephone. Her underwriting files are terrible . . . no documentation, no records of who did what, or why she did what she did. Agents love her, and they send her good business—she has the best loss ratio in your branch office.

Ruth is the best customer service rep you have ever seen. Some of your customers stay with you because of her. She seems to really care about them. The rest of the people in your office are really turned off by her. She steamrolls them, she is abrupt, she talks down to them, and always places her priorities over everyone else's. A couple of your other good people have left recently, and the word is that Ruth is the cause.

Ruth, Kim, Jerry, Charlie, Lois ... people. Or are they problems? They are people, with problems, and the problems are yours. They probably do not even know that they are causing you problems. And the problems are all just a little bit different. Or are they?

Performance Problems

Performance problems exist when an individual employee is not meeting agreed upon goals or objectives—production goals, project deadlines, error ratios, oversights, incomplete work, and the like. The employee is not doing the job the way it should be done or as well as it should be done. If the supervisor were to draw a picture of how the job would look when done to satisfaction, the individual with the performance problem would be able to see that his or her current performance did not match the standards of the supervisor.

Discipline Problems

Discipline problems occur when individuals conduct themselves in such a way that their behavior is a source of irritation to others. Their behavior gets in the way. It may not keep the misbehaving individuals from performing their own jobs at agreed upon standards, but it may keep them from doing more. Or it may distract others. Absences and tardiness are discipline problems. Unwillingness to cooperate, being overly competitive, too talkative, violating dress codes or no smoking rules are also examples of discipline problems.

It is necessary to differentiate between performance and discipline problems only insofar as it is necessary for you to avoid the mistaken notion that strict adherence to only one or the other is important.

The object of this chapter is to suggest some principles and some practical techniques for use in handling both performance and discipline problems.

IS THERE A PROBLEM?

The first step in basic problem solving is the recognition of the problem. How do you know when you really have a problem?

There is no need to make this complicated. It is simple: any deviation between what you want to happen and what is actually happening is a problem. The "you" is you, the supervisor. The "what you want to happen" is often expressed in formal terms—objectives, progress reports, performance standards, policies, procedures, or standards of conduct. What you want to happen can be expressed informally through your desire for customer good will or teamwork in your unit. If people are not doing what you expect or if they are doing something that you do not want them to do, your job as supervisor is to take action.

Six Possible Causes

There are six common causes of performance or discipline problems:

1. Employees do not have the ability.
2. Employees do not know how to do it.
3. Employees do not know what is expected of them.
4. Employees do not know that they are not performing or behaving up to job standards.
5. Employees cannot meet standards because of existing obstacles—in the job, the organization, or in their personal lives.
6. Employees "do not want to."

The six causes have six solutions. It would be an oversimplification of the human condition to indicate that any solution will neatly provide the precise answer to a specific situation you face at any given time. However, you are well advised to learn some of these guidelines and concepts of human behavior so that you have a beginning point when dealing with each individual. The trial and error method is too costly and the intuitive method too "iffy."

Learn the principles first. Principles do not go out of style like fashions. Last year's fashions and last year's new techniques may not be acceptable this year. Some practices have been outlawed. State regulations and federal laws required us to change some of our methods. The supervisor who is committed to the goals of getting along with others and helping them to grow will have little difficulty in changing times.

Six Possible Solutions

Here are six possible solutions to the six common causes of performance or discipline problems.

Possible Causes	*Possible Solutions*
1. Employees do not have the ability.	1. a. Transfer employees to positions in which their abilities match the job to be done. b. Terminate employees. This is usually an unpleasant task for the supervisor, but often the alternative is a deterioration in the mental and physical well-being of the employees and decline in the productivity and morale of the organization. Any thought of termination should prompt a review of the requirements of fair employment, as covered in the companion volume to this text, *Essentials of Supervision.*
2. They do not know how to do it.	2. Provide necessary training and, of course, test it as it progresses to determine its effectiveness.

3. They do not know what is expected of them.

3. Provide written goals, objectives, standards of performance, and standards of behavior. Some supervisors and managers do not write these things down. Nonetheless, goals and standards should be reduced to writing in order to reduce guesswork, assumptions, and errors in communication. One test of good supervision is to get the *same* answer from both supervisor and worker when both are asked what is expected of the worker.

4. They do not know that they are not performing or behaving up to standards.

4. Provide an effective feedback system. There are very few people who do not really care what others think of their work. How sad it is to watch competent employees develop feelings that no one cares how well they perform! Give feedback whenever you observe performance or its results. Give feedback in every available way: verbal and written, formal and informal.

5. They cannot because of existing obstacles in the job, the organization, or in their personal lives.

5. Change the structure, change the job, or provide employees with counseling and resources to cause changes in themselves.

If personal problems exist outside the organization that adversely affect the individual's performance on the job, you have many alternatives. You can ignore them, accept them and their consequences, recommend professional assistance, or in less traumatic situations such as lack of transportation, babysitting, and other practical living problems, you may be able to offer common-sense advice.

In those situations on the job where the job structure or the resources available get in the individual's way, changes should be made. There may be too many people reporting to one person, with the result that none receives adequate attention. Conversational noise, lack of telephones or terminals, lack of necessary privacy or too much privacy (being shut-off from colleagues), may all hold down productivity.

6. They do not want to.

6. It is human nature to resist doing those things which others tell you you "have to" do. You, the supervisor, must change "have to's" to "want to's" by improving reinforcement, or by lessening punishment, or by a combination of the two. Of the six common causes of problems, this may be seen as the most difficult to tackle.

FOSTERING BEHAVIOR (CHANGE) IMPROVEMENT

Manage Consequences, Not People

This maxim is an oversimplification, but is the key to this chapter. It does not say that the subject of supervision and management is not the person. Rather it attempts to direct your attention to the need to strengthen some behaviors and discourage others. It suggests that supervisors are well advised to consider the consequences of a person's actions as the key to future behavior.

The ABCs of Behavior

The result that follows the behavior is more likely to have a lasting effect on the occurrence and frequency of future behavior than is the event which precedes the behavior. Here are the terms used to discuss this rule of human life:

a. *antecedent* is that which precedes the behavior
b. the *behavior* or act itself
c. *consequence*, which comes about as a result of the behavior

Examples:

The spouse who prepares an exceptionally elegant meal, but receives no comments whatsoever from the partner is not likely to repeat the performance.

The baby learning to walk who receives hugs and kisses and whoops of joy from adults is sure to try it again and again.

Drivers who do not know the penalties for speeding are likely to drive faster than those who know that 56–59 m.p.h. will cost, say, $60; 60–64 m.p.h. will cost $95, and so on.

Determine Which Behavior the Consequences Favor

Do the consequences of an individual's behavior favor the desirable behavior, or do they favor the unacceptable behavior?
Consider this:

One of the employees in an insurance agency has been assigned a new job—telephoning households in the area in an attempt to get the expiration dates of Auto and Homeowners policies. The rejection rate is high—over 75 percent of the people called refuse or are not qualified to give the information. At the end of four weeks the individual is many, many calls behind. In spite of being "chewed out" by the boss the individual continues to get further behind in telephoning.

For many individuals, the consequences favor continuing the unacceptable behavior. The employee's behavior is unacceptable to the boss, but it is preferable from the individual's viewpoint.

Consider Special Conditions

There are certain conditions the supervisor must consider when evaluating consequences—those consequences which favor the person versus those which favor the organization; those which are certain to occur versus those which are doubtful; and those which will happen in the immediate future versus those which will take place in the distant future. In a nutshell, *personal, certain, and immediate* consequences have more impact on an individual's future behavior.

Rearrange or Manage the Consequences

This is your challenge—to manage consequences so that they favor the desired behavior.

Here is an example:

> Using the same illustration as above, the effective supervisor might have the telephone marketer create a chart to put up on the wall for all to see. The number of successful expiration dates would be posted at noon and at the end of each day. Incentives might be cost-effective: $.50 per X-date, with a $2.00 award for exceeding previous highs and a percentage of commissions for every X-date that becomes a customer. Other possible reinforcers include recognition and praise from the supervisor—such simple things as a verbal pat on the back, tickets to an event, or a special luncheon.

Punish the Offender

There is no quicker way to make your point when you catch someone engaging in unacceptable behavior than to "lay on" the punishment right then and there. It is immediate, it is usually personal, and it usually makes you feel good.

If the subject of this chapter is the successful handling of discipline and performance problems, and punishment will do that in a very short time, should supervisors punish? For some the answer is *yes;* for others, *never.* Consider the flip side of punishment—the possible harmful consequences:

- revenge
- sabotage
- employee quits, but stays on the job
- mere compliance rather than total personal commitment

There have to be better ways. We will look at three of them.

IMPROVING PERFORMANCE

Reinforce Desirable Behavior

Catch people doing things right![1] This meets a basic need of all humans—to have someone who is significant in their lives express gratitude for who they are and what they accomplish.

This is not only the simplest but also the easiest behavior change method available to the supervisor. It does require, however, that both supervisor and employee know what is expected of the individual.

The most powerful feedback is specific: it cites a particular action or accomplishment. Ironically, "You always do a good job" is fainter praise than "You did a good job on the Consolidated Motors application." The former probably comes across as flattery (or worse), but the latter shows that you have noticed the employee's efforts and judged the results.

What happens if the individual worker does not do the job completely right? As supervisor, you help the worker to improve by reinforcing the "almost rights." Positive reinforcement on the "almost rights" usually leads to "absolutely-right."

Does it seem as if we are belaboring the obvious? If so, count yourself lucky. You recognize that positive reinforcement has more power than punishment in fostering change. Chances are you learned this within your family, schools, and work experiences. On the other hand, reservations about this approach may reflect your own experiences and observations. Many of us, unfortunately, learned to equate being strong with being tough.

You can deliver negative feedback without it being punishment. Here are two guidelines. First, state the facts as objectively as possible. ("There are three errors in these calculations and two omissions in the file.") Second, ask questions to let the employee tell what the facts mean. For instance, "Are you aware that there are three errors in calculations?" Going on, "How serious do you think these errors are?" The employee who reaches the conclusion "I goofed" quibbles less than the employee who is told, "You goofed." Your challenge is to give the facts (objective feedback) without the resentment-causing overlay of criticism and demeaning comment.

Ignore Undesirable Behavior

If the behavior is neither self-destructive nor critical in your eyes as supervisor, you would be well advised to set out on a plan to change some behavior by ignoring it. A supervisor, especially a new one, often thinks that to overlook undesirable activities or actions is evading managerial responsibilities. This is an unsound view. Removing the reinforcement for any behavior will cause it eventually to disappear. Building an environment in which people are caught doing things right, and where nit-picking does not take place, addresses itself to the other half of your job—getting things done.

The disadvantage to using the technique of ignoring behavior is that it usually takes a long time to affect the desired change. When behavior is unacceptable—either self-destructive or causing a significant impact on the goals of the work unit—confrontation is necessary.

Confront the Unacceptable Behavior

Make sure it is the *behavior* that is confronted, not the individual employee as a person.

Your objective remains the same—help people to grow, develop, and improve. If you come to the confrontation with a desire to win or with a desire to put the person in his or her place, you will lose. You both may lose.

In most instances, confrontation will be with a competent, valuable individual whom you do not want to lose. To be successful, you need a personal, caring commitment, and communication skills. You have to care—there must be respect for the individual employee as a person and as a valuable employee; as a competent performer and as an employee with potential for growth, development, and improvement within the organization. If you do not have these positive feelings about the employee, take time to review his or her assets and contributions. Delay confrontation until you have the good as well as the bad in sight.

Steps for Effective Confrontation

1. Do it immediately, as soon after the unacceptable behavior takes place as possible under the circumstances.
2. Identify the behavior and hold it up against the acceptable standards.
3. Use *behavioral* terms such as "you have been late twice this week," not generalities—"you have a bad attitude." If you cannot use specific behavioral terms to describe what it is that has caused the confrontation, then the wrong supervisor is conducting the confrontation.
4. Share your *feelings* too. It is not only okay to tell the employee that you are displeased at the behavior, but show him or her. Yell, and pound on the desk, if that is how you feel, but do it in private.

   Many supervisors believe that any confrontation should begin and end with words of praise. Such sessions have been called "praise sandwiches." Supposedly, the employee does not hear the words of praise, because he or she knows that the real message is what comes in between. This skepticism is justified when the supervisor's praise is inappropriate or insincere. However, beginning and ending with honest appreciation for what the employee does do well should not seem phoney or contrived. On the contrary, it shows that you value the employee and his or her contributions and are concerned about a minor problem that you believe can be solved. Your honesty and sincerity will come through to the employee. Remember, the criticism is of the behavior, not of the person.
5. Get agreement on what the individual will do differently.
6. Help the employee set specific goals.
7. Ask for a commitment to change.

8. Follow up. Look for signs of change, and provide positive reinforcement for new behavior.

Summary

The goal of this chapter is to assist you in handling discipline and performance problems. When problems occur, you should seek to manage the consequences of behavior by reinforcing desirable behavior, ignoring undesirable behavior, and confronting the unacceptable. When necessary, criticize the results of the behavior, not the person. Catch people doing things right.

As you turn now to the cases, find practical solutions for the supervisor in each situation. "Improve communications" or "Change his attitude" are not solutions. They may be goals, but they are too far removed from "doable" actions. If you decide that better communications will resolve a problem, you must specify *who* will take *what action when, where,* and *with whom,* and explain how this action will improve communication. Be specific.

CASE: LOIS TARDEE

Lois Tardee was a policy and endorsement clerk-typist in the home office of an insurance company. She had been in the job four years, ever since graduating from high school. She was one of sixteen people in the same work unit, all doing the same work, preparing and mailing personal lines policies and endorsements.

Pam Dalton was the supervisor of the work unit. She had been promoted from the ranks of clerk-typist less than a year ago. The productivity of the work unit had been average-to-good, and its morale seemed good.

Dalton regarded Lois Tardee as one of her key people, a work leader. Lois Tardee produced more policies and endorsements than any of the other unit members. She had the lowest error ratio and lowest reject ratio in the unit. Her work was always neat.

A few months ago Dalton began to notice that Tardee was coming in late, just a few minutes after everyone else was settled and busy working. It became noticeable because Tardee often made funny comments about being late again. Pam Dalton assumed that Lois was a night person and just could not get herself going in the morning.

Dalton did not say anything about it at first. Recently she noted that Tardee was late every day that week. This was too much for Dalton. After thinking about it over the weekend, she called Tardee into her office Monday morning with the intention of calmly, rationally discussing the matter with her. She expected Tardee to see the error of her ways and make a firm commitment to change her behavior. That is not what happened.

Dalton started out by telling Tardee that she had to start coming in on time. Tardee said that she was in early that morning. Dalton agreed that she had arrived on time that day, but that she had been coming in late often during the past few months.

Tardee said she remembered being a couple of minutes late once in a while, but it certainly was not the big deal her supervisor seemed to be making it out to be. Tardee said that even when she was one or two minutes late, it did not affect either the quantity or the quality of her work, because she knew she put out more and better work than any of her peers. Tardee went on to remind her boss that she, Tardee, was the one who always stuck around at night, after the others went home, when there was a rush policy or endorsement to get out, and that she did so on her own time.

Dalton agreed to all Tardee said. She acknowledged that Tardee was the top performer in the group. Dalton said that this was not what she called her in to talk about. She said that by coming in late Tardee was setting a bad example for others, and that if Dalton allowed it to continue, others might want the same preferential treatment, and that would hurt productivity and morale. When she asked Tardee if she would make every effort to be on time in the future, Tardee agreed to "try my best."

The next day, Tuesday, Tardee arrived five minutes early. From her office Dalton watched her come in.

Wednesday, Tardee was also five minutes early. Dalton could see her and the clock at the same time, from her chair in her office. Secretly, Dalton was delighted that their "little chat" had paid off.

Thursday, Tardee was two minutes early. Dalton noted it.

Friday, when Tardee was ten minutes late, Dalton met her at the door.

Questions:

1. Drawing on your knowledge of motivation, explain why Lois Tardee was often late to work.
2. Explain the action that you recommend Pam Dalton take. Provide reasoning to support your recommendations.

CASE: CHARLES (GOODY) GOODHUE

Charles "Goody" Goodhue was a claims adjuster with the Comprehensive Mutual Assurance Company in its Mid-State Branch Office. Goody had been with Comprehensive Mutual over sixteen years in his present position. He was very popular with his colleagues, because he always had time for everyone, and because he went out of his way to acknowledge and to chat with all the other employees.

Marie King was Goody's supervisor. She was transferred to the Mid-State Branch four months ago in a promotion from another smaller branch.

The Comprehensive Mutual had recently become very aggressive in the market place, and the Mid-State Branch had enjoyed a solid increase in business. Marie King had seen a resultant increase in claims volume. Her staff members were putting in overtime almost every day just to stay even. Three weeks ago Marie decided to do a case-load study to measure work load and individual productivity before hiring additional claims people.

It came as no surprise to Marie that, after one week's study, Goody

Goodhue was lowest on the productivity scale when compared to others handling the same line of business. Goody handled fewer cases, and he seemed to make more errors. In checking with home office claims examiners, Marie learned that they had come to expect "little goofs" from Goody. Home office people knew that these were innocent oversights on Goody's part, because he had always been a loyal, well-intentioned "sweetheart of a guy."

In checking with agents, Marie learned that they all liked Goody. He had good relationships in every office. Any who had reason to comment on any minor problems were quick to forgive him.

Marie decided to discuss work load and errors with Goody, but only one issue at a time. Two weeks ago she arrived an hour before normal starting time. Goody was there. He had the coffee on and was over at the desk of another early arriver talking about the previous night's ball game. In Marie's office, Goody was surprised to learn that Marie didn't think he was carrying his load. He explained that he took a little more time to handle a case, because "people are important," and he felt it was more important to be sensitive to the policy holder or claimant than to play the numbers game of a large case load. Marie agreed to a need to treat people fairly and equitably. She pointed out to Goody that others seemed to be getting the same results as Goody but were handling far greater numbers of claims. Goody agreed to try to speed things up.

One week later Marie again met with Goody before regular office hours. She began the discussion saying that the reason for this meeting was to talk about the problems Goody was causing with his errors. She had two examples from the past week. Goody readily admitted the omissions. They were just oversights, he said, and anytime they had occurred before, no one had complained. The home office had either called Goody for the missing information in the past, or sent the file back to him to be completed. Goody agreed that this was inconvenient and probably caused a little extra work. He tried to get Marie to see that they were not malicious mistakes, nor did they indicate incompetence on his part. Marie said that the increased work load made these errors too costly now. Goody agreed to take more care in the future.

Goody asked Marie how he was doing in terms of the numbers of cases he had handled during the past week. Marie said she believed things were better now, and she was glad he was concerned.

One week later Marie received a telephone call from the head of the underwriting unit asking why a large claim that was not covered was actually paid the previous day. Marie's investigation found that it was Goodhue's case; there was no coverage; a check had been mailed and evidently cashed by the claimant. Later, in her office, Goody admitted that he must have overlooked something, but if he did, it was in the interest of handling more and more cases. He said it really was not his idea to "put so much stress on speed that a guy could not even stop to think."

Question:

1. What actions should Marie King take to improve communication with Charles Goodhue?

CASE: JERRY KALLER

Jerry Kaller had been a Marketing Representative for the Olympus Insurance Company for two years. He had applied for the job while working as an Underwriter for the same company. He was the chosen candidate because of his technical insurance skills and because of his interpersonal skills with agents and peers.

As a Marketing Representative, Jerry had the responsibility to produce property and liability business from his assigned sales territory. The company did business through independent agents. Jerry's agents thought highly of him. They often invited him to go on sales calls with them. They called him on technical questions. There was no question that Jerry was effective in helping his agents to bring business into their agencies, and to the company.

After his last performance evaluation Jerry received a substantial salary increase. His bottom line result was unmatched among marketing representatives as his premium volume far exceeded the goal. It was further noted that the numbers of agency calls Jerry had made exceeded the average for the company.

There were a number of towns and cities in Jerry's territory without Olympus agents. Jerry's boss, Tim Farraday, believed that Olympus should acquire two or three new agents in each sales territory each year if their growth objectives were to be met. As Farraday saw it, many of the present agents had "plateaued out," or reached volume levels that made it unlikely they would be able to send increasing volumes of business to Olympus. Uncertainty was compounded by the growing rate of agency mergers or buy-outs.

Jerry Kaller agreed with the reasoning that new blood was needed, although he had never prospected or cold-called before. Farraday explained that Jerry would probably have to call on at least fifteen prospective agents before he found one that needed Olympus and that met company standards. Farraday urged him to begin prospecting early in the new year so that he could reach his goal of three appointments in the year.

In January Jerry called on twenty-two cold prospects. None reacted favorably. A recent issue of an insurance trade paper had an article about agents representing fewer companies, and all of the twenty-two January prospects said they had too many companies.

At their monthly meeting Tim told Jerry not to be disappointed, and that it would all come if he just kept at it. None of the fifteen prospects Jerry called on in the first part of February showed any real interest in representing Olympus. In the meantime, some of Jerry's agents had called asking him to stop by. He did not call on any more prospects in February.

At their next monthly meeting Tim reprimanded Jerry in a nice way, saying that Jerry had not been doing what they had agreed he would be doing. Jerry protested that he was ignoring his present good agents, and that he probably would not be too successful appointing agents at that time because of the industry trend to represent fewer companies. Tim insisted that Jerry keep trying and reminded him why the company needed new agents. Tim told Jerry that other Olympus fieldmen had been making appointments. He contended that there were many agents "out there" who needed the Olympus, even if they did not know it yet. Tim asked Jerry to give him a written plan of where and how often he would be prospecting in March.

At the end of March's monthly meeting, Jerry reported that he had called on ten prospects the first week, according to the plan. He called on ten the second week, also according to the plan. In the third week he recalled one of the second week's agents who had indicated some interest in Olympus. Jerry then called back on this same interested agent in the fourth week. When Jerry and Tim discussed the interested prospective agent, Tim was less enthusiastic than Jerry. He knew the agent and did not think it would make a good appointment for them at the time. As a side note at their monthly meeting, Tim pointed out to Jerry that premium volume was below goal for the first quarter.

At the April meeting Jerry reported that he spent the first three weeks calling on his present agents attempting to bring up the volume, and only prospected two days the last week. He told Tim that he was sure Tim was more concerned with the bottom line than with his activities, including prospecting. Tim told him both were important, and that prospecting had to be done.

Of the thirty calls on prospects Jerry made the next month, three were recalls on a new prospect in a desirable marketing area. On the fourth call the agent agreed to contract with Olympus. Jerry telephoned Tim. Tim said, "Jerry, I knew it would happen. It's about time!"

The following month Jerry reported four prospecting calls, one per week, but said he had spent a lot of time with the staff of the newly appointed agency getting them started.

At the next month's meeting Jerry reported premium volume starting to come back; but he made no prospecting calls.

Questions:
1. Assume that Tim Farraday has asked your help in understanding the behavior of Jerry Kaller. What would you say to Farraday?
2. Assume that Jerry Kaller has asked your thoughts on improving communication with Tim Farraday. What would you say to Kaller?
3. What actions do you recommend Farraday take as of the end of the case? Provide reasoning to support your recommendations.

CASE: THE NEW MODEL 550

Mary Lou Williams was office supervisor for a large insurance agency located in downtown San Francisco. The agency had a total of sixty-two employees and wrote commercial lines business almost exclusively. Its clients included some of the largest firms in the San Francisco Bay area.

Mary Lou joined the agency about ten years ago. She progressed through a variety of clerical jobs and became a customer service representative. About two years ago she was asked to become office supervisor, replacing a man who retired. As office supervisor, Mary Lou was responsible for the eight-person word processing unit, the receptionist, and the mail clerk. Very little supervisory attention was required by the receptionist and mail clerk. As a result, Mary Lou concentrated on training, coaching, and supervising the work of the eight word processing specialists. They prepared a variety of documents and reports, the most important of which were proposals for clients and prospective clients and "coverage portfolios" given large commercial insureds. Accuracy was a critical requirement in their work. Meeting deadlines was a constant problem. Overtime was occasionally necessary. Under Mary Lou's supervision, the word processing unit had attained an excellent reputation for accuracy and cooperation in meeting deadlines. In her eyes, effectiveness was the direct result of participative supervision and teamwork.

Each Monday morning, the word processing unit members gathered around Mary Lou's desk for what they called "our work planning meeting." Members reported on their work in progress and mentioned any equipment problems they had. Mary Lou described incoming projects. A general discussion followed and usually led to consensus on how the major jobs should be allocated. Very rarely did Mary Lou make work assignments that did not result from the Monday morning discussion. From time to time other matters of common interest were discussed at the meetings.

Mary Lou received notification yesterday that a new word processing system would be delivered in ten days. The new system would be significantly superior to the models presently used in the unit. Its memory was larger, its operating speed on most kinds of work was higher, and it offered improved interface with the agency's computer system. Word quickly spread that "we're getting a new model 550."

By noon today, the five most senior word processing unit members have been in to see Mary Lou. Each said, in effect, "I think that I should get the new model 550." Their reasons were all different:

> Dinah was the first one in to see Mary Lou: "I have the oldest unit here—I bet it's the only model 150 left in the city—so I'm sure that you will give me the 550. Everyone knows how much I deserve it."

> Mildred came in soon after Dinah. She told Mary Lou that there was one overriding consideration: "My equipment is in far worse shape than any other unit we have. You know that I have more downtime than anyone else, and that hardly a week goes by without a service call on my system. Now, at last, we can get rid of that lemon and I can show you what I can really do."

> Lavaida, the most senior employee in the unit, suggested that it was only fair that seniority be the basis for deciding who should receive the new equipment. She also mentioned that her attendance record was the best in the agency "and should be rewarded in a way that will inspire others."

> Alberta offered this argument: "I do the most difficult reports and proposals. Every Monday morning, whenever you list a 'monster' proposal, the group always says, 'Alberta is best at charts and tables,

so give it to her.' If I do the toughest jobs, I should have the best equipment."

Billie based her claim on the fact that her equipment was not compatible with the other office equipment. Billie and the unit she used had come from a smaller agency acquired a few months ago. Billie pointed out that she disliked "being an oddball, with oddball equipment." She argued that she was being held back in her career by "being kept out of the mainstream."

These five requests left Mary Lou feeling bewildered. She knew that if she took the problem to her manager, he would only ask her to recommend which employee should be given the Model 550. She discarded the idea of assigning the new equipment to herself since she spent most of her time supervising and spent little time on projects. She wondered about giving the problem to the unit members at the next Monday morning meeting.

Questions:
1. List the pros and cons of asking the unit members to resolve the problem.
2. What action do you recommend Mary Lou Williams take? Provide reasoning to support your answer.
3. Role-play the conversations between Mary Lou and unit members and/or role-play a unit discussion of who should get the Model 550.

Note: This case was inspired by a classic, "The New Truck Dilemma," in Norman R. F. Maier, Allen B. Solem, and Ayesha A. Maier, *Supervisory and Executive Development* (New York: John Wiley & Sons, Inc., 1957), pp. 20–37.

CASE: RUTH WARNER

Ruth Warner had been an employee of the Professional Service, Inc. insurance agency for the past eleven years. During the most recent four and a half years she has been a Customer Service Representative. Ruth's boss, Arthur Owens, PSI president, considered Ruth one of the main reasons for the success of the agency. Owens had received many unsolicited favorable comments from customers about how well Ruth handled problems for them.

Owens regarded Ruth as a person who got things done. He had no concern about Ruth's handling of customers. He had, however, overheard confrontations between Ruth and other agency employees. She seemed to dominate them. She interrupted and was curt and abrupt in many of her dealings with them. She was heard to talk down to them as though she and she alone knew the correct way to do things. Owens had never interfered in these discussions, because Ruth was usually right. Nonetheless, he often wished that she behaved a little less abrasively.

Two months ago, two other Customer Service Representatives left within a week of one another. During the exit interviews one said she was leaving for more money, and the other said it was for a better opportunity with another agency. Experienced CSRs were hard to find. Owens replaced only one of them to date, and service has been suffering because of the vacancy.

Last night just before closing time, another CSR told Owens she was leaving. Owens invited the woman to sit for a moment and let him collect his thoughts. He explained that he thought he had been paying top dollar, and that he had pretty much allowed the CSRs to run their own show. He said he knew that it had to be something more than money or opportunity. He asked her outright if Ruth had anything to do with her decision to leave. The woman nodded yes, then quickly went on to say that she could see why the owner would consider Ruth a valuable employee, but that she could not face working with her for the rest of her life.

Note: Questions and directions are deliberately omitted. As in most supervisory situations, you must decide what the facts mean and what action, if any, is appropriate.

Chapter Note

1. Kenneth Blanchard and Spencer Johnson, *The One Minute Manager* (New York: Berkley Books, 1981), p. 38.

CHAPTER 8

Time Management

Time management is a key activity that will affect every aspect of supervisory performance. Practiced skillfully, it can give you more time for the tasks that only you can do. Indeed, if we cannot manage time effectively, we are not apt to be proficient planners, organizers, communicators, problem solvers, or leaders.

USING SUPERVISORY TIME—QUIZ

Let's start with a quick quiz. After you complete the quiz, we will review each of your answers and then explore each point.

1. Most supervisors and managers believe that they have enough time to do their jobs.

    _____Agree   _____Disagree

2. Time management has both a technical and an emotional aspect.

    _____Agree   _____Disagree

3. Time is

    _____Similar To   _____Different From
           _____Identical With

    such resources as money, staff, equipment, and supplies.

4. Time management is

    _____More Important   _____Less Important

    to the supervisor than to clerical and technical employees.

5. Most intuitive estimates of how supervisory time is spent are

    _____Accurate   _____Inaccurate

6. Time management is more directly related to the supervisory functions of planning and controlling than it is to those of directing and organizing.

    ____Agree   ____Disagree

7. The member of management who usually has the greatest impact on how employees use their time is

    ____The Chief Executive   ____The Supervisor
    ____The Middle Manager

8. The supervisory skill of delegation is uniquely related to time management.

    ____Agree   ____Disagree

9. Rapid, widespread and continuing change

    ____Increases   ____Decreases
    ____Has No Effect On

the need for skillful use of supervisory time.

10. Time effectiveness and time efficiency are

    ____Identical   ____Similar
    ____Different

11. Analysis is more important than synthesis in time management.

    ____Agree   ____Disagree

12. Your unit or department objectives should affect your use of time.

    ____Agree   ____Disagree

13. Procrastinating or putting off necessary tasks, usually

    ____Wastes   ____Saves
    ____Has No Effect On

the supervisor's time.

14. The supervisor's goal should be to

    ____Eliminate   ____Control

all interruptions.

Now, let's look at your answers. First, we'll give the preferred answer and then comment on the specific point being examined.

1. Most supervisors and managers believe that they have enough time to do their job.

    ____Agree   __X__Disagree

Most supervisors and managers feel rushed. For example, in polls of thousands of managers and supervisors, 99 out of 100 believe that they do not have enough time to do their job.[1] This has to be a compelling statistic!

In another survey of managers, approximately half of those questioned ranked time management as their main challenge, ahead of communication, listening, and coaching.[2] Indeed, respondents reported that unless they planned their time, they might either not get to perform some tasks at all or would perform them incompletely or ineffectively.

2. Time management has both a technical and an emotional aspect.

    X Agree   _____Disagree

You may learn how to analyze your present time use and discover that you are wasting supervisory time in doing routine technical work that others can do, in socializing too much, and in reading less-than-vital mail. This analysis, while necessary, will not of itself be sufficient to improve your time management. You will also have to resolve to follow through with appropriate corrective action such as delegating technical work and the screening of junk mail.

3. Time is

    _____Similar To   X Different From

                    _____Identical With

such resources as money, staff, equipment and supplies.

This is admittedly a "teaser," but we hope that you chose "different from." Time is generally unlike other resources in that it is uniquely irreplaceable. For example, you and the other supervisors in your organization generally have the same amount of time available. Let's assume that the office opens at 8:30 a.m. and breaks for lunch at noon. You all have a unique, never to be duplicated, three and a half hour period in which to accomplish your supervisory tasks. How much each of you achieves during this time will depend largely on how skillfully you use your time.

Subtle, but perhaps critically important in the long run, is the overall philosophy or mind set you adopt on the subject of your use of time. The effective supervisor approaches time management affirmatively and proactively not negatively. Such a supervisor thinks of making or creating "discretionary" time in order to accomplish tasks.

Other resources can be easier to supervise. For example, you can probably add an employee to your staff if you can show that the increasing business warrants it. You can add a word processor to your unit if you can demonstrate its value through cost/benefit analysis. In other words, resources like staff, equipment, budget, supplies, and floor space are expandable or contractable to meet the needs of the unit. Not so with time. Every person gets the same amount of it and, once it passes, it is gone forever.

4. Time management is

    X More Important   _____Less Important

to the supervisor than to clerical and technical employees.

Time management is important for all employees but, especially, for the supervisor. As a supervisor, you are accountable for your unit's results and must direct the achievement of these despite staff turnover, absenteeism, training, and retraining requirements. Today, management expects you to be time proficient. This expectation can be expressed in the desire for a favorable ratio of supervisors to technical and clerical staff. Other things being equal, a ratio of one supervisor to fifteen employees (1:15) is probably better than 1:10. In the former case, the cost of the supervisor's pay and benefits is being spread over a larger number of employees. This ratio can also indicate, at least in a general way, whether supervisors concentrate on supervisory or technical tasks. Generally, the larger the number of employees you supervise, the less likely it will be that you perform many technical tasks.

Of course, we must be careful in applying such rules of thumb. Some objectives and some employees require close supervision and a small span of control. But many insurance jobs permit a larger span and, indeed, prosper under more general supervision.

A special challenge to you as supervisor is the often fragmented and sporadic nature of supervisory activities. Often you can devote no more than a few minutes to a particular task before your attention is challenged by something more immediate and compelling. This pattern of many short demands calls for the development of habits that increase your skill and give you the time for your uniquely supervisory tasks.

    5. Most intuitive estimates of how supervisory time is spent are

            _____Accurate   X Inaccurate

Supervisors and managers are frequently off the mark in this regard unless they periodically log their time or keep some type of an operations diary.

Supervisors tend to underestimate expended time after the fact. For example, a supervisor may later recall that he spent a total of two hours the previous week in setting up vacation schedules. Actually, he might have spent twice that with blocks of time spread out over a week.

This is one reason that most time management authorities recommend that supervisors and others first analyze their time through a one or two week time log in order to identify areas for potential improvement. Later in this chapter, we will describe in more detail how you can log time.

    6. Time management is more directly related to the supervisory functions of planning and controlling than it is to those of directing and organizing.

            _____Agree   X Disagree

The better answer is *disagree*, for isn't time management helpful in everything you do? Superficially, it might appear that time management is more directly related to planning than to organizing and directing. Failure to plan ahead can often result in glaring evidence of time mismanagement. For example, failure by a supervisor or manager to identify objectives beforehand can lead to later waste of time on non-critical activities.

In the same way, failure in a control function can often lead to later time misuse. For example, a supervisor might fail to follow up on the effects of a coding procedure change with resultant errors and need to redo the work.

The relationship of time management to planning and controlling is often highly visible and, indeed, sometimes dramatic. However, it can also be critical in organizing. Let us again consider the situation in which failure to identify priorities led to misuse of staff. An office manager, because the analysis was inadequate, might miscalculate the interest of commercial producers in a new pricing program. When the response proves lower than expected, valuable technical staff can be underused and time wasted until corrective action is taken.

An example of the directing function being related to time management could be the failure to properly schedule installation of additional computer terminals. Maybe the system is not fully operative so the supervisor may have to devise some makeshift alternative. To summarize, time management is of equal and direct value in performing all four supervisory functions. Furthermore, failure to use time skillfully in one function can have a later negative impact on sequential or "downstream" activities. If a supervisor lavishes time and attention on setting unit objectives, and then hastily misassigns the work to staff, poor work performance may result. In turn, the supervisor is likely to divert time to checking for errors or giving closer supervision.

7. The member of management who usually has the greatest impact on how employees use their time is

    ____The Chief Executive   X_The Supervisor
    ____The Middle Manager

The supervisor is the only member of management who usually directly supervises significant numbers of operating employees. He or she usually sets the objectives that are the unit's main tasks. In larger companies, the chief executive may be many management layers and hundreds of miles away from a particular unit or department. Consequently, that manager's influence on employee time management can be tenuous. Similarly, the middle manager's impact may be diffused, particularly when he or she supervises such diverse functions as supply, mail, communications, and word processing.

Hence the unit supervisor will usually be the role model, teacher, and coach for how the department uses its time. He or she will be the appropriate example for how to set and follow up on priorities. The supervisor uniquely can teach the staff how to eliminate redundant tasks, how to combine like activities, and how to simplify some work so that it is more "doable." This influence, hopefully benign, meets the expectations of today's employee. That employee expects the supervisor to be a competent time manager and to display a helping attitude, particularly in an environment characterized by high demand for performance and tight control of staff size and expenses. Understandably, the supervisor seen wasting time cannot credibly ask staff members to use theirs wisely. Further, since time management is a skill, it must be exercised or it will deteriorate. Your continuing good example here is important to your subordinates if they are to monitor their time use. Later in this chapter, you will learn how to use time effectively and also how to train employees in this skill.

8. The supervisory skill of delegation is uniquely related to time management.

    X_Agree   ____Disagree

If you can delegate to your staff, you and they can accomplish more. As a supervisor, you know that you are effective in proportion to the collective results produced by your employees, not by your own work as an individual technician. If you are to achieve the fullest desirable group results, you must be able to delegate.

In supervisory and management training programs, the subjects of time management and delegation are frequently treated together because of their logical relationship. Thus, one author on time management quotes a former company president's painful remembrance, "I was so busy doing things I should have delegated, I didn't have time to manage."[3] Another author notes that the failure to delegate authority when warranted can limit the supervisor's effectiveness.[4] Other authors cite a feeling of insecurity and a failure to train or develop employees as mental blocks to delegation on the part of the supervisor or manager.

In general, if you suspect that work quantity and quality deteriorate significantly when you are not physically present, then you should rethink your delegation practices. Later in this chapter, we'll examine the subject of delegation in more detail and give you some tips on how to improve it.

Let's briefly review some of the key points made up to now.

1. The overwhelming majority of supervisors and managers do not believe that they have time to do their jobs.
2. Time management has both technical and emotional aspects.
3. Time is a unique resource that requires skillful management. In a sense, you create discretionary time.
4. Time management is probably more important to you than it is to technical and clerical staff.
5. Your intuitive estimate of how you spend time is probably inaccurate.
6. Time management is a skill that supports all the supervisory functions.
7. The supervisor, of all an organization's managers, can have the greatest influence on employee time use.
8. Time management and delegation are uniquely related. Rarely will you find a good time manager who is not also a skillful delegator.

We're ready to return to the quiz answers now.

9. Rapid, widespread and continuing change

    __X__ Increases   ____Decreases
              ____Has No Effect On

the need for skillful use of supervisory time.

Since as a supervisor you are often at the forefront in introducing change to your group, you must be able to absorb and even anticipate change with a minimal time loss. Such changes could include upgrading the role of underwriting assistants or other paratechnical employees, adding a new job into your department, or implementing a change in procedures. Invariably, such change will cause some temporary dislocation or inconvenience and you must be prepared to absorb these. You will probably use such time-saving tactics as determining beforehand the content, duration, and format for training the paratechnical staff, revising procedure descriptions to add the new task, and creating a job description for the new position.

10. Time effectiveness and time efficiency are

       ____Identical   ____Similar
            __X__ Different

Effectiveness connotes the value of the result. It means doing the right thing. Efficiency refers to the energy or resource expended in obtaining a result. In managing time you will be using both concepts. However, time effectiveness is what you should ultimately pursue. Let's look at several examples. Assume that you are concerned with the time it takes to issue a boiler and machinery policy endorsement. You might improve verification time efficiency by storing and retrieving data in the unit's micro-computer. However, you might go further and conclude that it is no longer vital to verify some data. You could improve time effectiveness by eliminating some verifications, not by doing them more quickly. You would thus aim at doing the right thing as well as doing things right.

Another example would be to analyze what your underwriters do and find that 30–35 percent of their time is spent in non-judgmental tasks that could be delegated to underwriting assistants. Reassigning the work to assistants would be time effective. The underwriters' morale will probably improve since they will be freed from less challenging tasks. In turn, the assistants should find the new tasks stimulating and enriching.

Your efforts to improve the efficiency of the tasks would be devoted to the way they are performed by the underwriting assistants. It may be that the assistants perform the tasks less efficiently than the underwriters. However, time effectiveness dictates that these tasks not be done by underwriters.

11. Analysis is more important than synthesis in time management.

_____Agree   _X_Disagree

Another close call. Aren't they both necessary? Certainly analysis is important in time management. As we just saw, you had to analyze underwriters' tasks in order to determine whether they should be delegated. You must analyze how your time is spent in order to decide how it can be better allocated. But you also have to use synthesis in managing your time, that is, you have to combine components or elements into a whole. You will create personal and unit plans that pull together a variety of resources and apply them against a complex of requirements. Thus both techniques will help you make or create precious discretionary time.

12. Your unit or department objectives should affect your use of time.

_X_Agree   _____Disagree

The critical objectives set for your unit serve as the ultimate criteria on how you and your staff should be spending your time. These objectives frequently include:

1. Amount of premium or commission income.
2. Other key productivity indices such as desired unit costs or process "turnaround" time.
3. Expense control of such items as telephone and supplies.
4. Staff training and development accomplishments.
5. Required performance on indices of customer satisfaction.
6. Desired performance on such measures as staff turnover, absenteeism, and tardiness.

If you or your staff log your time for a week and find that the great majority of the time is not spent in supporting unit or department objectives then you will have to take the necessary corrective action. Other aids that you can use are the position guides and performance standards for you and your staff. Standards can be particularly helpful in spelling out the main results desired from technical and clerical jobs. Naturally, these have to be related to your objectives and performance standards.

13. Procrastinating, or putting off necessary tasks, usually

    __X__ Wastes   ____Saves

                 ____Has No Effect On

the supervisor's time.

One definition that captures the sense of the word "procrastinates" is "to put off intentionally or reprehensibly something that should be done." Notice that what you postpone is a necessary task. Procrastinating is bound to create anxiety. You are likely to have the undone task gnawing away silently at your peace of mind.

Let's assume that your boss has asked you to make some recommendations on the non-salary budget items for your unit of fourteen people. The job is admittedly a big one. You may not know just how to begin, so you delay action, finding seemingly rational excuses to do lower priority tasks. Anxiety then builds and drains away your energy and lowers your normal sense of fulfillment in doing your job. Eventually, you force yourself to start on the assignment and you experience a noticeable feeling of relief.

Later in this chapter we'll give you some practical tips on doing the "doable" things right away, avoiding procrastination, and even giving you time for some of the less critical but fun activities that can make the job more enjoyable for you and your employees.

14. The supervisor's goal should be to

    ____Eliminate   __X__ Control

all interruptions.

It would be unrealistic for you to expect to eliminate all interruptions. As a supervisor it will be your responsibility to absorb and to plan around interruptions. You might even say that dealing with interruptions is your job as a supervisor. Let's assume that it is early on Monday morning, minutes after the office opens. One of your ten raters calls in, telling you that he is ill with flu and will not be in at all. Another phones and says she'll be delayed because of car trouble. Your manager calls and asks to meet with you in fifteen minutes. These are necessary interruptions to your job. You are going to have to make some quick decisions, possibly including reassigning work in order to get your unit back on the track for the day.

Of course, there are some interruptions that are not as important as those just described, such as the fellow employee who wants to have a friendly chat about yesterday's ballgame. While you don't want to hurt that person's feelings, you find yourself with some important tasks that must be done right away. How do you handle this type of interruption?

We will not forget this happy kind of interruption in giving you some ideas that successful supervisors use to deal with interruptions; those arising from the job itself and those stemming from the social relationships that accompany the job.

Now, let's summarize the later key points we've developed through the quiz.

1. The continual demands of change require the supervisor to manage time skillfully.
2. The supervisor must be able to distinguish between time effectiveness and time efficiency.
3. Analysis and synthesis are both useful techniques for managing time.
4. The unit or department objectives should generally determine the supervisor's time priorities.
5. Often procrastination uses more time and energy than doing a task right away.
6. The supervisor should learn how to control interruptions.

THE MAJOR STEPS OF TIME MANAGEMENT

Now that you're familiar with the key definitions and terms, let's take a closer look at how we go about managing supervisory time. We'll follow several major steps. At least in the beginning, you should follow the steps consciously. After a while, you'll do them more or less automatically.
The steps are:

1. Analyze how you spend your time.
2. Identify and set your priorities.
3. Determine what should be done and what should not be done.
4. Replan your allocations of time.
5. Make and follow a daily "to do" or task list.
6. Do what is "doable" now.

1. Analyze How You Spend Your Time.

Earlier you learned that your intuitive estimates of how you spend your time are probably inaccurate. Invariably, such estimates are much too low. For whatever reason, the time spent on a particular task becomes understated in unaided recall.

Coming to grips with your use of time must begin with a time log or some type of time record. A time log need not be elaborate or cumbersome. The one shown in Exhibit 8-1 has been used by thousands of supervisors and managers with excellent results.

Notice that time is listed in 15 minute increments vertically on the log, starting with the morning and going through the day. This particular log identifies various tasks and activities horizontally across the page. You may change both the time periods and the task categories to suit your needs. For example, at the present, the "Other" category, "Special Projects" may not be a factor in your job. If so, relabel it to some task that does fit your situation, such as "Work Measurement" or "Word Processing Applications."

How are you going to use the log? You should keep it handy and check off

Exhibit 8-1
How Am I Spending My Time?

Time	Routine Work	Handling Mail	Talking to People in Person	Meetings	Talking to People on The Phone	Training	Other (include Special Projects)
8:15							
8:30							
8:45							
9:00							
9:15							
9:30							
9:45							
10:00							
10:15							
10:30							
10:45							
11:00							
11:15							
11:30							
11:45							
12:00							
12:15							
12:30							
12:45							
1:00							
1:15							
1:30							
1:45							
2:00							
2:15							
2:30							
2:45							
3:00							
3:15							
3:30							
3:45							
4:00							
4:15							
4:30							

the time periods through the day. To illustrate, let's assume that you start work at 8:15 a.m. and spend most of the first fifteen minutes talking to people on the phone. You check that block to show the dominant activity for that fifteen minute period. In effect, you "round off" your self-observation by noting only the dominant activity for the period. Since you will keep the log for many days, the "rounding errors" should disappear.

At the end of the day, you can total your times for the various tasks. Let's assume that you work eight hours a day and, by day's end, your time log looks this way:

Talking to people in person	2.5 hours
Talking to people on the phone	1.5 hours
Routine work	2.0 hours
Meetings	1.0 hours
Handling mail	1.0 hours
Total Time for Day	8.0 hours

While we'll describe various analyses that you can make later, for now let's assume that the "routine work" and "handling mail" categories catch your eye. You're surprised that you have used that much time for those things. The two categories account for nearly half your day. You know that your intentions are good. You do some technical work such as underwriting or billing to "help out" your staff, even though you actually have enough employees to get the job done.

You have to admit that you enjoy doing some technical work occasionally. After all, you started your carrer as an underwriter, or clerk typist, or claim processor. However, your conscience asks a persistently unsettling question, "How much such work should I be doing?" Remember that with a large supervisory span of control, such work should probably occupy only a fraction of your day.

Now, what about the hour spent on mail handling? You also have some misgivings here. Intuitively you know already that one of your staff could screen your mail and thus save you time.

These, then, are your thoughts at the end of the first day of keeping your time log. For how long a period should you log your time? We recommend that you log time for two weeks of a representative period, trying to avoid both rush periods and times of low or unusual activity. The patterns and trends you identify at the end of the period will surely have greater validity for you than those based on the analysis of a single day.

Let's assume that by the end of two weeks you find that you have spent the equivalent of three days (out of ten) in routine technical work. In other words, you have used thirty percent of your time in doing something that you are probably paying one of your staff to do. At the end of the measured period, you also find that you've spent a day on handling mail, a task that may be delegable at least in part. To summarize, of the ten work days you measured, four of them were spent in activities that someone else could probably do. This is not an untypical finding. No wonder we mentioned earlier that 99 out of 100 supervisors and managers believe that they have insufficient time to do their jobs. Time analysis will often show that they have drifted into doing work that takes them away from their supervisory role.

In addition to categorizing time used by tasks and activities as we did in our example, you might consider several other kinds of analysis:

Who Initiates? Indicate whether you or someone else initiates a particular task or activity. For eample, when you checked off that you attended a supervisors meeting for 45 minutes, you could also enter an "M" for "My Manager" next to each check to show that your department manager called the meeting.

Later in the day, you might have called a 15 minute meeting of some of your staff. Here you could enter a "ME" next to that checkmark to indicate that you initiated that activity. Still later in the day, several of your employees might ask for clarification on how a new procedure affects their jobs and you take thirty minutes for this explanation. You could code this activity with an "E" for employees.

Just as you analyzed the amount of time spent in various activities, you can study the patterns of demands for your time. Not surprisingly, your immediate manager will often be most influential here. Certainly your employees will justifiably require much of your time. However, you might be surprised at the amount of your time that is demanded by supervisors and managers of "user" departments of the product or service you produce. Perhaps your analysis will lead to some action steps. You might find, for instance, that whenever an occasional problem occurs, you have a chain of phone calls with three other supervisors. You might decide that meeting with them in person will save you all time each time the situation arises. Incidentally, you want to code these demands, particularly if they are significant. You might use such categories as "OM" for other managers. "OD" for other departments, "A" for agents, "P" for policyholders, and "C" for claimants, and so on.

Product or Task Classification Another approach to classification is to reflect the specific, unique tasks that your unit performs or the items handled. For example, let's assume that you direct eight commercial property underwriters, five of whom underwrite commercial packages, two of whom process non-package commercial coverages, and one of whom underwrites inland marine risks.

Let's assume that under the time log category "Talking to People in Person" you spend ninety minutes during the day talking to the package underwriters. Alongside the time checkmarks, you may want to code "CP" to show that during that time you were working with your commercial package people. At other times during the day you could code your entries "CF" and "IM" to represent time spent on commercial fire and inland marine matters. At the end of each day or week, you can get a good idea of how much of your supervisory time each activity is demanding. Your analysis may show a recurring need that can be met in another way. You might decide that a senior underwriter should handle some questions, or that particular training is warranted.

Whatever categorizing approach you use, your analysis reflects the facts, not your impressions, of where your time goes. Incidentally, this data can be useful until you believe it is time for you to compile an updated analysis. You are now ready to go to the next step in managing your time.

Identify and Set Your Priorities

As was pointed out earlier, the relatively limited number of supporting objectives that you have for your unit or department should largely dictate how time is used within the unit. These objectives may make use of such key indices as sales, income, underwriting loss ratio, productivity, expense control and staff performance. Your position guide and performance standards should also help in setting your priorities.

Not least will be the emphasis that your immediate manager places on what the department or office is to accomplish. For example, if he or she insists on tight control of such expenses as telephone, photocopying, and mail, then you will have to respond appropriately in setting your priorities. Perhaps your organization has a hiring freeze and it may be impossible to replace those who retire, terminate, or leave during the fiscal period. If so, your priorities will have to reflect this constraint.

Now that you have asembled the various documents and inputs, you are ready to determine your priorities. A key tool to use here is the "80/20 rule" which states that generally 80 percent of the value of the results we achieve as supervisors come from 20 percent tasks.[5] Hence, we should concentrate our attention on these critical tasks. Some examples might be:

- 80 percent of the branch's premium income comes from 20 percent of its agency plant.
- 80 percent of absenteeism may be caused by 20 percent of an organization's employees.

Why not take a few moments and jot down where the 80/20 rule might be applied in your department or unit. In any case, you will identify the "vital few" tasks that you should focus on as against the "trivial many" activities that can ensnare the unwary supervisor.[6]

Up to this point you have completed two major steps:

1. You analyzed how you spend your time.
2. You identified and set your priorities.

You are now ready to take the next step.

Determine What Should Be Done and What Should Not Be Done

In this step, you want to apply this criterion to two areas:

- The unit or department
- Yourself

Let's take them in order. First, you want to meet with your staff, either individually or in a group, and assure them that you want to help them work smarter rather than harder. You also want to point out your desire to keep the department a pleasant place to work. You want their ideas on such points as:

1. Should a certain task(s) be done at all?
2. What processes take too much time?
3. What steps can be saved?
4. Is there a better way for performing the job?
5. What can be done more efficiently?
6. Is there unnecessary duplication of effort?

These questions are particularly important if you have a large supervisory span of control. In such a situation it is unlikely that you can know the details of your employees' jobs. Further, it may be that considerable time has passed since job procedures were last reviewed and a few unnecessary, contradictory, nonproductive activities could have crept into the work processes. These can often frustrate and demoralize employees.

Now let's assume that you have obtained the employees' comments, suggestions, and recommendations to these and other questions that might apply to your specific operation. The likelihood is high that some of what your staff members are now doing, through no fault of their own, is redundant, misapplied or obsolete.

Replan Your Allocation of Time

Assuming that you have the authority or can obtain approval, you can help your staff and yourself by taking several immediate actions:

1. From the viewpoint of time effectiveness, you can *eliminate* unnecessary activities outright. It may be that a particular inspection report is no longer required for certain risks but that the desk guide has not been updated to reflect this fact.
2. Next, you can *simplify* some processes or tasks.
3. You can also *combine* processes or tasks where applicable.
4. Finally, you can *reassign* tasks, perhaps to employees in support positions.

Make and Follow a Daily "To Do" or Task List

You are at the point where you know what work you personally should be doing. You should take the unit objectives and priorities and break them down into smaller time periods including "doable" daily tasks. If you do not do this, there is a danger that the annual objectives will appear so large and difficult that you won't know where to begin.

A clear danger is to make no daily task list, just doing what needs to be done from moment to moment. You can probably guess what will happen. Later, at the end of the week or some other period, you will suspect that you have dissipated your own and your staff's time with often trivial, low payoff activities that do not support your objectives or reflect your priorities.

Exercise Here is an exercise that will give you a chance to practice setting up a "To Do" or task list. Assume that you are a first-line supervisor of ten telephone claim representatives. It is now 8:20 a.m. on Monday. The workday will start in ten minutes. In these few minutes, you have to plan your day.

On the following list of six tasks, show the priority, 1 through 6, that you would assign in the blank on the left. Number 1 would represent the highest priority, number 6 the lowest. After you complete the list, we'll review the answers and add some pertinent comments.

____A. Meeting with one of your senior employees to briefly discuss a retraining schedule required by a procedural change to be implemented in several weeks.

____B. Responding to a phone call from your company nurse who tells you that she may send one of your staff home because of a cold.

____C. Meeting with one of your newer claim representatives who would like to see you this morning. This employee has had a tardiness problem, but recently has showed some improvement.

____D. Submitting a brief written recommendation to your boss on how you can reduce unit photocopy expense. The deadline is tomorrow afternoon and you believe that your boss may be out of the office until late tomorrow morning.

____E. Giving your boss a tentative vacation schedule for your staff. The deadline is Wednesday noon of this week.

____F. Conducting a six-month performance appraisal meeting with your newest claim representative, scheduled for 10:45 a.m.

Now, let's review your answers.

__1_B. Responding to a phone call from your company nurse who tells you that she's going to send one of your staff home because of a cold.

You should do this first in order to keep the operation moving. You will probably have to reassign or reschedule the work normally done by the sick employee.

__2_C. Meeting with one of your newer claim representatives who would like to see you this morning. This employee has had a tardiness problem, but recently has shown some improvement.

This should be your next task. You would want to determine why the employee wants to see you. The visit may be connected with his or her attempt to improve performance on tardiness, or it may concern a difficulty on the job. Note that it would have been easier to assign a priority to this request if you had originally asked the claim representative why he or she wanted to see you.

<u> 3 </u> F. Conducting a six-month performance appraisal for your newest claim representative, scheduled for 10:45 a.m.

You will probably do this third, depending on how much time the two preceding tasks take. While the work reassignment normally should not take long, the appraisal meeting could be time consuming.

Actually, you should have done the detailed preparations for the performance appraisal earlier. This morning, you would make time for a quick rereading of the file before beginning the appraisal interview.

<u> 4 </u> D. Submitting a brief written recommendation to your boss on how you can reduce unit photocopy expense. The deadline is tomorrow afternoon and you believe that your boss may be out of the office until late tomorrow morning.

You should probably do this next since the deadline is tomorrow afternoon, that is, Tuesday. This could require concentration on your part. If feasible, while you are doing this work, you might have one of your employees answer your phone calls.

Also, as a courtesy, you might want to give the report to your boss earlier, perhaps this afternoon, assuming he or she is in the office.

<u> 5 </u> E. Giving your boss a tentative vacation schedule for your staff. The deadline is Wednesday noon of this week.

You should do this task fifth since its deadline is Wednesday noon, two and a half days away. Conceivably, you could continue working on this tomorrow, assuming that you had some discretionary time then.

<u> 6 </u> A. Meeting with one of your senior employees to briefly discuss a retraining schedule required by a procedural change to be implemented in several weeks.

You will do this task last since its deadline appears several weeks away. You expect the proposed discussion to be brief. Therefore, while you might be able to hold it off until tomorrow, you would probably want to meet with your senior employee before day's end if at all possible.

How did you do? This scenario seems typical, especially for a supervisor with a relatively large span of control and particularly on a Monday morning. In all likelihood some sort of "emergency" will appear during the day, requiring you to reschedule some of your tasks for later in the day or the next day. One of the major benefits of the daily task list is the flexibility it gives you to make or create discretionary time. You can work on your day's plan, respond to emergencies, and then return to your plan. In a sense, you analyze your day beforehand, then synthesize or combine the varied tasks into a whole for the overall day's plan.

Your next logical question is when to prepare your daily "To Do" or task list. Two general approaches are used largely based on personal preference. Some supervisors and managers prefer to prepare the list at the end of the previous day; others would rather make the list early in the morning as we saw in the earlier quiz example. There are some pros and cons to both approaches. Let's look at a few of them:

Make the List at the End of the Previous Day

Advantages

- Your tasks are probably still fresh in your mind, so you will have the advantage of continuity as you schedule your next day.
- You may be one of the last people to leave your office daily. Phone and other distractions could be at a minimum, allowing you to concentrate.
- You may do your best mental work later in the day, so such planning might be easier for you then.

Disadvantages

- You may have had a rough day and be mentally fatigued or emotionally unsettled. The thought of planning your next day, particularly if it is to be another demanding one, can be demotivating. You may prefer to do something that is more relaxing for you
- Staying late, particularly with flexible hour scheduling, may mean having to answer all of the phones, leaving little or no time for planning.
- You may do your best thinking in the morning.

Make the List Early in the Morning

Advantages

- You have had a chance overnight to relax and think about matters other than work. However, your mind will often work away on problems, even while you sleep. You may discover that suddenly you have an answer to today's scheduling problem that was not apparent yesterday.
- If you arrive early enough, you can do your planning before the phones start ringing and other activities begin.
- You may be a "morning person" and at your best at that time of day. Hence, you will probably make a better daily plan then. If you are such a person, you should also do your more demanding mental tasks before noon if that is possible. In the quiz example, we saw that the supervisor had scheduled both the talk with the tardy employee and the performance appraisal during the morning. Since such activities can often be demanding, it is probably wise to do them when you are at your peak.
- You have a chance to consider items placed on your desk after you left the day before.

Disadvantages

- On weekdays, you have been away from the job for some twelve to fourteen hours so you may have to allow yourself time to resume thinking closely about job tasks.
- Sometimes, particularly with flex hours, each new arrival to the office can get into a conversation with those already there, thus dissipating what is intended to be an advantage. In such instances, you may have to tactfully but firmly communicate the desired result to those involved.

• Even "morning persons" have rough mornings once in a while.

The choice as to whether you want to schedule yourself the day before or the same morning is ultimately up to you and can stem from your personality, temperament, energy level at certain times of the day, and other factors.

As you develop your daily to do list, you may want to categorize your activities by priorities so you can concentrate on high payoff actions during the day. Here's one categorization used by many supervisors and managers.

Prioritize Items to Be Done
1. *Must be done* (these should be done completely before undertaking the next category)
2. *Should be done* (these should be done completely before undertaking the next category)
3. *Can be done*

The first category, what must be done, includes both important and urgent tasks. The former are typically activities that support your unit objectives. The latter are things that call for your immediate attention though they may be of lower relative importance. The "should" category contains responsibilities of lower urgency or value. Some may become "musts" in a few days. Items are placed on the "can be done" list with the understanding that they will be done only after the other two lists are completed. As a daily to do chart, the list should not contain more items than you can expect to accomplish in the day. Carrying "can do" projects from list to list is discouraging and gives them a negative cast. Your to do list should be challenging but feasible.

Incidentally, we'll look at the question of urgency in more detail later. For example, in the recent quiz, we saw that things came under this *must be done* classification. They were:

1. Reassigning the work of the sick employee.
2. Meeting with an employee at his or her request.
3. Conducting the scheduled employee performance appraisal.

For that day, the other two categories were:

Should be done—
4. Composing and writing the recommendation (due tomorrow) on reducing photocopy expense.
5. Developing and writing a tentative staff vacation schedule (due in two days). This is placed second because you could do it tomorrow.

Can be done—
6. Discussing the retraining schedule which will be needed in several weeks.

Another possible categorization is:
Top priority tasks
Medium priority tasks
Low priority tasks

Some supervisors also assign priority numbers to tasks, such as 1,2,3, and so on. You can experiment with various approaches and finally select the one that works best for you. Again, a critical point to remember is to do all in the "must" category before starting the "should" category; otherwise, you could find yourself at the end of the day with key tasks undone.

"Cushion" Time   As you plan your day you should also leave yourself a "cushion" of an hour or so each day to absorb the various emergencies or crises that arise even in well run departments. This time can also be used occasionally for planning the rest of the week's activities or planning ahead for a longer period. However, you may find that in a large unit with many activities, responding to many changes, that planning ahead for a week or so is all that may be feasible.

You now have analyzed your time, set your priorities, determined what should be done and drawn up a daily task list. You are now ready to perform the fifth and last major step of managing your time.

Do What Is "Doable" Now

To some supervisors and managers, this step may seem trite, obvious, and even anticlimatic. And yet time management authorities identify procrastination as the graveyard of many good intentions by supervisors. Why is this so?

There are a variety of reasons, including the understandable temptation to postpone tasks seen as difficult or distasteful, the subconscious desire to actually encourage interruptions and be diverted from necessary tasks, the lack of organization skills, and the tendency to drift into trivial activities. What can you do about this tendency to procrastinate? We defined it earlier as putting off intentionally or reprehensibly something that should be done. Here are a number of approaches that have helped others:

1. Concentrate on completing "must be done" tasks before beginning "should be done" ones, etc.
2. Scrutinize "emergencies" or "crises" until you determine that they are bona fide. Otherwise, stay with your plan and do not divert your attention.
3. Schedule a time cushion or buffer in your day to provide time for responding to genuine emergencies and to give you an opportunity to change pace.
4. Once you have handled an emergency, return to your daily task quickly, giving it your undivided attention.
5. Break large, formidable tasks into doable sub-tasks.
6. Start the job, even if you can only make a beginning.
7. As you complete demanding tasks, reward yourself. Perhaps a piece of candy or a cup of coffee is all it takes. Save an enjoyable task, such as reading an employees' club bulletin, as a reward for completing a "must" activity. A psychological reward can be crossing the completed job off your list.

8. Get your staff's ideas on how to do tasks and delegate wherever it is possible.
9. Establish a "quiet hour" if possible within your unit. A quiet hour is a period set aside for difficult work, usually early in the day. Telephone calls are intercepted and "Do Not Disturb" signs literally or figuratively hung on doors.

You'll find that these actions benefit you because procrastination can often use more mental energy than prompt action does. Very often, the undone tasks will remain in the back of your mind, diverting your full attention from the job at hand, and reducing the fun and satisfaction you get from your work.

TEACHING TIME MANAGEMENT

Often it will be necessary for you to teach your technical or clerical staff how to manage their time. How do you go about this? Essentially you can teach them some of the techniques you learned yourself:

1. You can communicate department objectives to them and show them how they can support these through their efforts.
2. You can show them how to analyze their time through a time log and follow up with them on any necessary improvement.
3. You can enrich their jobs by delegating challenging, interesting tasks to them rather than hoarding such "stretching" activities for yourself.
4. You can show them how to use the "must-should-can be done" classification of work priorities.
5. You can demonstrate to them how their periodic reports to you on their time use can set up a natural communication link between you.

Earlier we described "one on one" sessions between you and your staff as you both tried to identify unnecessary or counter-productive job procedures. You can also use group sessions to teach them how to manage their time. For example, you can show them how to complete a daily "To Do" List in a group session. You may also choose a group session to instruct them on how to incorporate time management into the performance standards for their job.

At least in the beginning, you should ask your employees to give you frequent feedback on tasks that you have delegated to them. Once you have assured yourself that they can do these tasks, the follow-up conversations can be fewer and farther apart.

MAJOR TIME PITFALLS AND
HOW TO CONTROL THEM

There are four major pitfalls to managing time. They include a lack of knowledge and lack of resolution or will to apply one's know-how. In each case, we will identify some reasons why the pitfall exists along with the ways you can control the error or tendency. Take a moment and see if you can identify some of them. The four pitfalls are:

1. Failure to get started in improved time management.
2. Failure to recognize that interruptions are an inherent part of the supervisor's job.
3. Inability to say no to requests.
4. Repeatedly handling the same piece(s) of paper.

Did you identify them or some of them? Let's examine each in detail.

Failure to Get Started in Improved Time Management

Why do you think this form of procrastination occurs? There are several reasons, some of them understandable. They are:

1. The supervisor or manager refuses to admit that he or she needs to improve his or her time management.
2. The force of habit.
3. The challenge appears overwhelming.
4. Fear of failure.

As you can see, there are elements of both knowledge (or its lack) and the willingness to use that knowledge interwoven among the reasons. How can you get started? For one thing, you can review the earlier tips on combatting procrastination, particularly the one that urges a start even if it is a modest one. Waiting for the perfectly representative two week period is likely to be procrastination! If you resist completing a one or two week time log, log a day or two and then analyze the results. This can help address the emotions of fear and the sense of being overwhelmed by the task. Even this small sample can be helpful in getting you started. You might set a goal to save a certain amount of time each day or week.

Failure to Recognize That Interruptions Are an Inherent Part of the Supervisor's Job.

Why does this come about? There are several reasons:

1. You and/or your employees do not accept the fact that interruptions are part of your job(s).
2. You or they do not know how to deal effectively with interruptions.
3. You or they may know how to deal with interruptions but you fail to take specific corrective action.

Again, these reasons include knowledge and the willingness to apply it. How can you address these so-called reasons? To begin with, both you and they (through your teaching) can accept the fact that interruptions are part of your job. As a supervisor you have already learned that your daily job demands constant response to a variety of people and situations including such emergencies as reassigning the work of a sick employee. You learned also that much of your day can be spent in relatively fragmented and discontinuous activities.

Regarding your employees' perceptions, you can teach them that the many daily phone calls they receive from claimants, agents, or others are not interruptions at all but rather are the very reason for the existence of their jobs. A tactic which you or your employees can use is to analyze "bona fide" interruptions for a week, or some other period, in order to see if there is a pattern.

You and your employees can learn how to deal effectively with interruptions. For example, you both can learn how to distinguish between "important" and "urgent" requests and how to respond to them. In general, you should give priority to the urgent. In the earlier exercise it was probably more important to respond to the employee who requested the meeting than to be certain that every single task usually performed by the absent employee be reassigned that day. Certainly with the latter, some urgent tasks such as returning phone calls, and sending letters, would become apparent as the day progressed and should be done expeditiously.

It might be necessary to respond to an important, but not urgent, problem by halting the discussion momentarily and asking for relevant documentation and the views of others who may be involved. Once you have been interrupted, it often seems easiest to dispose of a matter then and there. The fallacy is this: doing so encourages others to interrupt you. You and the members of your unit must take an assertive stand about interruptions. You should have ready such words as "I can't get to it right now," "Is it an emergency?" and "Send it on top of the other files and I will do it first." Instead of trying to dispose of the problem immediately, you might set up a way to address it at a specified time soon.

Inability to Say No to Requests.

Here are some reasons for the inability to say no:
1. Habit.
2. Strong need to please others.
3. The existence of an overly polite organizational climate or social norm.

As you know, social norms and organizational climates are slow and difficult to change. Changing a personal habit or reducing a strong personal need are beyond the scope of this book. However, focusing on end results and accepting the discipline of a "To Do" list are forward steps toward that end. We suggest a humble technique: saying no while seeming to say yes. By that we mean deferring action with a positive statement, such as "I'll do it as soon as I finish this," "I'll move it ahead of everything else and it will be the next item I handle," or "I'll give it top priority and you can expect an answer by four o'clock."

Repeatedly Handling the Same Piece(s) of Paper

As we saw in an earlier example, the typical supervisor is surprised how much time he or she spends in handling mail. Why don't we do this part of the job better? We have seen some of the reasons before. They are:

1. Habit.
2. Does not know a better alternative.
3. Desire to avoid priority tasks.

How can we overcome this pitfall or tendency? Let's start with the sometimes disarming influence of habit. We'll illustrate with a question. Did you ever notice what happens when you have been away from the office for a few days? If you have been out ten working days, it probably does not take you ten times as long to go through the stack of accumulated mail as your average daily reading time. Don't you simply zip through the nonessential items when you feel time pressure? Put another way, doesn't the daily mail often take more of your time than it deserves?

Another step you can consider is having someone else screen the incoming mail and handle those items that he or she is capable of processing. Next, you can ask your staff and others to mark memos and other correspondence "For Your Information Only" if action is not required.

Further, on documents that you will refer to later, you can underline, make marginal notations, or highlight key points with a special marker so that you won't have to reread the entire letter or memo. Where feasible, on requests that require a written answer, you can write your reply on the original message, making a photocopy if a copy is required.

To summarize this chapter, you have learned the key time management definitions, how to manage your time, and how to avoid major pitfalls. You are now ready to take the most important step: putting your knowledge into action. It takes commitment and discipline, but the results are far-reaching.

Chapter Notes

1. R. Alec Mackenzie, *The Time Trap* (New York, New York: American Management Association, 1972), p. 1.
2. William F. Simpson, CPCU, "How Managers See Their Role," *The National Underwriter* (Property and Casualty Insurance Edition), 24 September 1983, pp. 37 and 46.
3. Mackenzie, p. 45.
4. Martin M. Broadwell and William F. Simpson, CPCU, *The New Insurance Supervisor* (Reading, Massachusetts: Addison-Wesley Publishing Co., 1981), pp. 162-164.
5. Alan Lakein, *How To Get Control of Your Time and Your Life* (New York: New American Library, 1973), pp. 70-73.
6. Mackenzie, p. 52.

CHAPTER 9

Developing Teamwork

A supervisor speaks:

Like everyone else, I was shocked when Ned resigned. His work was excellent
and he seemed to have a career ahead of him in this organization. He seemed
to get along well with everyone. No, wait a minute. What I mean is that I
never saw Ned argue or disagree with anyone. I know that the others teased
him about going to concerts all the time. Now that I think back, I guess he was
always out of it when the conversation turned to movies or television
programs or sports. I noticed a few weeks ago that Ned began bringing his
lunch and eating by himself when the others went to the cafeteria. Maybe I
should have done something then.

Ned said that he was offered a better job in another company . . . but I wonder.

Sound familiar? Recall your own work experiences. Have you ever felt out
of place within your organization somehow? Have you ever hurt inside because
"they" did not understand you? Have you ever found yourself "going along"
with the group when it meant going against your own beliefs and preferences?
If so, you have felt the force of the social group when it is against you.

There is another side to the story. The group can fill your days with
excitement and pleasure, even when the work situation is difficult. The vignette
above portrays the bad side: we hope that you experience the uplifting power of
the group in every job you ever have.

As a supervisor, can you do anything about the social groups that form
within your unit? Do you think that the supervisor quoted above should have
done something when he saw that Ned was pulling away from the group? Your
supervisory role will present you with a stream of problems and opportunities
that rest on the powerful forces within employee groups. Such groups are
usually called informal groups or, more loosely, work groups. Together they
comprise an intricate and influential superstructure called the informal
organization.

THE ROLE OF GROUPS

Groups Satisfy Needs

Your study of motivation made clear that people have needs that can only be satisfied through others. (Needs and motivation were treated at length in *Essentials of Supervision*, and that discussion will not be repeated here.) No matter how challenging and satisfying a person's job may be, the days are incomplete without opportunities for self-expression and the exchange of facts and feelings with others. Achieving status and influence requires the presence of others. While two-person relationships meet some of our needs, we usually meet social needs through groups.

Groups Influence Organizational Results

Work groups have enormous influence over the results achieved within organizations. In a sense, management decisions must win the approval of informal groups. If employees unite in resisting managerial demands, dismal results are inevitable. On the other hand, surpassing results occur when employees, banded together, make the formal goals their own.

Within a unit or department, employee groups will, almost inevitably, establish informal standards of output. Groups decide what constitutes a good day's work and exert great pressure on members to comply. They will pressure slow workers to come up to the socially-set standard. They will also, in most instances, exert strong pressure against an employee whose production is annoyingly high.

Groups "Control" Behavior

Work groups encourage and support much daily behavior. They can foster hard work, humor, and helpfulness. On the other hand, they can encourage lateness, laziness, and laxness. They can heap praise on the innovator or they can punish the employee who does something extra for the supervisor. They can dictate the wardrobe and the wisecracks that are acceptable at the office. It does not seem too serious an exaggeration to say that groups control workplace behavior.

Illustration: Getting New Partitions

Helen was concerned about the appearance of her unit. To her it seemed crowded, messy and lacking in privacy. She requested that partitions be placed between the desks. She did not tell members of the unit because she was unsure that her request would be approved. Approval came on Friday and the partitions were installed on Saturday. When Helen saw the new look of the unit on Monday, she waited for unit members to express their approval. At first they said nothing. Then they asked why she thought that talking had gotten out of line. No explanation by Helen could overcome their belief that she had partitions installed to reduce conversation. The group defined the partitions as a kind of punishment. Helen had them removed after three weeks.

What mistake did Helen make? She failed to recognize how tightly knit the social group within her unit was. To unit members, being able to consult one another was more valuable than having a more private work area. While their conversation was minimal, the opportunity to talk was a key element in the existence of the group. Once the group defined the meaning of the new partitions, the odds were against Helen substituting a new meaning.

It would be wrong to conclude that groups usually resist changes such as the one Helen made. If she had communicated her thinking earlier, the group might have welcomed both the partitions and the added privacy they afforded.

NORMS

Standards of Behavior

Norms are standards of behavior expected of members in good standing within a group. Just as formal organizations have written and unwritten performance standards, social groups have norms of expected behavior. Norms are not unreachable ideals. They are standards of everyday conduct and performance that members are to use as rules for living and working with others.

Range of Behavior

Norms do not usually specify a single standard or level of behavior. Instead, they define a range of acceptable conduct. For instance, assume that an agency provides one hour for lunch. The support staff in the agency constitutes a strong employee group. The group may maintain as a norm that members may take from one hour to an hour and a quarter for lunch. No comment is made when members return up to an hour and fifteen minutes after lunch began. However, those who return too late are likely to be told, somehow, that they are out of line.

Enforcement

Norms are *enforced.* If a member violates a norm, he or she will be the recipient of a range of actions designed to correct the infraction. Norm-enforcing behavior can be mild, such as the humorous joking that groups often use as a first measure. At the other extreme, violations of group norms are sometimes punished with acts of violence against the person or property of the norm-breaker. In between are a vast array of enforcement behaviors, including simple requests, teasing, pranks, confrontation, hostility, ridicule, exclusion, and isolation.

The person on the receiving end of enforcement faces a difficult choice. The major alternatives are:

- Conform
- Leave the group
- Become a fringe member

The selection of a response is not always a conscious decision. Confusion is normal when we find that fellow employees disapprove of our actions. We feel the heat of this disapproval and make our way toward new behavior only with difficulty.

Members of a group show uniformity in many ways: beliefs; values; interests; goals; and perceptions. Norms are different from these other uniformities. Norms hold their special significance because of the enforcement mechanisms that support them. It is a matter of definition: if expected behavior is enforced, that expectation is a norm. The implication for you, as supervisor, is readily apparent: you pit yourself against a force of great collective power when you seek to change behavior that is subject to a group norm.

Typical Norms

Groups can establish norms about any matter of mutual interest to members. However, there are some subjects that are so commonly covered by norms that you can expect to find them in any work group:

- Quality of work
- Quantity of work
- Helping others
- Accepting dress
- Acceptable language
- How feelings are to be expressed
- How disagreements among members are to be resolved
- Symbols of status within the group
- Cooperation with other groups, especially management

It is difficult to use the word *always* when talking about human behavior. Nonetheless, we can say that ongoing work groups "always" have norms about work performance. How long, how hard, and how fast members work are too important for a work group to leave in the hands of management.

Sometimes the output norm is restrictive, and the group establishes a ceiling on an employee's output. This is often the case when employees perceive that the amount of available work is somehow limited. It is also accompanied by mistrust of management: "If we do any more today, they will expect it every day." Those who break restrictive output norms are called ratebusters or worse, and unmistakably strong behavior is often directed toward them.

Not all work groups curtail output. In fact, many establish output norms that exceed formal standards. Indeed, a group may set as its norm "Do the best you can" and show disapproval of any member who holds back. Some work groups make it a cardinal sin to withhold help from coworkers who face deadlines or workload peaks.

Neither Good nor Bad

Group norms should not be regarded as good or bad. They have advantages or disadvantages depending on the situation. As supervisor, you should see their existence as unavoidable. Viewing norms as bad and trying to sweep them away is surely a misguided effort. Rather, you should accept them as necessary and normal aspects of group formation. Your approach should be to work toward integrating norms with the goals of your organization, not to hope for their disappearance.

Norms Control Individual Behavior Group norms keep people "in line." For most employees, norms and their enforcement make some behavior unthinkable. Norms also lead employees to behave in ways that they would not do otherwise; for example, by staying late to get work out on time. In this sense, then, norms exert control over individual behavior. It is true that some individuals will violate or ignore group norms. They do so at a price, often an enormous one.

Norms Can Control the Expression of Feelings Directly or indirectly, norms govern the expression of feelings within a group. Life in some groups is crisply businesslike and members learn that they are not to talk about their troubles. Elsewhere, employees are free to express themselves and to reveal as much of themselves as they want. Sometimes it is a violation of group norms to criticize others, including management. In other situations, groups seem to encourage complaining and criticizing.

Variability

The variability of norms deserves emphasis. Just as no two persons are identical, no two groups are alike. Groups differ in the number of norms they form and in the latitude allowed in meeting them. Norms differ in their strength or importance in general, and in how much leeway is given to high-status members in complying with them. Norms are relatively permanent, yet they evolve over time and new ones arise when warranted by new developments.

Influencing Norms

What can you, as supervisor, do to influence the norms that exist within the work groups in your unit? You cannot, of course, force a group to change its norms but you can intervene in the group process and influence the group to reevaluate its perceptions and beliefs. You can provide information and encourage rethinking, but you cannot change a norm directly. For that matter, neither can the group leader change a norm directly. Norms result from the group process and are not the doing of any one person.

In general, group members must see a need for change if they are to revise group norms. In turn, this means that you foster change by providing information that group members see as relevant. You may occasionally welcome the presence of an external threat or problem if it prompts groups to unfreeze norms and adopt new ones. Creating contact with others (such as members of other units) is another way you can add to the forces for change directed toward a group.

Jane was the newly appointed supervisor of a rating unit of six employees. Each member of the unit had at least two years of experience. However, each specialized in rating only one or two types of policies. They did not help one another—the norm was to do only the work assigned to you. Nonetheless, the unit members comprised a single, tightly knit group.

Jane wanted to rearrange the unit, cross train all raters, and prepare them for the introduction of automated rating in a few months. She considered adopting a cross-training program by simply doing it in a straightforward way. She decided instead to take another route. She explained the changes that were expected within the unit. At first the changes were seen as a threat. After a few days, Jane asked the members of her unit to make recommendations for things they could do to prepare for change. Jane was patient. She supplied whatever information they requested. She recognized their difficulty in sorting through the information and their feelings about the future. She reassured them that their jobs were secure, but made no attempt to soft-pedal the effects of automated rating on the unit.

In a few weeks' time, the informal leader of the unit proposed to Jane that she consider cross training the raters on additional policies. It need hardly be said that the cross-training program went smoothly since it was "their idea." Was Jane manipulative in allowing the group to reach her conclusion? In this case the answer is a clear *no* because she was willing to consider any action they proposed. Clearly, her patience was rewarded as the group moved to change its norm of doing only the work assigned.

COHESIVENESS

Cohesiveness refers to the tightness of the interpersonal bond that holds group members together and allows them to act together to achieve goals. Like its norms, the cohesiveness of a group is vital information to you as supervisor.

Hallmarks

The hallmarks of a cohesive group are these:

- Strong positive feelings toward other members
- Many shared beliefs and values
- Subordination of individual needs and goals
- High satisfaction from membership
- Norms exert great influence over members
- Loyalty
- Strong sense of group identity

Members of a cohesive group are well aware that they form a group. The group is important to them, and they are likely to say so. The sense of loyalty is high—unfair treatment of one member will be considered unfair treatment of all. While members may disagree within the group, they will protect one another from outsiders. While subgroups may exist within it, the sense of belonging to the group is clear.

If cohesiveness is low, a group is likely to have subgroups of considerable strength. It may be difficult for an observer or even a group member to define the group as fringe membership may be common. Loyalty is low and members may be indifferent to some of the group positions. Norms are weaker than they are in cohesive groups. (Do not look for neat cause-and-effect relationships in understanding groups. It is enough to note that cohesive groups are likely to have strong norms.)

Forces for Cohesiveness

While there are many forces at play, some factors clearly contribute greatly to group cohesiveness. For one thing, the more common the backgrounds of members, the more likely a cohesive group will exist. Similarities in age, family situation, ethnic background, education, and financial position make for a cohesive group.

Opportunities for interaction have an important bearing on the development of cohesion. Most important are the opportunities for communication that arise because of the work flow and physical closeness to others.

The existence of a common threat or enemy promotes cohesiveness. Groups that are not normally cohesive often become so when facing a major problem. (An arrogant supervisor may find that his behavior may be the force that unifies unit members!)

The Pros and Cons of Cohesiveness

Which would you rather have, a cohesive group or a loosely knit one within your unit? This is hardly a moot question, since your behavior figures into the development of cohesiveness. From your supervisory point of view, there are pros and cons to be weighed.

You will see a cohesive group as an asset if the group works to help you achieve your objectives. A unified social group can drive performance and spur healthy innovation. On the other hand, a cohesive group constitutes an enormous, unyielding obstacle if its goals are contradictory to yours or if the group fights change.

Loosely knit groups are more easily influenced by outside forces, including your own efforts to stimulate change. You can follow a "divide and conquer" strategy when the group lacks cohesiveness. However, weak groups are not as coordinated or easy to predict as cohesive groups; and change may require reaching members individually.

Clearly, your efforts to foster or discourage work group cohesiveness should be based on a careful appraisal of the circumstances. Within that appraisal, special attention should go to the need for and likelihood of change. The kind of group you prefer today might be a hindrance in the future.

GROUP STRUCTURE

Informal groups develop an internal structure. We will examine two key aspects of this structure, leadership and membership. Both aspects show how members develop roles and statuses within a group. These roles and statuses comprise a structure that is marvelously rich and significant. As supervisor, you "read" the informal structure in tailoring your communications to others. The more sensitive you are to the informal positions of unit members, the more you will be seen as a good communicator.

By and large, the informal structure is stable. Change in a group's structure is gradual and evolutionary, unless a sudden or drastic change occurs in the group's environment or membership. From your point of view, the structure of a work group is relatively constant and predictable.

Leadership

Nature of Informal Leadership   The person who emerges as a group's informal leader is the one who is the most liked, or most respected, or is best able to help the group achieve its objectives. This immediately suggests that leadership is a complex process, and that leadership may shift as circumstances and needs change.

As in the formal organization, leadership effectiveness is determined by forces in the leader, the followers, and the situation. Unlike the appointed leader, the informal leader's status results from a kind of consensus. One cannot seize informal leadership—it must be granted by the group members.

The leader often is the person who best lives up to group norms and lives by group values. Ironically, a leader is given greater leeway in complying with the group norms. An outright violation of a critical norm may cost a person the leadership position, yet occasional deviation is permitted. It seems that allegiance to norms and shared values helps one to achieve high status and leadership responsibility within the informal group; but the requirements are loosened for those who have made it.

Multiple Leaders   Informal leadership is not always vested in one person. It is possible for a group to have a number of leadership roles that supplement that of the dominant leader. For example, Bill might be the overall leader of a unit of claims adjuster. However, Janice exercises the leadership role over the group's annual picnic, Christmas party, and other social events. Roger is the key person in dealings with the accountant group that shares office quarters with the adjusters. Bill did not delegate his authority to Janice and Roger in any official manner. Rather, their special talents allowed them to emerge as leaders for specific functions. In effect, the group executed an intricate process of weighing the talents of members and allocating leadership tasks in ways that best use these talents.

This pattern of shared leadership contrasts with the normal image of leadership in the United States. In general, we hold a "Superman" view of leaders. We expect managers and supervisors to take charge and to be effective regardless of the problem or circumstances at hand. Strangely enough, we are far more flexible in assigning leadership duties within our informal groups and in what we expect our informal leaders to accomplish.

Your Relationship to the Group Leader   As a supervisor, you should not look on the work group leader as an adversary or rival. Your role is that of task leader. Other leadership roles should be left to the group to provide. You should not try to be the informal leader as well as the formal task leader. You cannot and should not conform to all group norms; and conformity is the customary path to informal group leadership.

Should you treat the informal leader differently from the way you treat other group members? Yes! Failure to show recognition of the leader's special status is likely to be harmful to your relations with group members. Ignoring the leader means risking that the group members will feel slighted or that you will seem ignorant in their eyes.

The informal leader can be an excellent ally. There are many steps you can take to win his or her cooperation. You can give the leader early notification of important news. You can ask the leader's opinion on matters of importance within the unit. You can send messages through the leader, especially those messages that cannot be issued through official channels.

Let's consider an example. Paula, a clerical unit supervisor, was concerned about staff member reaction to a new productivity measurement procedure about to be implemented in the unit. She held a unit meeting and explained the details of the new procedure. She sensed a negative undertone to the comments made by unit members. Paula asked Marge, whom she saw as the informal leader, "What's wrong?" Marge told her that the employees were afraid of losing their jobs and cited rumors (unfounded, incidentally) of staff reductions elsewhere in the company.

When Paula attended a supervisors meeting on the new procedures, she asked Marge to come along. When Marge assured herself that no staff cutbacks were planned, she took the message back to the unit. Despite the high esteem that Paula generally enjoyed, in this instance Marge had more credibility than Paula. Paula made use of Marge's leadership without lessening her own.

Membership Status

Not all persons in a group seem to be full-fledged members. A useful way of looking at the many possible membership positions is to use these categories:

- Leaders—persons of high status and influence
- Regulars—persons who are generally accepted and who take part in most of the group's activities
- Fringe members—persons who are not always included in the group or whose status and influence are low. Fringe members of one group may be regular members of other groups.

- Deviants—those who are tolerated but denied regular membership, often because they violate some important norms

In addition to these categories of membership, a work unit may contain *isolates*. Isolates is the term given to those who are deliberately excluded from an informal group. A group may cut a person off from its activities and interactions for many reasons, including prejudice. Outright exclusion is often the final punishment given to persons who violate important group norms. For instance, when a work group severely restricts output, the ultra-high producer is likely to be an isolate.

Is a person isolated because he or she violates the norms or does a person violate norms because he or she is rejected by a group? It is a chicken-and-egg matter. The point is that the person who is rejected by a work group is very likely to scorn its values and ways.

Sensitivity to the membership status of unit members can be valuable to you in supervising your unit. For one thing, caution is warranted when making work assignments and arranging the physical layout of the unit. In a sense you face a dilemma. Assigning leaders and regulars to work together may tap the resources of the group and will certainly please the people involved. However, it also perpetuates things as they are within the informal structure of the unit and offers no aid to the isolate.

You should be skeptical that harmony and tight teamwork will occur when assigning an isolate to work closely with a regular. However, one recipe for changing the unpleasant status of the isolate is to create opportunities for interaction with others. (The more we interact with someone, the more likely we are to develop a liking for that person.)

Isolates and fringe members may warrant special supervisory attention from you. You cannot assume that they "get the word" when messages pass along the grapevine. You cannot assume that they go along with the others when the group's voice is heard. They may want you to be generous with your ear and your time since they may not meet their social needs within the work group.

Conflict and Collaboration among Groups

Groups usually establish a network of mutual relationships. They create elaborate communications systems, including the infamous grapevine. Just as informal status exists within a group, groups have status rankings with respect to one another. The forces at play within a group, such as those that determine leadership, membership, and cohesiveness, also operate at the intergroup level. When contact among groups is plentiful, the resulting intergroup social system is wondrously intricate yet somehow understood well by its members.

Collaboration Cooperation and collaboration among groups are likely when:

- Members communicate with one another on a frequent basis
- Groups have common goals, values, and norms

- Overlapping membership is common
- Groups understand the functions and problems of one another
- Cooperation produces benefits for all

Conflict   Conflict among groups is likely when:

- Groups compete for resources
- Groups have different goals, values, and norms
- Groups attribute to one another things that pertain to the formal organization
- The formal organization promotes competition among units
- Higher level groups are in conflict and seek allies among lower level groups

Symptoms of Conflict   Among the signs of intergroup conflict are the following:

- Little communication among groups
- Groups distort information about other groups
- Stereotyping members of other groups
- Mistrust of other groups and their members
- Each group perceives that its leaders and ideas are superior to those of other groups

The conflict among cohesive groups is likely to be more severe than that between loosely knit groups. Strongly knit groups can mobilize efforts quickly whenever an outside threat is identified. You will recall that an external threat often raises the level of cohesiveness within a group.

Here is an illustration of intergroup conflict. Three inland marine specialists were housed in an insurer's regional office. They reported to the home office and not directly to the regional manager.

The three inland marine specialists had both underwriting and sales responsibilities. Certain inland marine policies could be sold separately from commercial packages, but most inland marine coverages were provided as parts of package policies. Package policies were sold by the regional sales department and were underwritten by the commercial lines department within the region.

The home office inland marine manager pressured the specialists to increase sales. They responded by saying "How can we sell when the regional sales department isn't selling commercial packages and the underwriters are rejecting more business than they are accepting?"

This seems to be a fertile situation for conflict between the specialists and the sales and underwriting groups. How can the conflict be prevented, minimized, or resolved?

Communication should be increased. The members of each group need to understand the position of each other group. In particular, the underwriter and sales units need a chance to learn how the specialists feel about the sales pressure they are getting. A meeting of representatives seems appropriate. Such a meeting should be carefully planned. It is foolish to call people together and simply tell them to get along better. An agenda should be developed to allow exploration of the sales problem, disclosure of feelings about it, and the search for action alternatives. Who will call and conduct such a meeting? Since the specialists do not report to the regional manager, the action is not likely to occur strictly within the chain of command. The most likely course of events is that the specialists present their problem to the regional manager and ask him to call a meeting.

Joint problem-solving is recommended. The specialists should see the problem as requiring a collaborative solution, not as a matter of getting others to do what they want.

A common goal should be established from a joint attack on the problem. There is no guarantee that a unifying goal can be found. After all, the sales and underwriting representatives may consider the problem "theirs" rather than "ours." Nonetheless, much effort should go into redefining the problem so that a common goal can be developed.

A Checklist for Analyzing Group Behavior

Can you predict how a group will react in a given situation? Sometimes your predictions can be quite good. You can probably better your predictive ability by following a structured guide. Like the experienced pilot who still uses a pre-takeoff checklist, you can reduce the chances that you will miss something. Here is a checklist to help you in understanding a group.

A. Who are the regular members of the group?
    1. Who shares in most activities?
    2. Who communicates with whom regularly?
B. Who are informal leaders?
    1. Who has the most influence?
    2. Who is respected and liked the most?
    3. Who is usually the spokesperson?
    4. Whom do others come to for help?
C. Who are the fringe members of the group?
    1. Who has low influence?
    2. Who takes part in some but not all group activities?
D. How cohesive is the group?
    1. What ideas and activities are shared by all?
    2. How often do members act on their own?
E. What are the norms of the group?
    1. What are the important "do's" and "don'ts" of the group?
    2. For what actions or ideas are people criticized or rejected?
    3. How are norms enforced?
F. How does this group fit into the larger structure of informal groups?

You can add questions of your own to this checklist. Through the use of disciplined (rather than random) observation, you can deepen your understanding of the informal organization and apply your insight in leading and directing others.

CHANGING THE INFORMAL SYSTEM

We have already considered some ideas that will help you to bring about change in the informal organization. Let us now ask in a more general way: what can you do to change the informal system? In one sense, you cannot change it by yourself. By definition, the informal organization is that spontaneously created system that forms around the formally designed organization. In another sense, you are a part of the informal organization. You belong to one or more informal groups, perhaps a group of supervisors or a managerial group. Although you do not (or should not) belong to the informal groups within your unit, your behavior is of central importance to those work groups. Let's consider some ideas useful in trying to bring about change within the informal organization.

Change the Formal System

Perhaps the easiest way to change the informal organization is to change the formal system. While formal requirements may be a step removed from informal behavior, changing them is clearly within your right.

Change Group Membership By reassigning employees or transferring them from your unit, you can force a change in a group's membership. This may lead to a change in its values, beliefs, and norms. A word of caution: the group may retaliate.

Change Work Flow or Procedures Physical closeness and work flow relationships are among the most important factors in group formation. You strengthen a group when you increase interaction opportunities. You usually weaken a group when you create obstacles to conversation and eye contact. Again, caution is advised. If a group is highly cohesive, members may maintain their activities and communications even if it means being away from their work stations and incurring your disfavor.

Develop or Revise Performance Standards A change in performance standards should lead to a change in group norms of quality and quantity of output. If members participate in standard-setting, they may promote changes that align norms and performance standards.

Change the Reward System Employees are acutely aware of the "real" reward system. Pay raises and promotions are important but infrequent rewards. On a daily basis, your more important rewards are recognition, work assignments, communication privileges, and inclusion in important discussions.

Revise Controls Control programs provide the feedback that employees use to adjust their performance and to spur their efforts. Controls that do not mesh with group standards will cause confusion or stress. In stipulating what performance you will and will not measure, you send important messages to the informal organization.

Intervene

You can intervene directly into the informal group to effect change. You might, for example, make a straightforward appeal that a group change its norm concerning the duration of coffee breaks. Obviously great skill is required in such direct intervention. Personal risk may be high. You take the chance that your request will be ridiculed and your judgment doubted.

You might attempt intervention through the informal leader of a group. Even if the leader is unwilling to carry your message, his or her opinion should be sought in advance.

TEAM BUILDING

The term *team building* refers to efforts to develop teamwork among organization members through planned participative activities. Although team building may appear under many different names, its essence is an open-ended workshop format. During workshop sessions, participants develop recommendations for solving problems of concern to them. In so doing, they improve their abilities to work together.

Team building activities do not usually aim at changing the informal organization. However, their influence echoes throughout the informal organization. A key distinction is that team building is structured around formal work units, not informal social groups.

The ideal unit or department would consist of employees who do their utmost within their individual jobs and also work together smoothly. The members of this ideal department would trust one another. They would join together eagerly to attack common problems and develop creative solutions. An impossible dream? This supervisor's paradise is not *too* far-fetched. Through team-building workshops, you can make progress toward this ideal.

Team building refers to planned, organized efforts to develop the collective problem-solving resources of a work group. The emphasis is on enhancing the group's ability to solve problems, as contrasted with finding a solution to a current problem. Team building is a participative endeavor. It takes for granted that employee involvement in solving a problem is itself a goal that ranks alongside the quality of the solution.

The workshop is the primary vehicle for team building. At its best, the workshop provides a productive mixture of structure and freedom in discussion. At its worst, the workshop allows "buzz groups" to talk on and on without purpose or guidance. A properly led workshop channels creative energy toward a well-defined goal and yet allows participants the freedom to influence outcomes.

Problems Addressed

A team-building workshop is established because some problem is known to exist. You will have an initial notion of a problem that serves as the reason for holding a workshop. Once the discussion is under way, that initial notion should give way to a revised concept of the problem. New problems may be identified and commitments made to work on them in the future. As leader of a unit team-building workshop, you serve as gatekeeper for the problems to be addressed.

Team building can address most work problems as long as they are within the knowledge and authority of the participants. It is essential that participants have, or can obtain, the information they need to solve the problems they decide to attack. That gives you a dual responsibility. You must see to it that needed information is obtained. You must also step in when employees choose a topic that requires facts and figures you cannot secure. Similarly, you must forestall the development of solutions that require authority you cannot access. Thus you may rule out some problem areas because, in your judgment, they will exceed the knowledge or formal power that can be brought forward.

Among the kinds of problems suitable for team building are these:

- Poor unit performance
- Lack of coordination within the unit
- Complacency
- Handling change

Note that these are (or should be) business problems, not interpersonal problems. The dividing line is often a blur, of course. Still, the team-building workshop addresses work problems, not personal and interpersonal ones. Personal and interpersonal change may result from a workshop, but they are not the explicit goals.

Workshop Format

The format that follows is a general model. It should be adapted and made more specific to fit each application.

Roles As unit supervisor, you serve as the *workshop leader.* You convene the workshop, structure small group activity, announce (and enforce) the timetable, lead the general discussions, summarize results, and adjourn the meeting. You also implement recommendations and follow-up on them.

Unless the unit is small (say, seven or fewer persons) the workshop will require forming *discussion groups* of no more than about seven persons. The main reason is to allow each unit member ample time to participate in the discussion. Keeping discussion groups small allows more ideas to be voiced and promotes the expression of feelings about the problem at hand. It also allows different topics to be discussed simultaneously if that is desired.

Each discussion group will have a *group leader* and a *group reporter.* The reporter takes notes during the discussion and reports the findings to the general workshop. If only the final conclusion is to be reported, one person might serve as both leader and reporter. In most instances, the group leader should be kept free of note-taking chores and allowed to concentrate on the discussion-leading role. Similarly, it is usually desirable that the reporter not have the added role of chairing the discussion.

Steps

1. Introduction.   As workshop leader, you convene the workshop and begin the proceedings. You describe the initial view of the problem to be addressed. You also give the ground rules for the meeting: such things as the facilities available, the meal and refreshment breaks, and the total time available for the workshop.

2. Define the Problem.   The initial statement of the problem should be explored at length and from as many angles as possible. In all likelihood it will be refined and restated. Perhaps underlying or related problems will be identified. Your responsibility as workshop leader is to see to it that the problem definition remains workable—that is, within the information and authority available to the unit. Ideally, the final statement of the problem should represent the unit members' view of it, not a management-only conception.

A vital part of the problem definition is clarification of the authority available to the group. Members should have a clear picture of what they can do on their own, what actions need your OK, and what needs higher approval. As the problem is progressively redefined, it will be necessary to return to the authority issue, perhaps repeatedly. The end result is, ideally, the definition of a problem that members of your unit see as important and can and want to do something about.

3. Problem Diagnosis Phase.   After the workshop group has agreed on the definition of the problem, the problem should be explored as fully as possible. Occasionally the problem may best be examined by the workshop group operating as a single discussion group. Usually the problem lends itself to separate inquiries and the unit is large enough to allow forming discussion groups.

Form Discussion Groups.   You divide the workshop into a number of discussion groups. Allowing participants to create their own groups is seldom wise. Instead, you assert control over the number and size of the groups. If the need is to generate as many new ideas as possible, very small groups are appropriate. If the need is to screen or refine ideas, groups of five to seven persons are preferable. Sometimes the number of separate topics or aspects governs the number and size of discussion groups.

Specify Discussion Topics.   All discussion groups may be given the same assignment: to explore the problem. On the other hand, each group may be given an individual assignment: to explore some aspect of the problem or to appraise it from a particular perspective. The discussion topics must be pinned down—vague assignments produce poor results.

Appoint Leaders and Reporters.   In many cases, you will want to designate the leader and reporter for each discussion group. In other cases you will want to ask the groups to select them. This self-selection is made easier by giving the groups a basis for selection.

Announce the Time Limit.   Failure to specify discussion time is a major error. You can always extend the time if necessary. Forgetting to give a time limit or terminating the discussion without advance warning is likely to annoy participants and douse their interest in later steps.

Discussion.   The discussion takes place within the discussion groups. You should move around the room, listening for a sense of the progress being made. Give a ten- or five-minute warning before announcing the end of the discussion phase.

4. Reports.   The workshop group reconvenes and the reporters give the high points or conclusions reached by their groups. You may encourage discussion as each report is given or, instead, ask that all questions and discussion be deferred until all reports have been received.

The goal at this stage is to reach consensus on the nature of the problem at hand. The problem should be fleshed out in whatever terms seem appropriate. For instance, one problem might be explored in terms of the reasons for its existence. Another might be presented as forces for and against change. Another might be structured as the search for the root cause of the problem symptoms. One value of the openness of the workshop format is that participants are free to select and combine approaches as they develop a workable idea of the problem facing the unit.

As consensus emerges, you summarize the final definition and diagnosis of the problem. Writing it on a flip chart or chalkboard is highly recommended. You then ask the group to turn attention to its solution.

5. Action Planning Phase.   A complete shift of attention should now take place. It is time now to develop action plans, not to go back over the diagnosis. The same general steps taken in problem diagnosis will be followed.

Form Discussion Groups.   The groups may be identical to or different from those created for problem diagnosis. If the problem now has some natural division, the number of segments may govern the number and size of groups. However, you should not allow the groups to be too large or too small for effective dialogue.

Specify Discussion Topics.   As before, the groups may be given separate assignments, such as planning the action to be taken at different times or in different areas. On the other hand, some problems are best handled by having all discussion groups generate solutions for later evaluation and intergration.

Appoint Leaders and Reporters.   Often new leaders and reporters are designated simply to give others a chance to serve in these roles.

Announce the Time Limit

Discussion

6. Reports.   Participants gather again as the full workshop group to hear the reports. The goal now is to develop a final action plan for solution of the problem. In all likelihood, the final plan will be a composite of ideas developed within the discussion groups. In leading this discussion, you should be alert to the practicality of the ideas that come forth. If a recommendation is too vague, or exceeds the authority that can be summoned, you should raise questions that make it more workable.

7. Summary When consensus has emerged, summarize the action to be taken. If the recommendations require action on your part, give an idea of when the unit members can expect you to report on the actions taken and their outcomes. Adjourn the meeting with an expression of appreciation.

Illustration

A large commercial lines department had contained an underwriting manager and seven underwriters, a supervisor of underwriting assistants and seven underwriting assistants, and a rating supervisor and six raters. The department was reorganized and a specialty lines unit created. Betty Dresser was promoted from senior underwriter to supervisor of specialty lines underwriting. Reporting to her were two underwriters, two underwriting assistants, and two raters. All had worked in the former department.

Since Betty had trained the raters and underwriting assistants, she believed that the work would go smoothly in her new specialty lines unit. However, she was keenly aware that the informal organization had been totally disrupted by the reorganization and new desk locations. The informal groups that had flourished in the old department no longer existed, including Betty's own group.

After Betty's unit had been in operation for a month, she concluded that there was confusion about the duties of the underwriting assistants. She considered doing a task analysis. Instead, she selected team building. She believed that all members of the unit recognized the confusion, and she thought that "their" solution would be more beneficial than any produced by job analysis. She also welcomed the opportunity for an activity that would promote understanding and team spirit.

Betty scheduled a meeting for 8:30 to 11:30 on a Monday morning. She said that the staff would discuss ways of resolving an apparent confusion about the duties of underwriting assistants.

The meeting introduction and problem identification phase took over a half hour, and Betty began to worry about the time required. However, the discussion seemed fruitful. The group developed the position that there were two related aspects of the problem. One was a work flow matter. The other concerned some tasks that could reasonably be done by either underwriters or assistants.

Based on this initial view of the problem Betty established two discussion groups. She gave each group one of the aspects. She assigned an underwriter to each discussion group and asked them to serve as discussion leaders. She announced that the groups would have twenty minutes for their assignments.

When Betty reconvened the staff as a single meeting, she put the key ideas on flip charts. The reports were similar. Each described the problem in detail and suggested some of the key decisions involved. The general discussion dealt with an overlap between the aspects and identified some changes in procedure that might be helpful. Betty believed that the discussion generated a number of useful ideas but many were left "hanging." She also noted a general enthusiasm for the search for better work methods. The reporting and discussion period took just under twenty minutes.

After revising the statements of each aspect of the problem, Betty reorganized the groups. It seemed to her that three of the employees were particularly interested in the work flow issue and the others were more interested in the task assignment question. Each group was asked to pick as leader a person who had not been leader before. Betty asked the groups to take twenty minutes to develop recommendations for dealing with the problems that had been identified. As she listened to the discussion, Betty realized that one group would need more time. She therefore waited until twenty minutes had gone by before giving a five-minute warning.

Betty found both groups eager to be first in presenting their recommendations. She tossed a coin to make the choice, and was teased about her "inability to make an executive decision." The reports revealed an overlap in the actions recommended. The discussion that followed focused on the problem previously defined as it wove together the action recommendations of the two discussion groups. The final result was a recommendation for four minor changes in work flow and procedures. All were within Betty's authority. As she thanked the unit members for their participation, Betty promised to assess the changes in a month and report the results to the unit staff.

Betty and her staff reaped many benefits from this team-building experience. Work procedures were improved. There was a dramatic demonstration of the close coordination required of employees in the three distinct roles: underwriters, underwriting assistants, and raters. Communication among them could only be enhanced by the workshop experience. There is a shared expectation that unit productivity will benefit from the changes adopted and from the team-building itself. Betty's leadership position was enhanced in no small part because she provided clear direction and control over the proceedings. Betty noted that the entire session took about two and one-half hours, and she later considered it a critical event in the development of an excellent unit.

Issues in Team Building

Commitment to Act Calling a team-building meeting is taken as a commitment to carry out the results. Do not conduct a team-building session if you are not sure that you can implement the recommedations that can reasonably be anticipated. Recommendations will often require you to obtain approval from higher management. You may want to pretest management's view of a team-building approach to a given problem.

Troublesome Individuals Occasionally work unit members have such strongly divided and firmly entrenched views that team-building only intensifies the conflict. Put another way: you may not have the discussion leadership skills to cope with antagonistic and unyielding persons.

Larger Issues Raised Despite your best efforts to confine a meeting to a problem within the accessible knowledge and authority of participants, discussion could get out of hand. Suppose that your organization faces a severe underlying problem, such as low salaries as perceived by employees. Team building workshops may only bring to the surface their feelings about the pay problem. You can hardly expect results with the immediate problem under such circumstances.

Time Required Clearly, team building workshops require time. Major problems often require a series of workshops and a major commitment of employee time. It is difficult to be patient, especially when people around you expect immediate or spectacular results.

Skill Required We have given a basic team-building model that most supervisors should be able to execute. Clearly, a measure of meeting-leadership skill is needed. Knowing when to speak and when to remain silent, and knowing how to handle the overactive and underactive participants may require skill that usually comes from considerable experience. Team building is not advised for you if you are shakey about your meeting-leadership skills.

SUMMARY

Learning to "read" the informal organization is essential to your success as a supervisor. The forces that exist within and among social groups are pervasive: they affect every one of your efforts to plan, organize, direct, and control organizational results.

Human behavior within work organizations is an inexhaustible field of study. We have had to content ourselves with highlights. Thus we have given major attention to norms, leadership, membership, and cohesiveness within groups. Each group develops its own mixture of these variables and thus each group is unique. For that reason, it deserves your careful analysis. A quick look could be misleading: take time to observe and interpret the facts about people at work.

As wondrous and powerful as they are, social forces are not beyond your supervisory reach. You cannot, of course, directly change the norms within groups or the relationships among people or groups. However, you can, through your own behavior and through your actions, trigger processes that lead to change within the informal organization. One particular technique for promoting change is the team-building workshop. The basic model presented here can be adapted to fit a variety of problems and situations. Although it focuses on a business problem, team-building often succeeds in making good its name.

Index